1872

WRITER

GERRY DUGGAN

ARTIST

NIK VIRELLA

COLOR ARTIST

LEE LOUGHRIDGE

LETTERER

VC's CLAYTON COWLES

COVER ARTISTS

ALEX MALEEV (#1) & LEONARD KIRK (#2-4)

ASSISTANT EDITOR

KATHLEEN WISNESKI

EDITORS

JAKE THOMAS & MARK PANICCIA

COLLECTION EDITOR MARK D. BEAZLEY
ASSISTANT EDITOR SARAH BRUNSTAD
ASSOCIATE MANAGING EDITOR ALEX STARBUCK
EDITOR, SPECIAL PROJECTS JENNIFER GRÜNWALD
SENIOR EDITOR, SPECIAL PROJECTS JEFF YOUNGQUIST
SVP PRINT, SALES & MARKETING DAVID GABRIEL
BOOK DESIGNER ADAM DEL RE

EDITOR IN CHIEF AXEL ALONSO
CHIEF CREATIVE OFFICER JOE QUESADA
PUBLISHER DAN BUCKLEY
EXECUTIVE PRODUCER ALAN FINE

MARVEL 1872. Contains material originally published in magazine form as 1872 #1-4; AVENGERS #80 and MARVEL COMICS PRESENTS #170. First printing 2015. ISBN# 978-0-7851-9877-2. Published by MARVEL WORLDWIDE, INC., a subsidiary of MARVEL ENTERTAINMENT, LLC. OFFICE OF PUBLICATION: 135 West 50th Street, New York, NY 10020. Copyright © 2015 MARVEL No similarity between any of the names, characters, persons, and/or institutions in this magazine with those of any living or dead person or institution is intended, and any such similarity which may exist is purely coincidental. **Printed in Canada.** ALAN FINE, President, Marvel Entertainment; DAN BUCKLEY, President, TV, Publishing and Brand Management; JOE QUESADA, Chief Creative Officer; TOM BREVOORT, SVP of Publishing; DAVID BOGART, SVP of Operations & Procurement, Publishing; C.B. CEBULSKI, VP of International Development & Brand Management; DAVID GABRIEL, SVP Print, Sales & Marketing; JIM O'KEEFE, VP of Operations & Logistics; DAN CARR, Executive Director of Publishing Technology; SUSAN CRESPI, Editorial Operations Manager; ALEX MORALES, Publishing Operations Manager; STAN LEE, Chairman Emeritus. For information regarding advertising in Marvel Comics or on Marvel.com, please contact Jonathan Rheingold, VP of Custom Solutions & Ad Sales, at jrheingold@marvel.com. For Marvel subscription inquiries, please call 800-217-9158. **Manufactured between 10/2/2015 and 11/9/2015 by SOLISCO PRINTERS, SCOTT, QC, CANADA.**

10 9 8 7 6 5 4 3 2 1

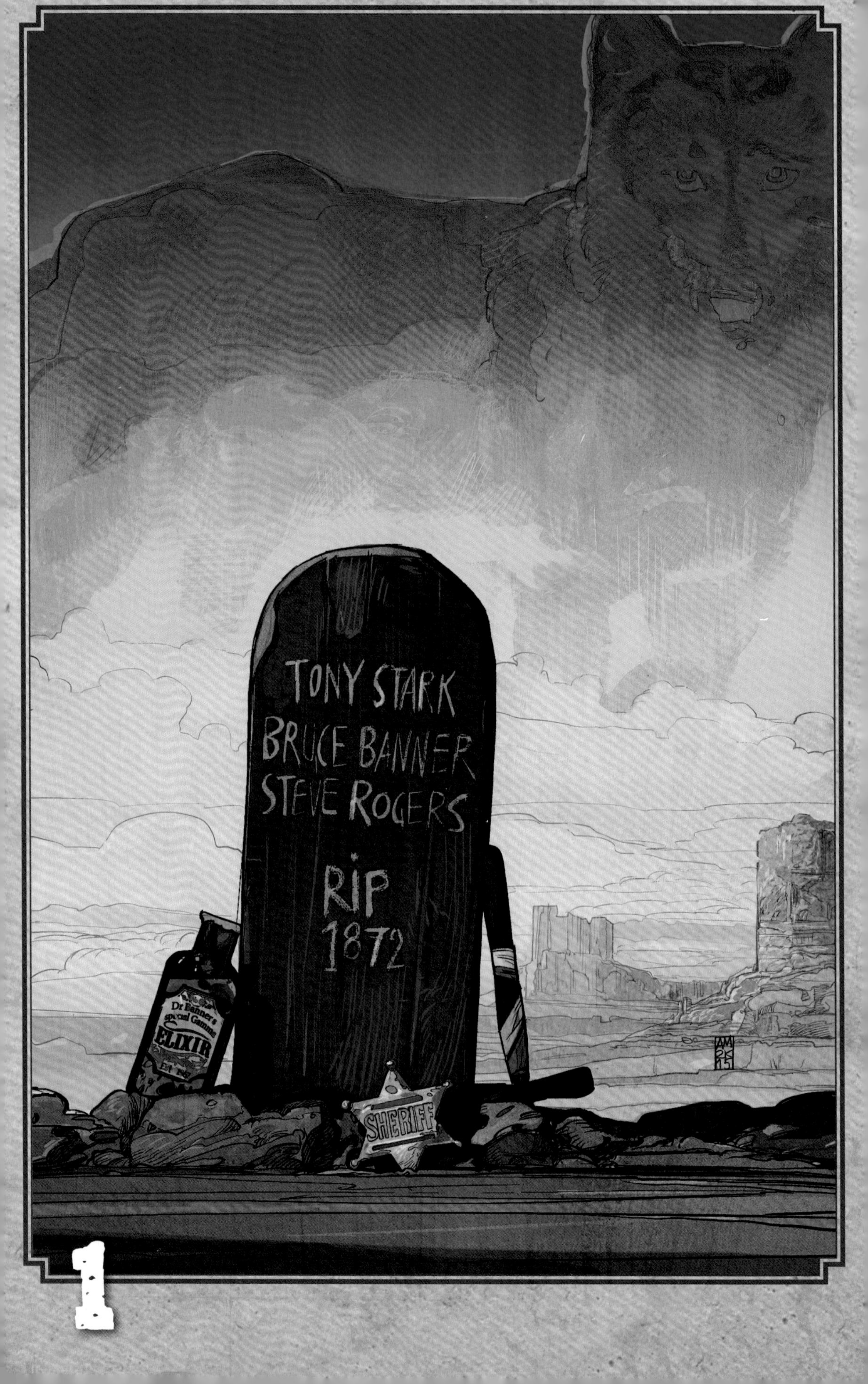
TONY STARK
BRUCE BANNER
STEVE ROGERS
RIP
1872
Dr Banner's special Gamma
ELIXIR
SHERIFF

1

SECRET WARS

THE MULTIVERSE WAS DESTROYED!

·

THE HEROES OF EARTH-616 AND EARTH-1610 WERE POWERLESS TO SAVE IT!

·

NOW, ALL THAT REMAINS ...IS BATTLEWORLD!

·

A MASSIVE, PATCHWORK PLANET COMPOSED OF THE FRAGMENTS OF WORLDS THAT NO LONGER EXIST, MAINTAINED BY THE IRON WILL OF ITS GOD AND MASTER, VICTOR VON DOOM!

·

EACH REGION IS A DOMAIN UNTO ITSELF!

1872

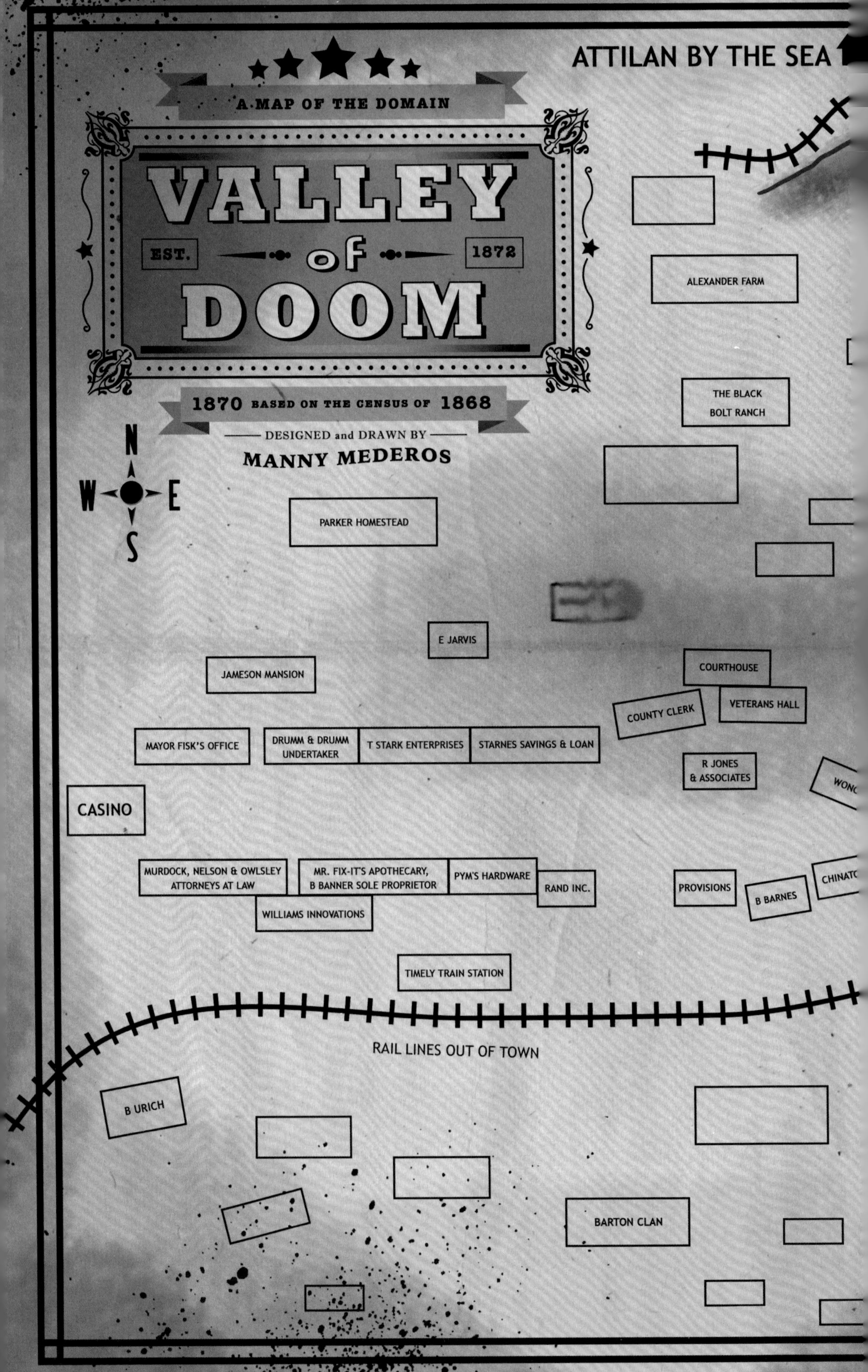
A MAP OF THE DOMAIN
VALLEY of DOOM
EST. 1872
1870 BASED ON THE CENSUS OF 1868
DESIGNED and DRAWN BY
MANNY MEDEROS
N
W
E
S
ATTILAN BY THE SEA
ALEXANDER FARM
THE BLACK BOLT RANCH
PARKER HOMESTEAD
E JARVIS
JAMESON MANSION
COURTHOUSE
COUNTY CLERK
VETERANS HALL
MAYOR FISK'S OFFICE
DRUMM & DRUMM UNDERTAKER
T STARK ENTERPRISES
STARNES SAVINGS & LOAN
R JONES & ASSOCIATES
CASINO
MURDOCK, NELSON & OWLSLEY ATTORNEYS AT LAW
MR. FIX-IT'S APOTHECARY, B BANNER SOLE PROPRIETOR
PYM'S HARDWARE
RAND INC.
PROVISIONS
B BARNES
WILLIAMS INNOVATIONS
TIMELY TRAIN STATION
RAIL LINES OUT OF TOWN
B URICH
BARTON CLAN

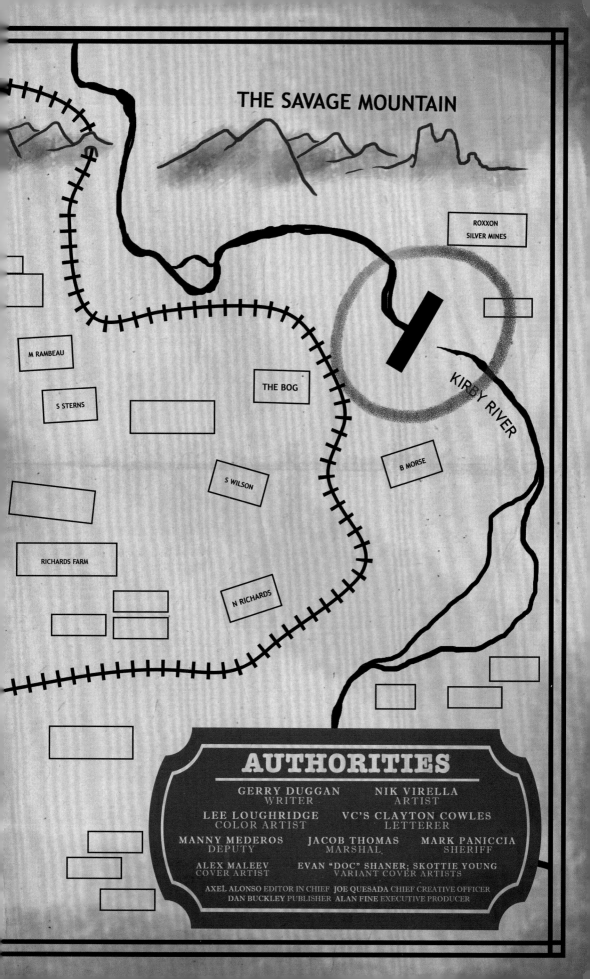

THE SAVAGE MOUNTAIN

ROXXON
SILVER MINES

M RAMBEAU

S STERNS

THE BOG

KIRBY RIVER

S WILSON

B MORSE

RICHARDS FARM

N RICHARDS

AUTHORITIES

GERRY DUGGAN
WRITER

NIK VIRELLA
ARTIST

LEE LOUGHRIDGE
COLOR ARTIST

VC'S CLAYTON COWLES
LETTERER

MANNY MEDEROS
DEPUTY

JACOB THOMAS
MARSHAL

MARK PANICCIA
SHERIFF

ALEX MALEEV
COVER ARTIST

EVAN "DOC" SHANER; SKOTTIE YOUNG
VARIANT COVER ARTISTS

AXEL ALONSO EDITOR IN CHIEF **JOE QUESADA** CHIEF CREATIVE OFFICER
DAN BUCKLEY PUBLISHER **ALAN FINE** EXECUTIVE PRODUCER

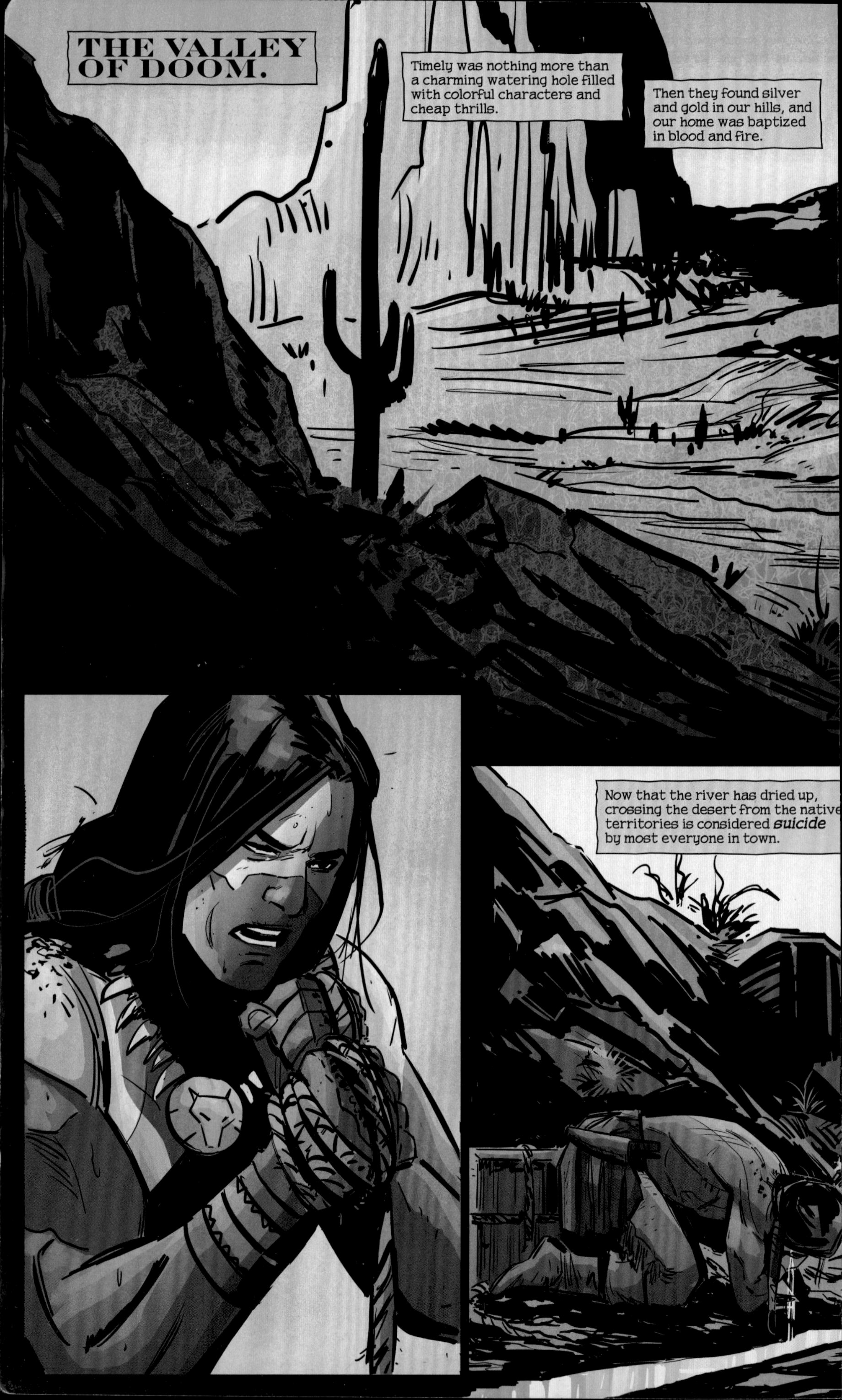
THE VALLEY OF DOOM.
Timely was nothing more than a charming watering hole filled with colorful characters and cheap thrills.
Then they found silver and gold in our hills, and our home was baptized in blood and fire.
Now that the river has dried up, crossing the desert from the native territories is considered *suicide* by most everyone in town.

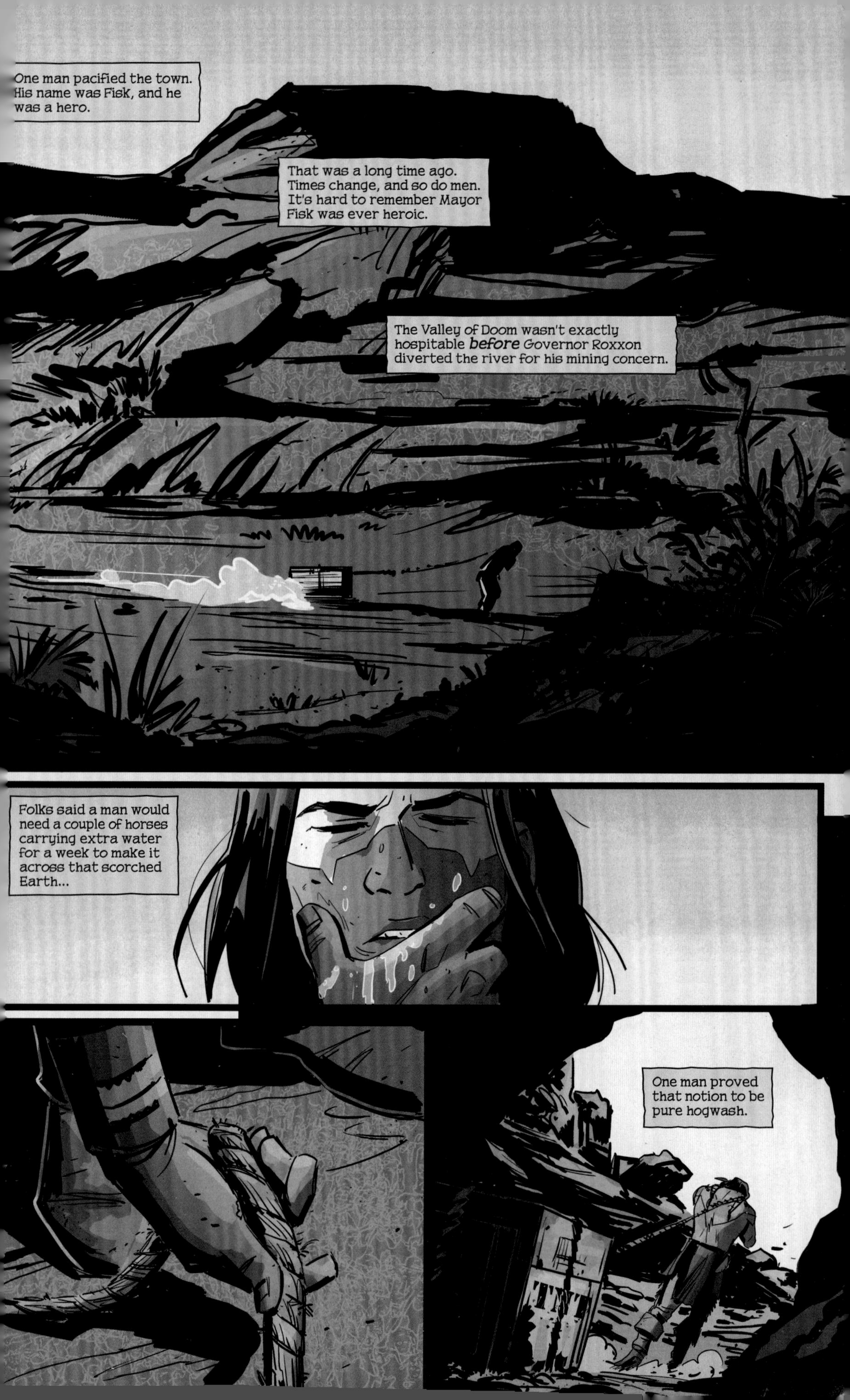
One man pacified the town. His name was Fisk, and he was a hero.
That was a long time ago. Times change, and so do men. It's hard to remember Mayor Fisk was ever heroic.
The Valley of Doom wasn't exactly hospitable *before* Governor Roxxon diverted the river for his mining concern.
Folks said a man would need a couple of horses carrying extra water for a week to make it across that scorched Earth...
One man proved that notion to be pure hogwash.

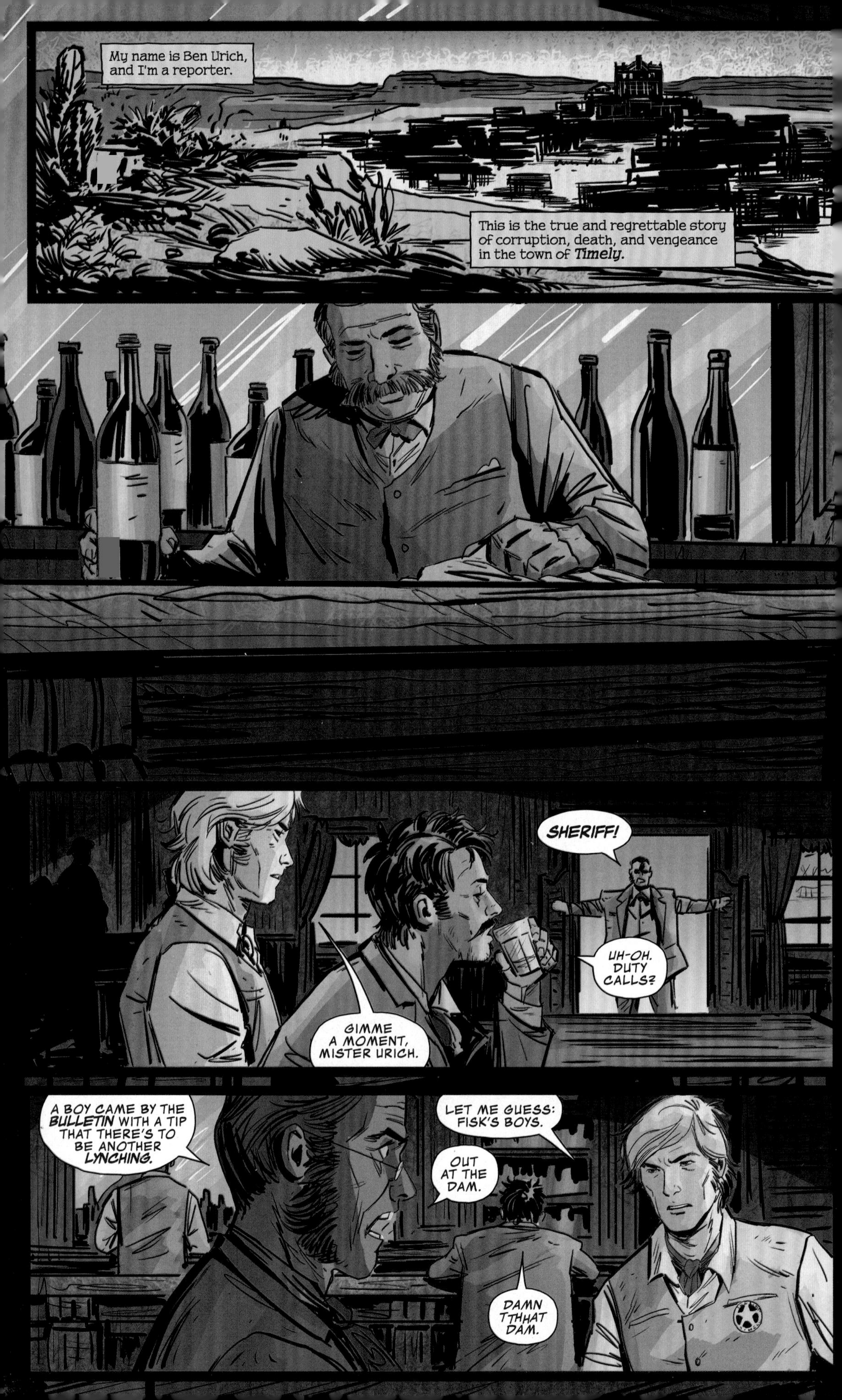
My name is Ben Urich, and I'm a reporter.
This is the true and regrettable story of corruption, death, and vengeance in the town of *Timely.*
SHERIFF!
UH-OH. DUTY CALLS?
GIMME A MOMENT, MISTER URICH.
A BOY CAME BY THE *BULLETIN* WITH A TIP THAT THERE'S TO BE ANOTHER *LYNCHING.*
LET ME GUESS: FISK'S BOYS.
OUT AT THE DAM.
DAMN TTHHAT DAM.

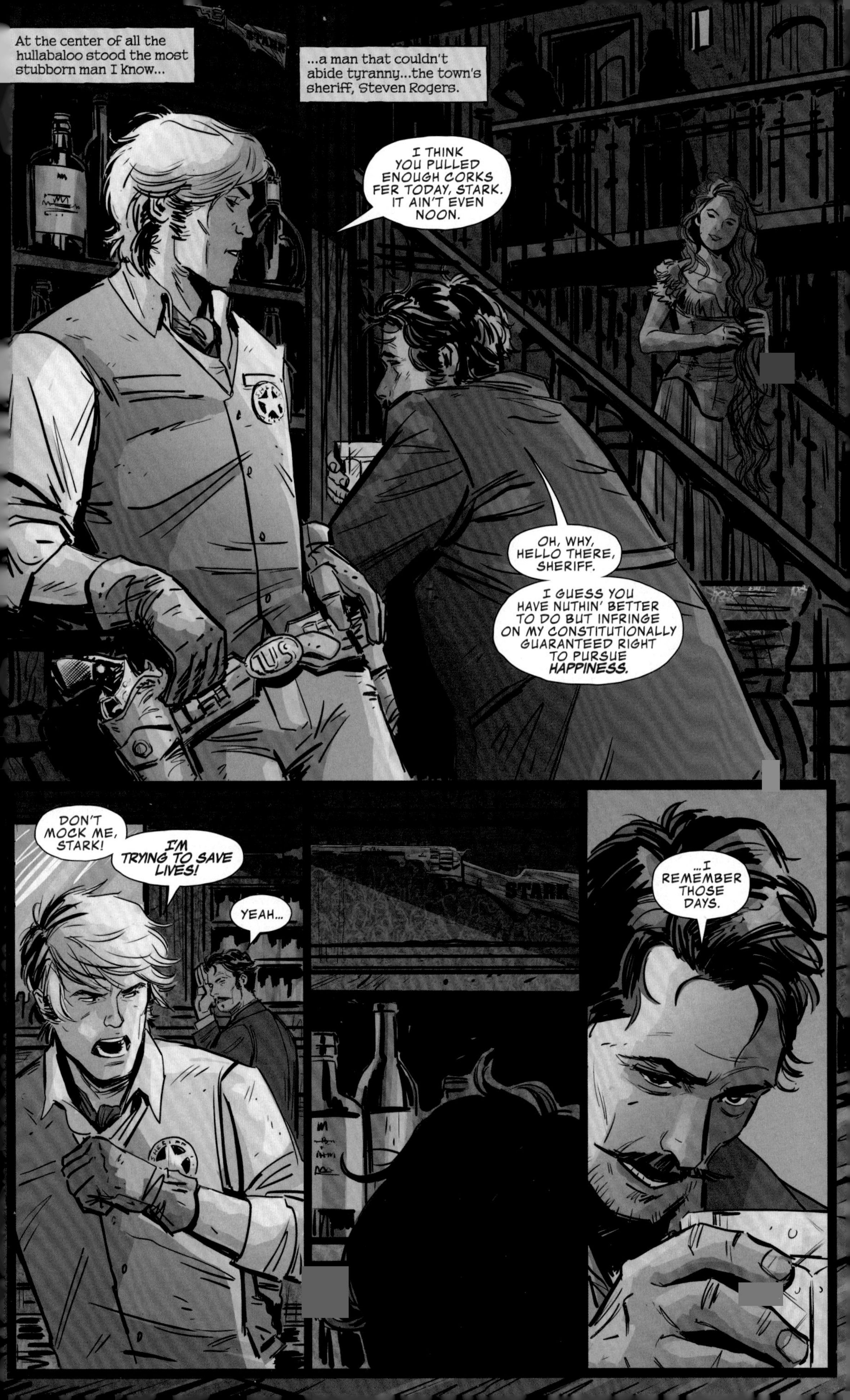
At the center of all the hullabaloo stood the most stubborn man I know...
...a man that couldn't abide tyranny...the town's sheriff, Steven Rogers.
I THINK YOU PULLED ENOUGH CORKS FER TODAY, STARK. IT AIN'T EVEN NOON.
OH, WHY, HELLO THERE, SHERIFF.
I GUESS YOU HAVE NUTHIN' BETTER TO DO BUT INFRINGE ON MY CONSTITUTIONALLY GUARANTEED RIGHT TO PURSUE ***HAPPINESS.***
DON'T MOCK ME, STARK!
I'M TRYING TO SAVE LIVES!
YEAH...
STARK
...I REMEMBER THOSE DAYS.

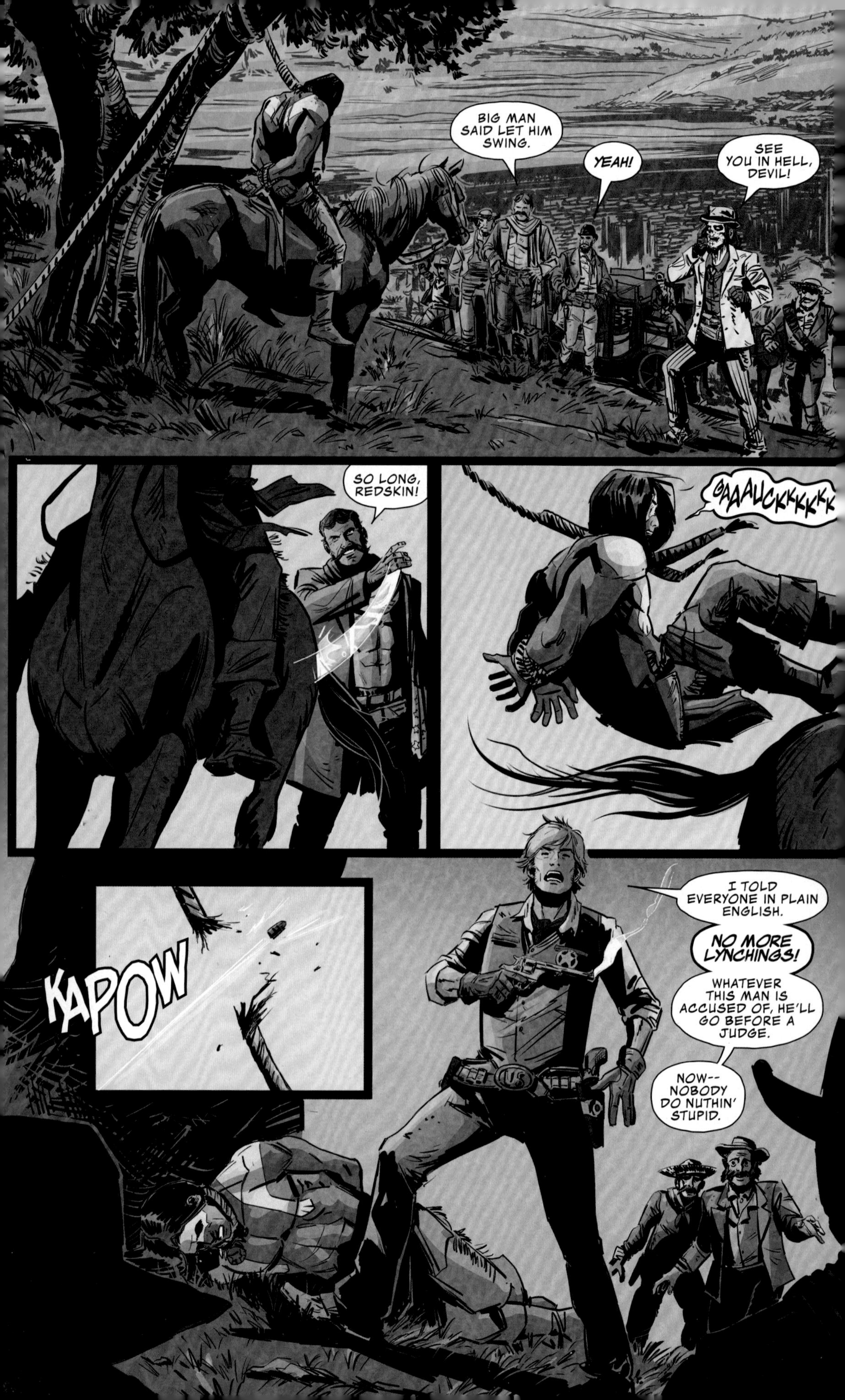

BIG MAN SAID LET HIM SWING.
YEAH!
SEE YOU IN HELL, DEVIL!
SO LONG, REDSKIN!
GAAAUCKKKKKK
KAPOW
I TOLD EVERYONE IN PLAIN ENGLISH.
NO MORE LYNCHINGS!
WHATEVER THIS MAN IS ACCUSED OF, HE'LL GO BEFORE A JUDGE.
NOW-- NOBODY DO NUTHIN' STUPID.

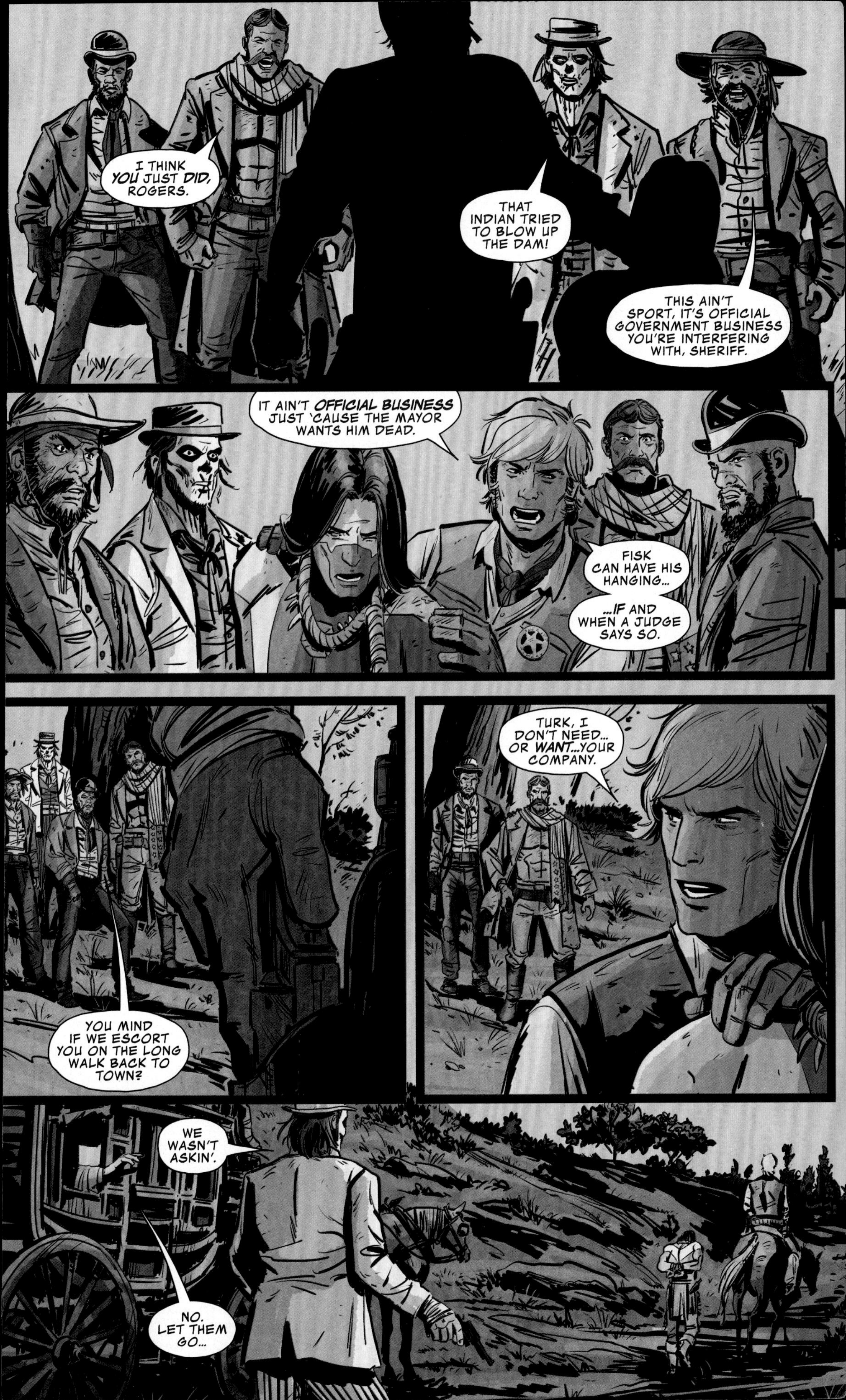
I THINK YOU JUST DID, ROGERS.
THAT INDIAN TRIED TO BLOW UP THE DAM!
THIS AIN'T SPORT, IT'S OFFICIAL GOVERNMENT BUSINESS YOU'RE INTERFERING WITH, SHERIFF.
IT AIN'T OFFICIAL BUSINESS JUST 'CAUSE THE MAYOR WANTS HIM DEAD.
FISK CAN HAVE HIS HANGING...
...IF AND WHEN A JUDGE SAYS SO.
YOU MIND IF WE ESCORT YOU ON THE LONG WALK BACK TO TOWN?
TURK, I DON'T NEED... OR WANT...YOUR COMPANY.
WE WASN'T ASKIN'.
NO. LET THEM GO...

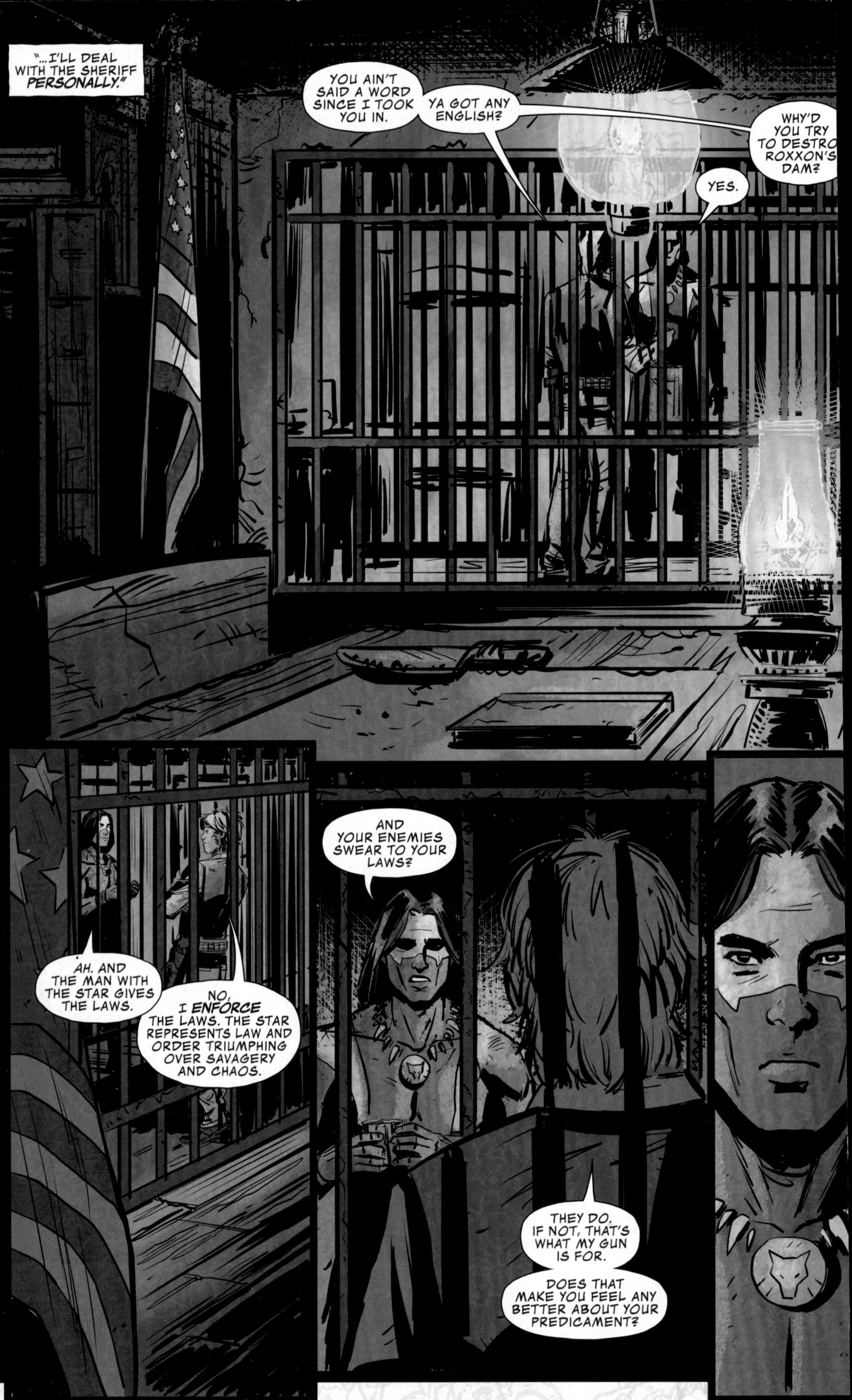
"...I'LL DEAL WITH THE SHERIFF *PERSONALLY*."
YOU AIN'T SAID A WORD SINCE I TOOK YOU IN.
YA GOT ANY ENGLISH?
WHY'D YOU TRY TO DESTRO ROXXON'S DAM?
YES.
AH. AND THE MAN WITH THE STAR GIVES THE LAWS.
NO, I *ENFORCE* THE LAWS. THE STAR REPRESENTS LAW AND ORDER TRIUMPHING OVER SAVAGERY AND CHAOS.
AND YOUR ENEMIES SWEAR TO YOUR LAWS?
THEY DO. IF NOT, THAT'S WHAT MY GUN IS FOR.
DOES THAT MAKE YOU FEEL ANY BETTER ABOUT YOUR PREDICAMENT?

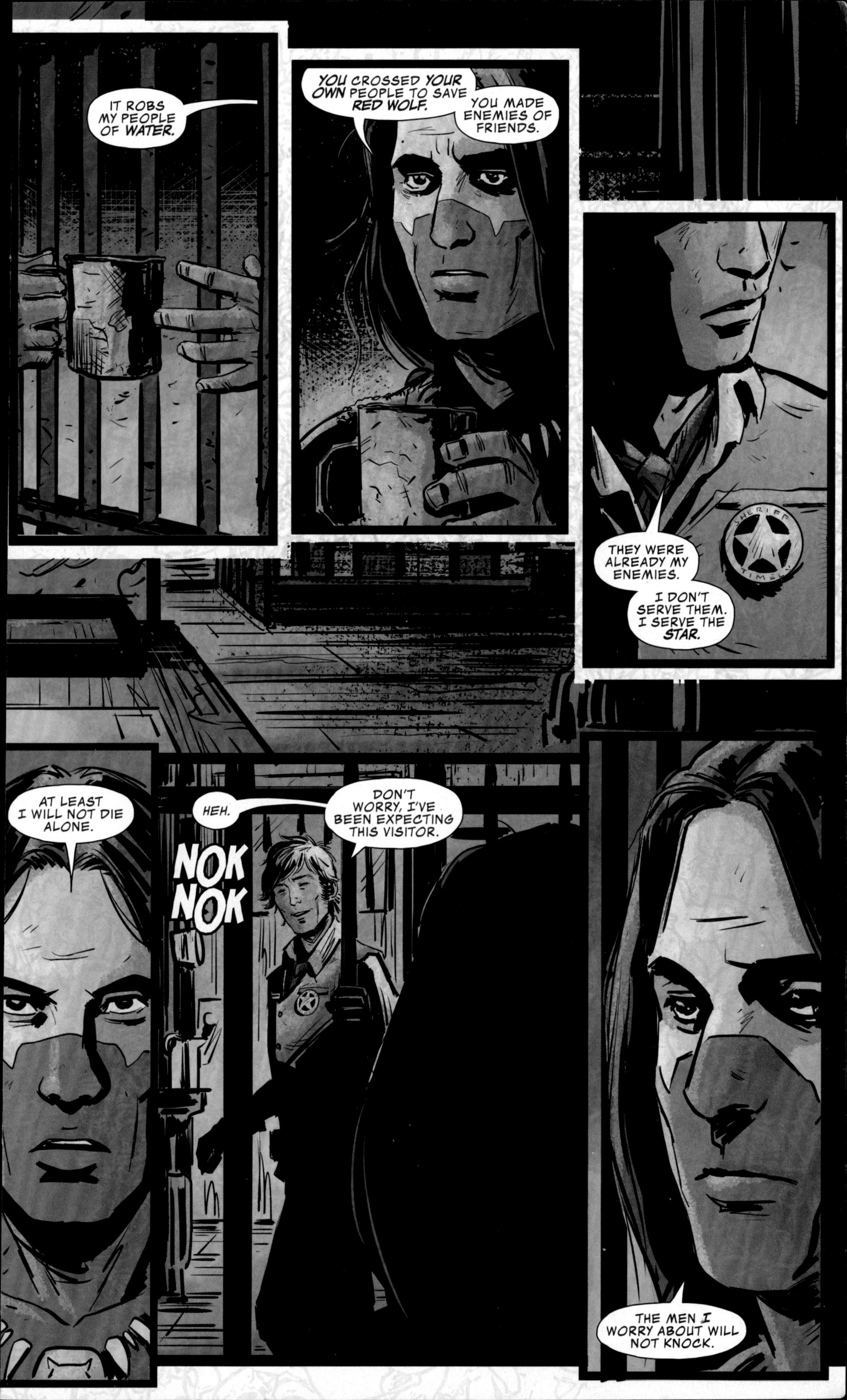
IT ROBS MY PEOPLE OF WATER.
YOU CROSSED YOUR OWN PEOPLE TO SAVE RED WOLF.
YOU MADE ENEMIES OF FRIENDS.
THEY WERE ALREADY MY ENEMIES.
I DON'T SERVE THEM. I SERVE THE STAR.
SHERIFF TIMELY
AT LEAST I WILL NOT DIE ALONE.
NOK NOK
HEH.
DON'T WORRY, I'VE BEEN EXPECTING THIS VISITOR.
THE MEN I WORRY ABOUT WILL NOT KNOCK.

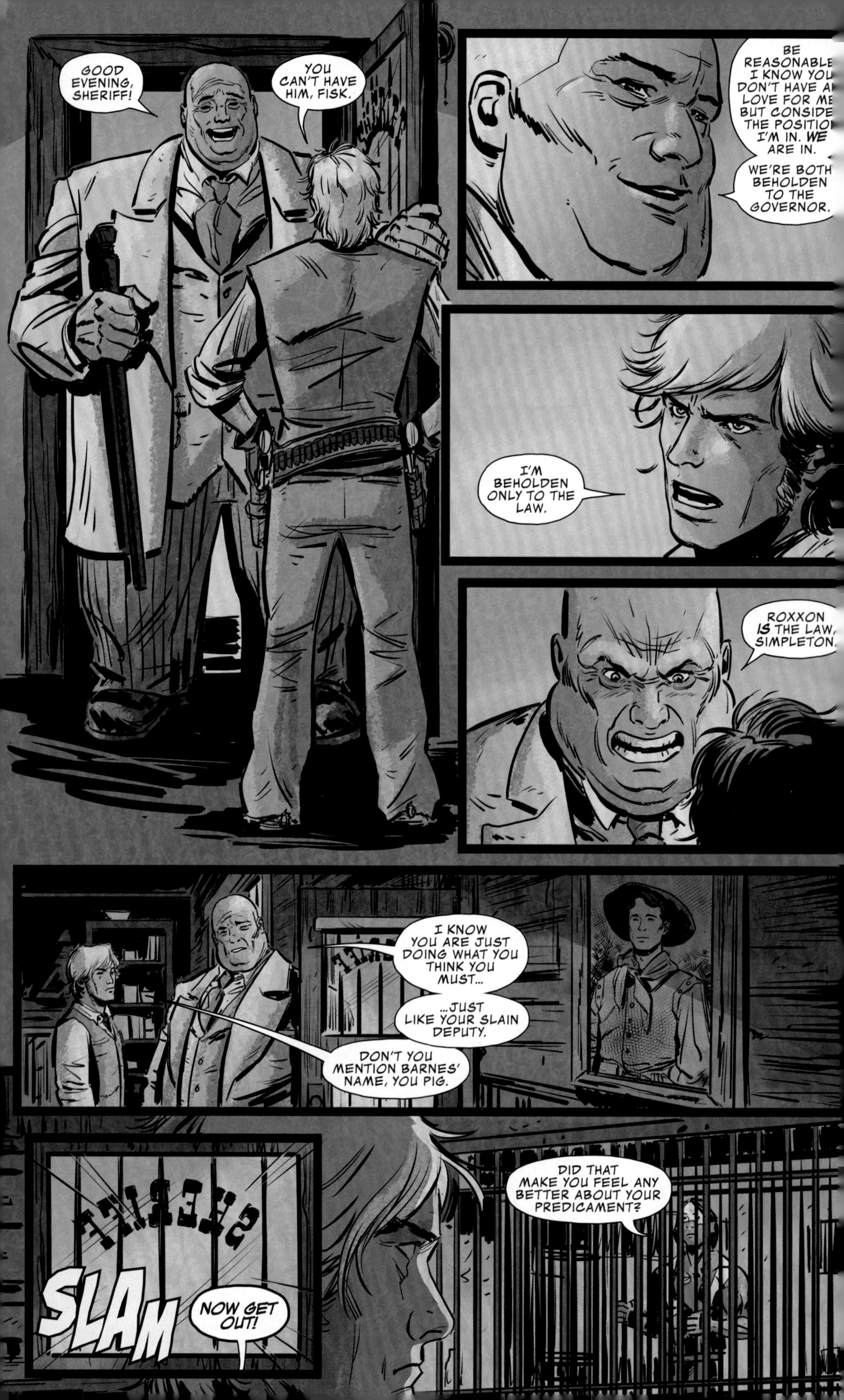
GOOD EVENING, SHERIFF!
YOU CAN'T HAVE HIM, FISK.
BE REASONABLE. I KNOW YOU DON'T HAVE ANY LOVE FOR ME, BUT CONSIDER THE POSITION I'M IN. WE ARE IN.
WE'RE BOTH BEHOLDEN TO THE GOVERNOR.
I'M BEHOLDEN ONLY TO THE LAW.
ROXXON IS THE LAW, SIMPLETON.
I KNOW YOU ARE JUST DOING WHAT YOU THINK YOU MUST...
...JUST LIKE YOUR SLAIN DEPUTY.
DON'T YOU MENTION BARNES' NAME, YOU PIG.
SLAM
NOW GET OUT!
DID THAT MAKE YOU FEEL ANY BETTER ABOUT YOUR PREDICAMENT?

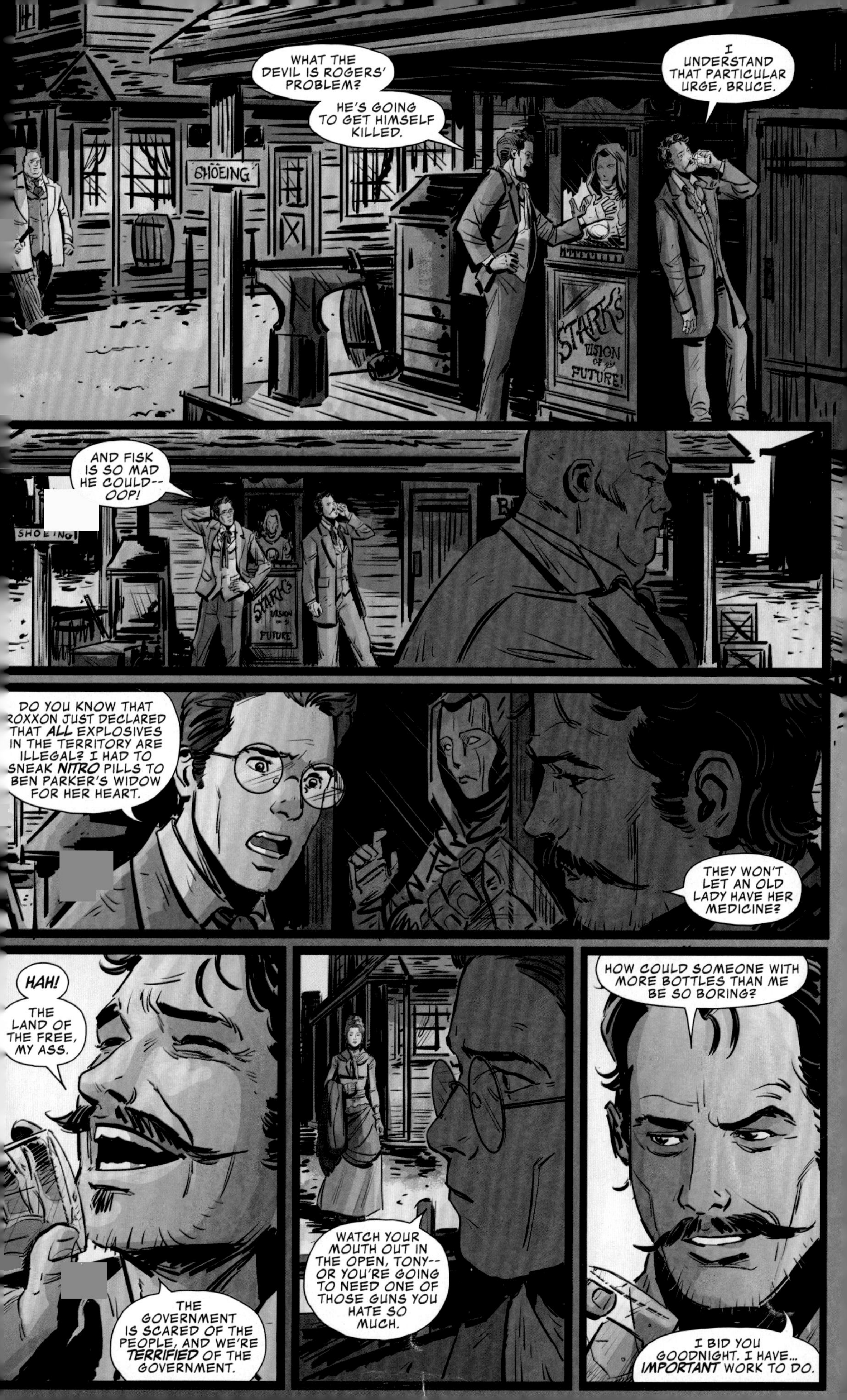

SHOEING
WHAT THE DEVIL IS ROGERS' PROBLEM?
HE'S GOING TO GET HIMSELF KILLED.
I UNDERSTAND THAT PARTICULAR URGE, BRUCE.
STARK'S VISION OF ye FUTURE!
AND FISK IS SO MAD HE COULD-- OOP!
SHOEING
STARK'S VISION OF ye FUTURE
DO YOU KNOW THAT ROXXON JUST DECLARED THAT ALL EXPLOSIVES IN THE TERRITORY ARE ILLEGAL? I HAD TO SNEAK NITRO PILLS TO BEN PARKER'S WIDOW FOR HER HEART.
THEY WON'T LET AN OLD LADY HAVE HER MEDICINE?
HAH!
THE LAND OF THE FREE, MY ASS.
THE GOVERNMENT IS SCARED OF THE PEOPLE, AND WE'RE TERRIFIED OF THE GOVERNMENT.
WATCH YOUR MOUTH OUT IN THE OPEN, TONY-- OR YOU'RE GOING TO NEED ONE OF THOSE GUNS YOU HATE SO MUCH.
HOW COULD SOMEONE WITH MORE BOTTLES THAN ME BE SO BORING?
I BID YOU GOODNIGHT. I HAVE... IMPORTANT WORK TO DO.

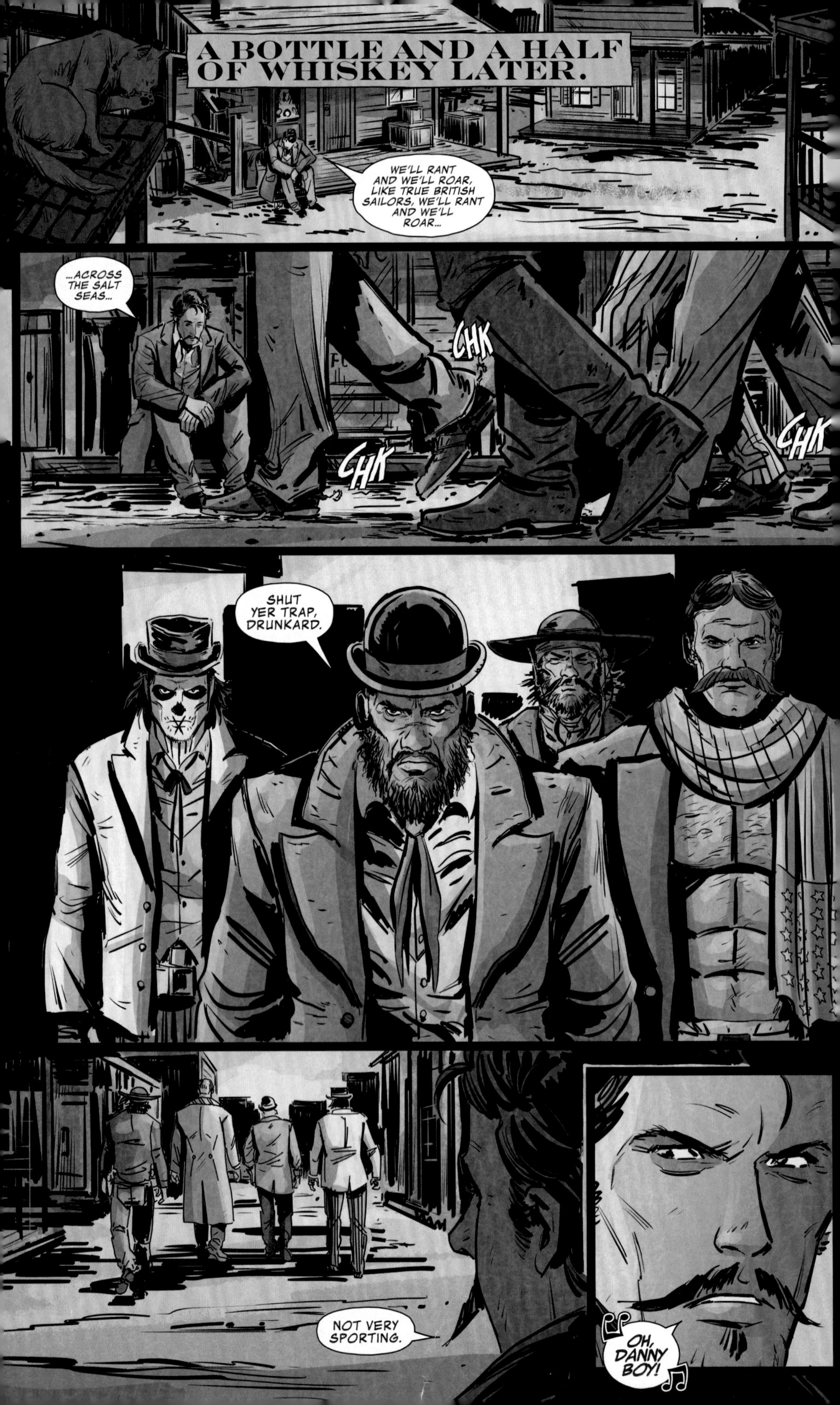
A BOTTLE AND A HALF OF WHISKEY LATER.
WE'LL RANT AND WE'LL ROAR, LIKE TRUE BRITISH SAILORS, WE'LL RANT AND WE'LL ROAR...
...ACROSS THE SALT SEAS...
CHK
CHK
CHK
SHUT YER TRAP, DRUNKARD.
NOT VERY SPORTING.
OH, DANNY BOY!

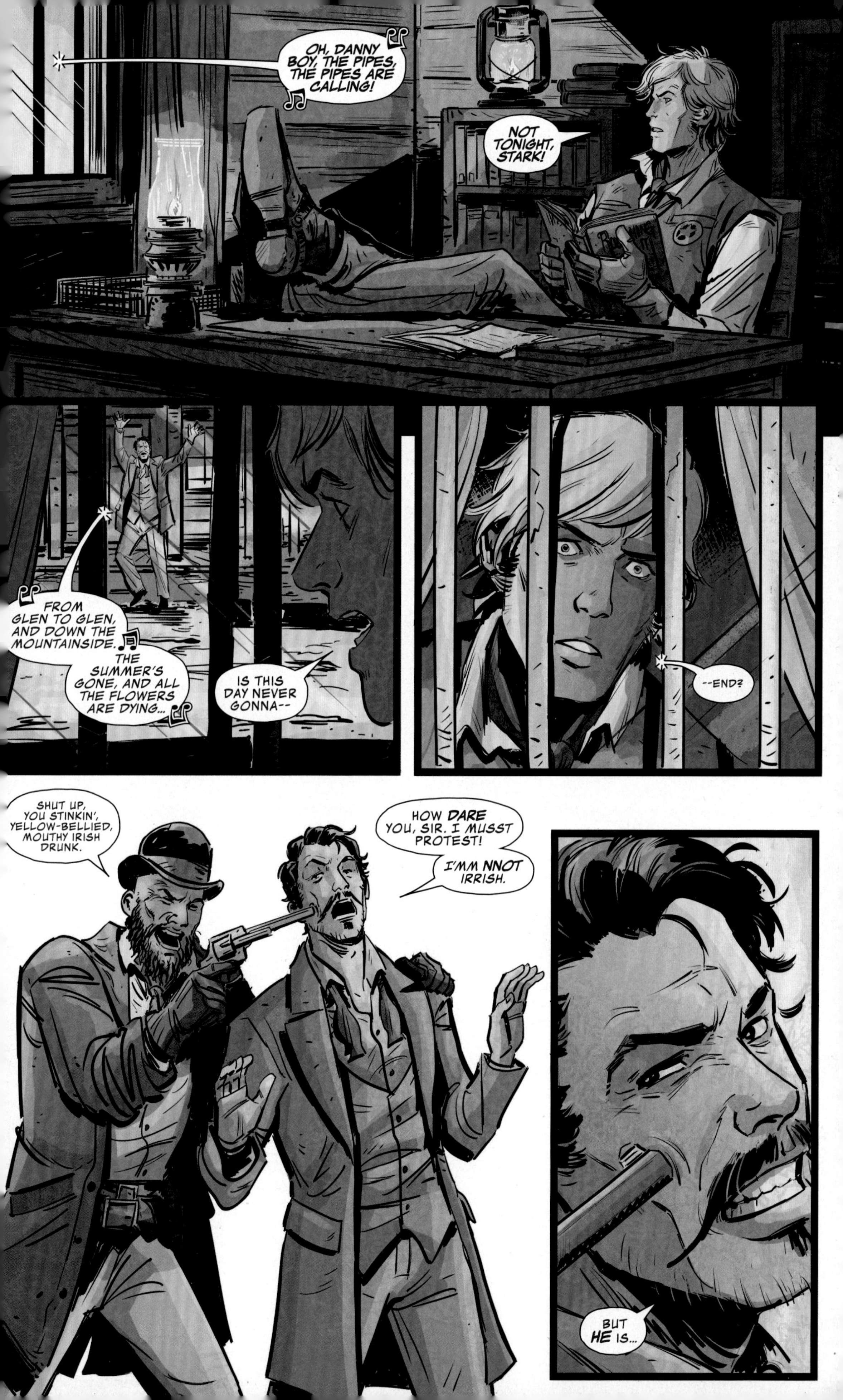
OH, DANNY BOY, THE PIPES, THE PIPES ARE CALLING!
NOT TONIGHT, STARK!
FROM GLEN TO GLEN, AND DOWN THE MOUNTAINSIDE.
THE SUMMER'S GONE, AND ALL THE FLOWERS ARE DYING...
IS THIS DAY NEVER GONNA--
--END?
SHUT UP, YOU STINKIN', YELLOW-BELLIED, MOUTHY IRISH DRUNK.
HOW DARE YOU, SIR. I MUSST PROTEST!
I'MM NNOT IRRISH.
BUT HE IS...

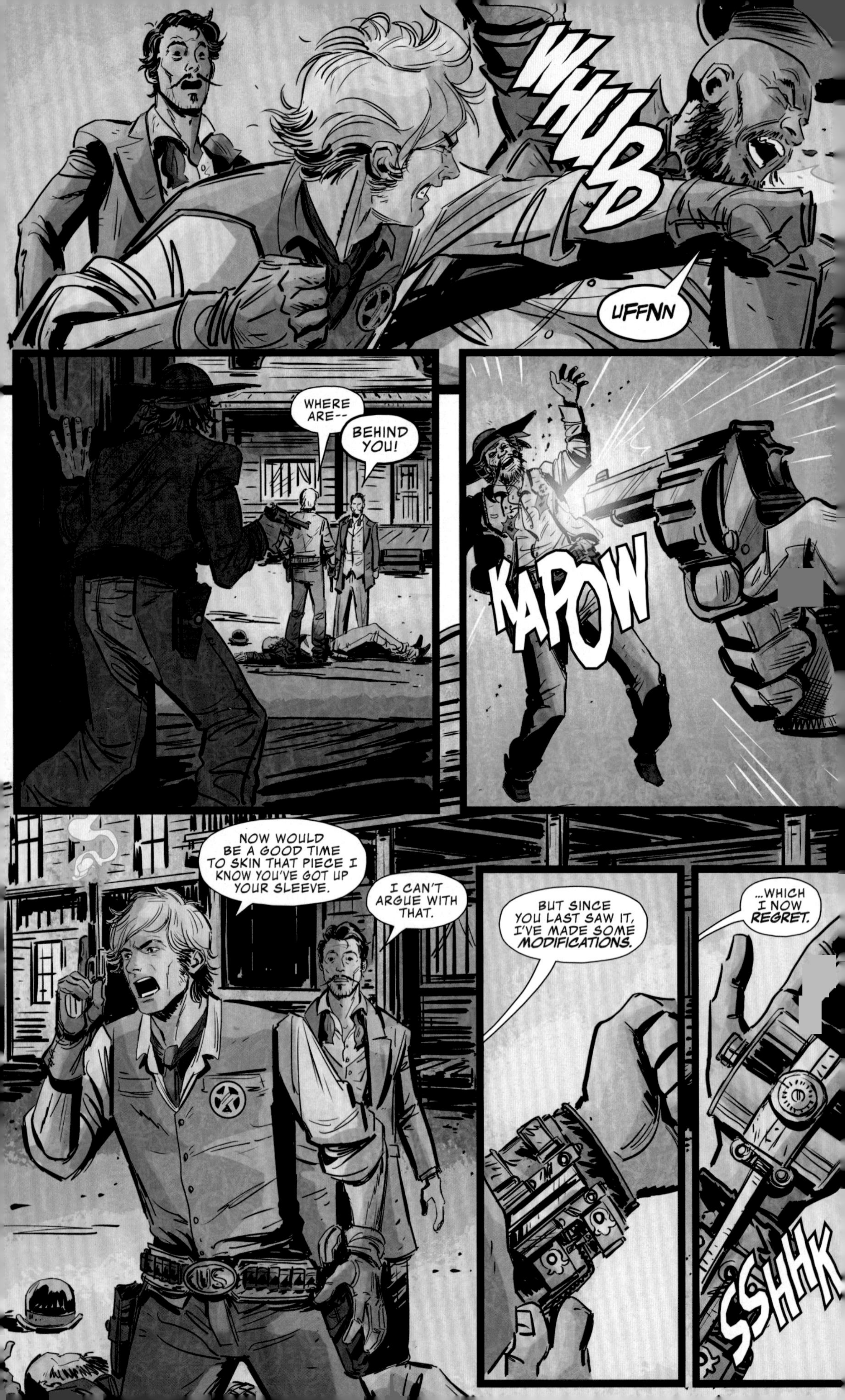
WHUB
UFFNN
WHERE ARE--
BEHIND YOU!
KAPOW
NOW WOULD BE A GOOD TIME TO SKIN THAT PIECE I KNOW YOU'VE GOT UP YOUR SLEEVE.
I CAN'T ARGUE WITH THAT.
BUT SINCE YOU LAST SAW IT, I'VE MADE SOME MODIFICATIONS.
...WHICH I NOW REGRET.
SSHHK

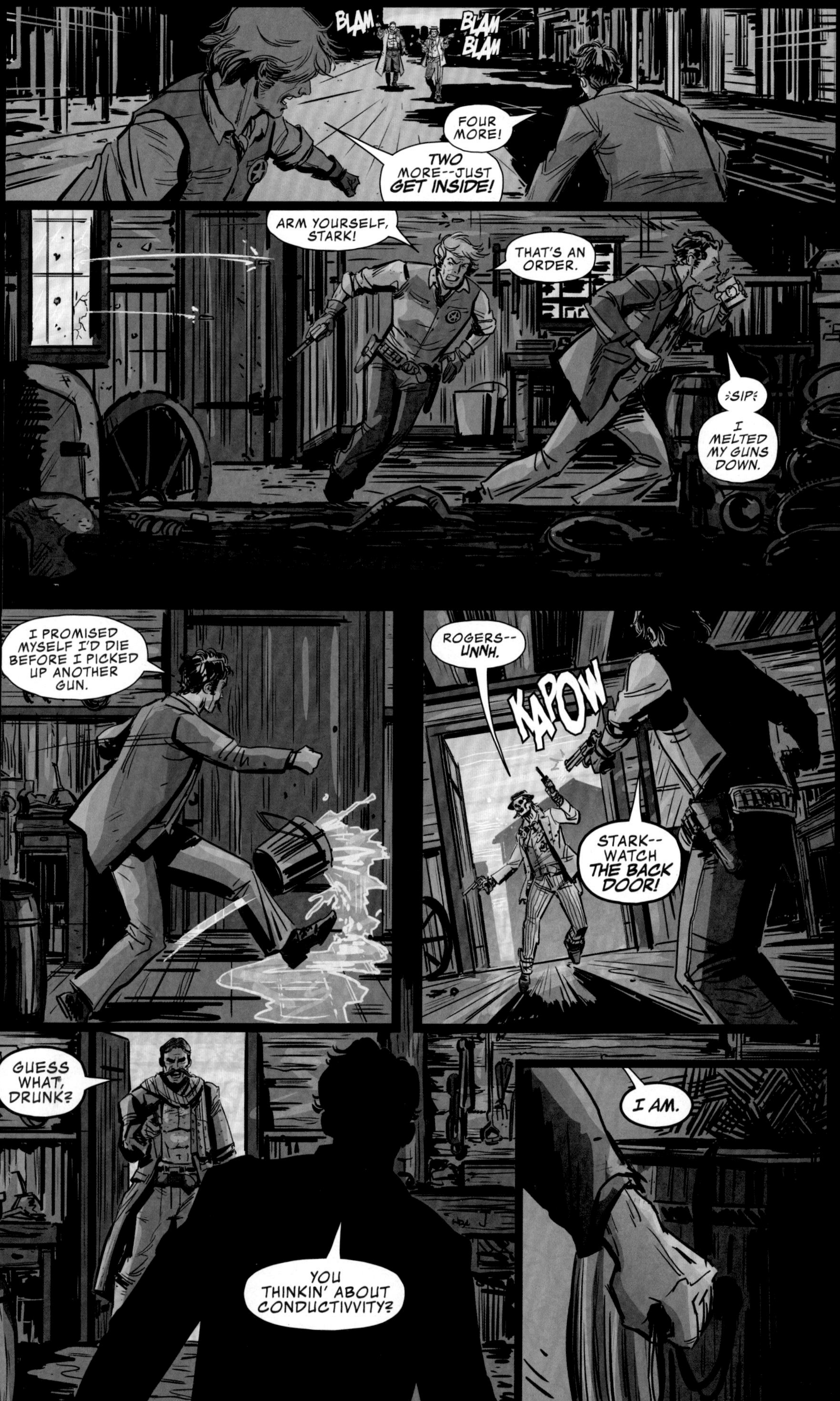
BLAM
BLAM BLAM
FOUR MORE!
TWO MORE--JUST GET INSIDE!
ARM YOURSELF, STARK!
THAT'S AN ORDER.
SIP
I MELTED MY GUNS DOWN.
I PROMISED MYSELF I'D DIE BEFORE I PICKED UP ANOTHER GUN.
ROGERS-- UNNH.
KAPOW
STARK-- WATCH THE BACK DOOR!
GUESS WHAT, DRUNK?
YOU THINKIN' ABOUT CONDUCTIVVITY?
I AM.

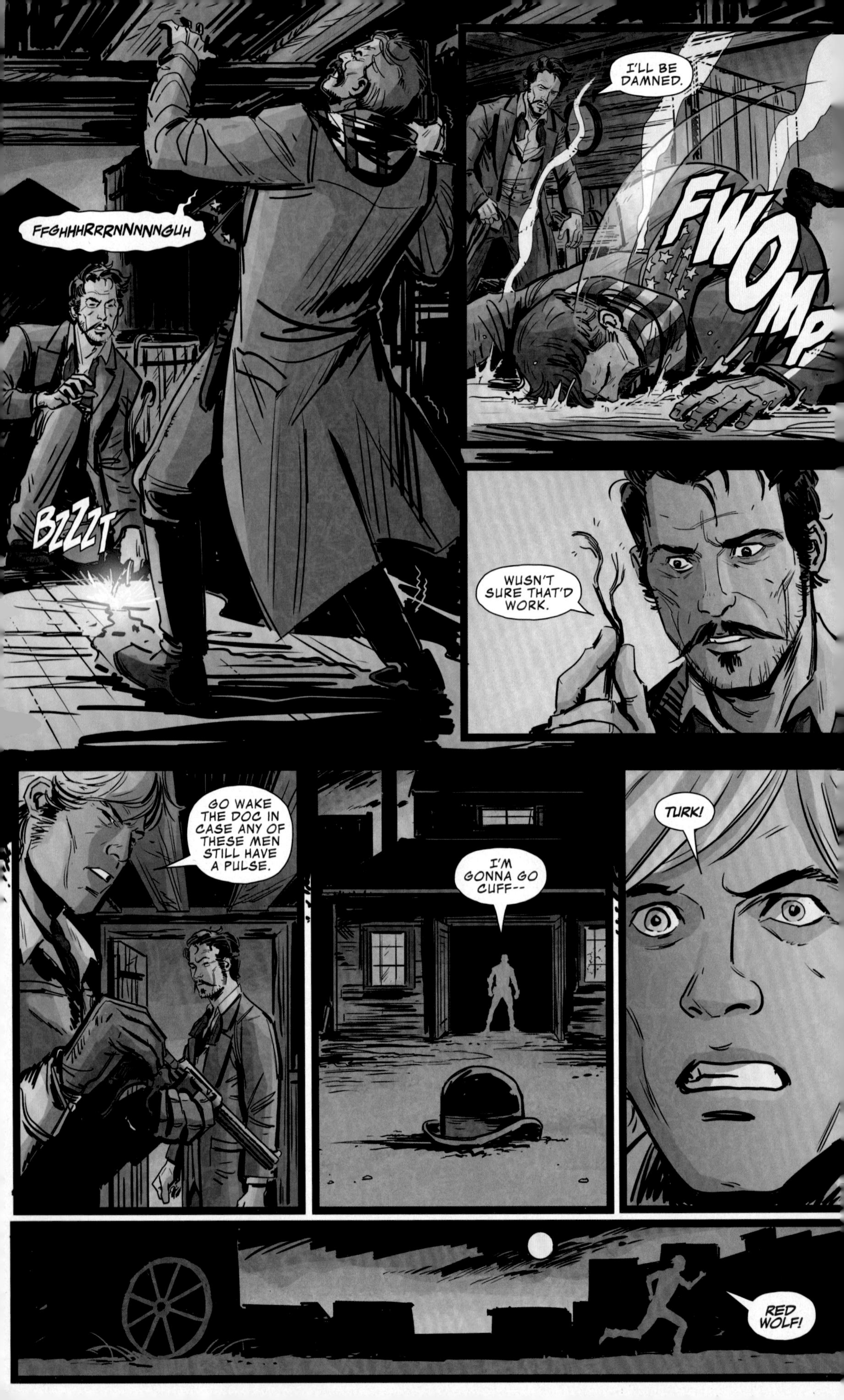
FFGHHHRRRNNNNNGUH
BZZZT
I'LL BE DAMNED.
FWOMP
WUSN'T SURE THAT'D WORK.
GO WAKE THE DOC IN CASE ANY OF THESE MEN STILL HAVE A PULSE.
I'M GONNA GO CUFF--
TURK!
RED WOLF!

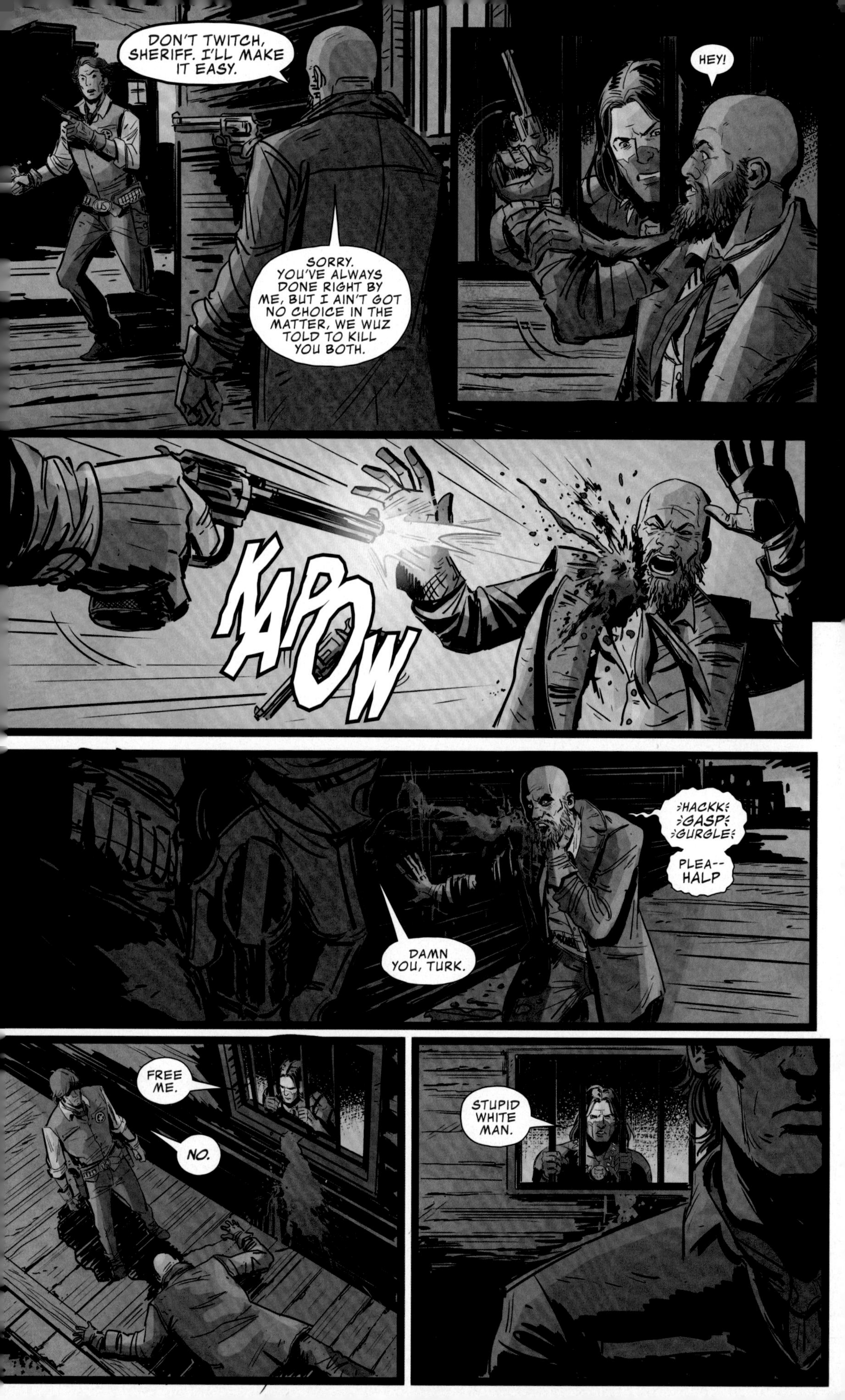
DON'T TWITCH, SHERIFF. I'LL MAKE IT EASY.
SORRY. YOU'VE ALWAYS DONE RIGHT BY ME, BUT I AIN'T GOT NO CHOICE IN THE MATTER, WE WUZ TOLD TO KILL YOU BOTH.
HEY!
KAPOW
HACKK
GASP
GURGLE
PLEA--HALP
DAMN YOU, TURK.
FREE ME.
NO.
STUPID WHITE MAN.

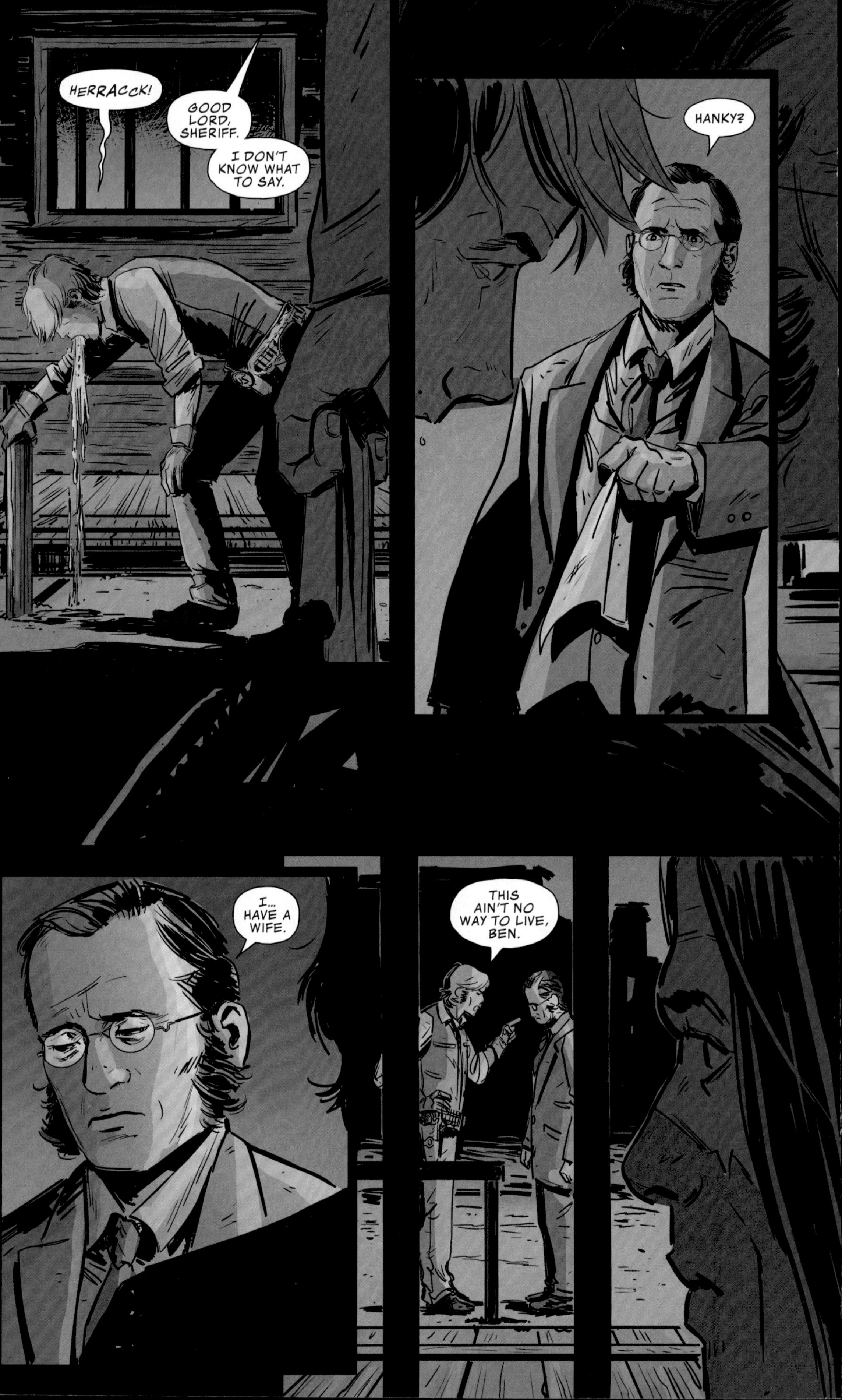
HERRACCK!
GOOD LORD, SHERIFF.
I DON'T KNOW WHAT TO SAY.
HANKY?
I... HAVE A WIFE.
THIS AIN'T NO WAY TO LIVE, BEN.

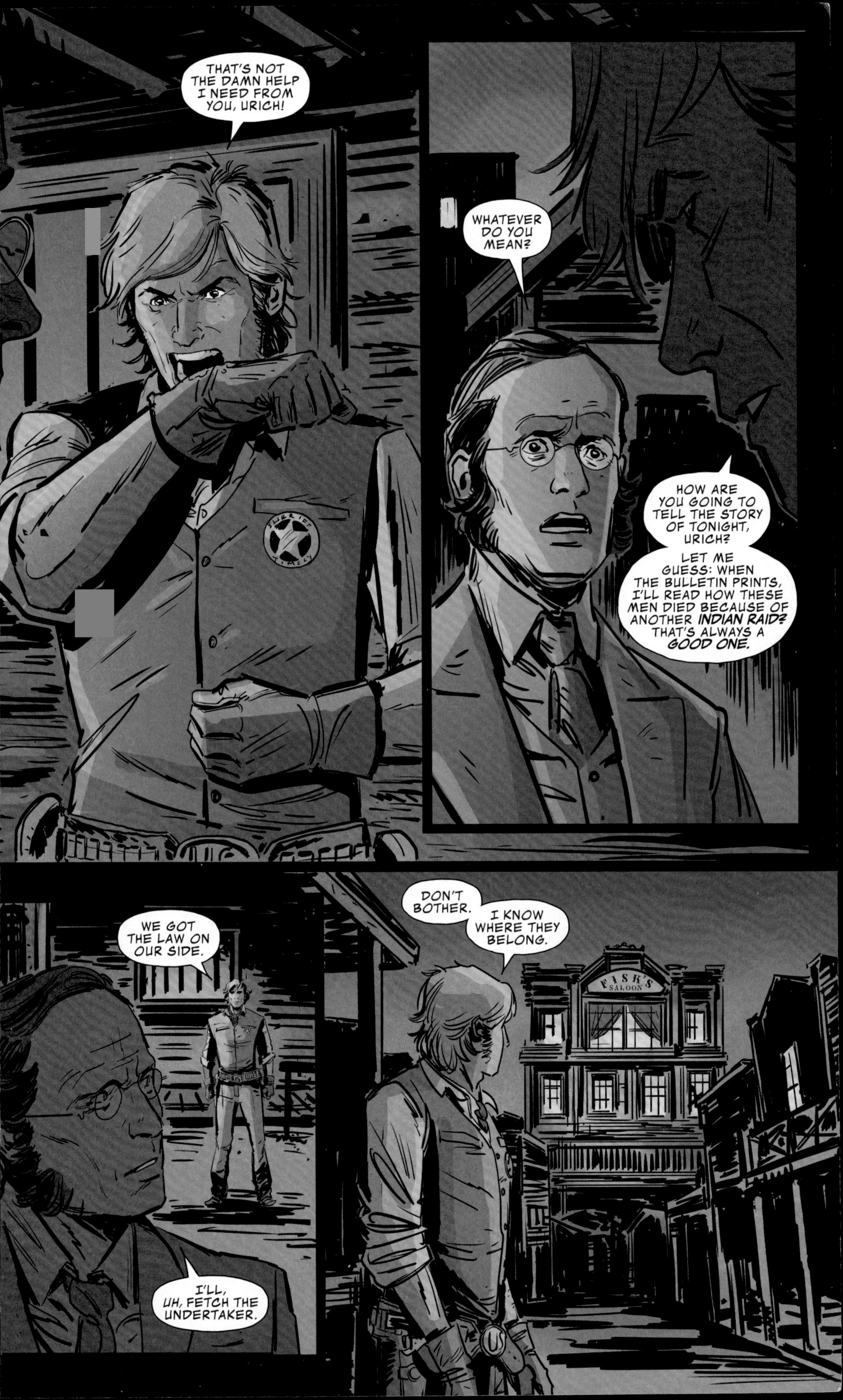

THAT'S NOT THE DAMN HELP I NEED FROM YOU, URICH!
WHATEVER DO YOU MEAN?
HOW ARE YOU GOING TO TELL THE STORY OF TONIGHT, URICH?
LET ME GUESS: WHEN THE BULLETIN PRINTS, I'LL READ HOW THESE MEN DIED BECAUSE OF ANOTHER INDIAN RAID? THAT'S ALWAYS A GOOD ONE.
WE GOT THE LAW ON OUR SIDE.
I'LL, UH, FETCH THE UNDERTAKER.
DON'T BOTHER.
I KNOW WHERE THEY BELONG.
FISK'S SALOON

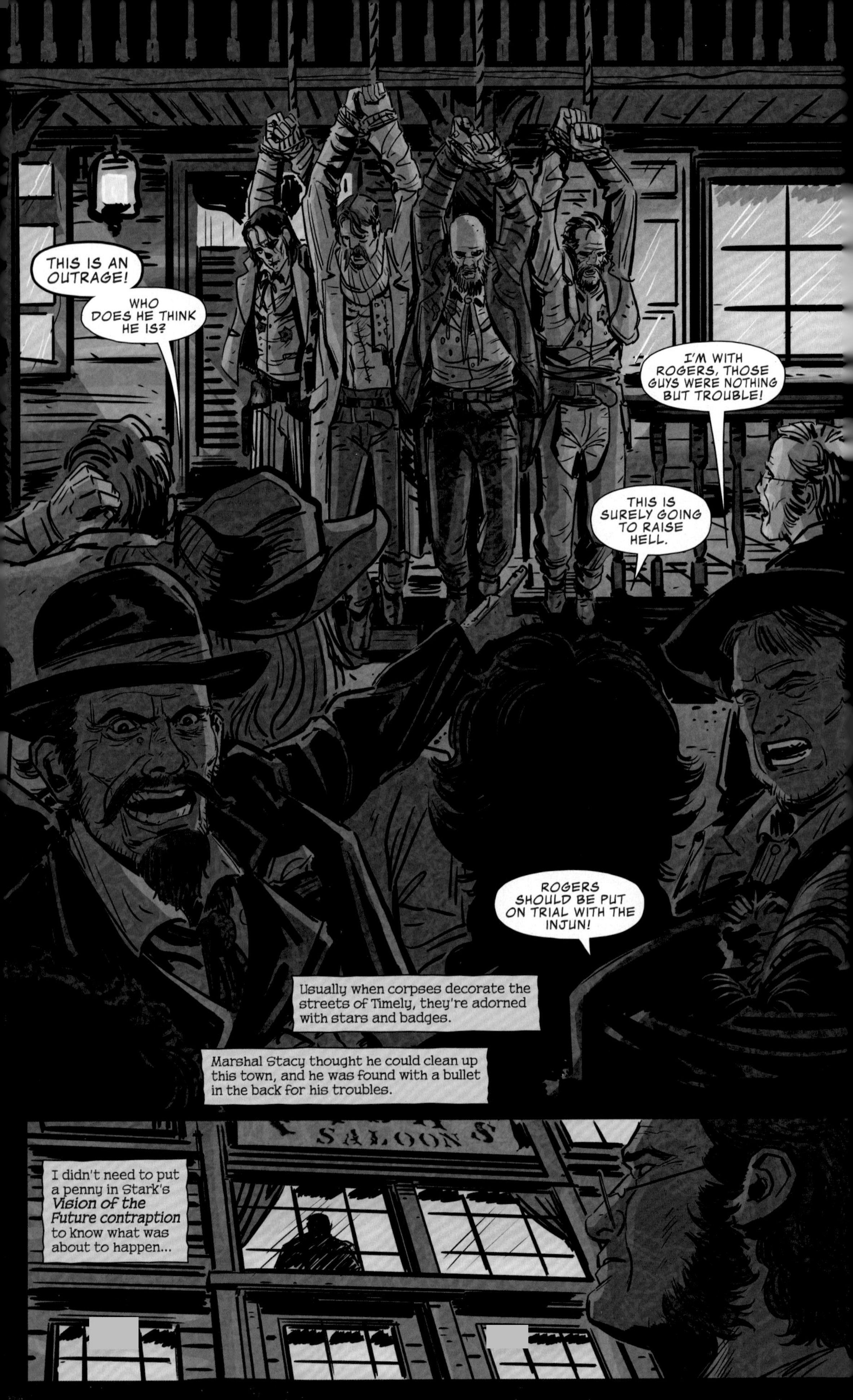

THIS IS AN OUTRAGE!
WHO DOES HE THINK HE IS?
I'M WITH ROGERS, THOSE GUYS WERE NOTHING BUT TROUBLE!
THIS IS SURELY GOING TO RAISE HELL.
ROGERS SHOULD BE PUT ON TRIAL WITH THE INJUN!
Usually when corpses decorate the streets of Timely, they're adorned with stars and badges.
Marshal Stacy thought he could clean up this town, and he was found with a bullet in the back for his troubles.
SALOON
I didn't need to put a penny in Stark's *Vision of the Future contraption* to know what was about to happen...

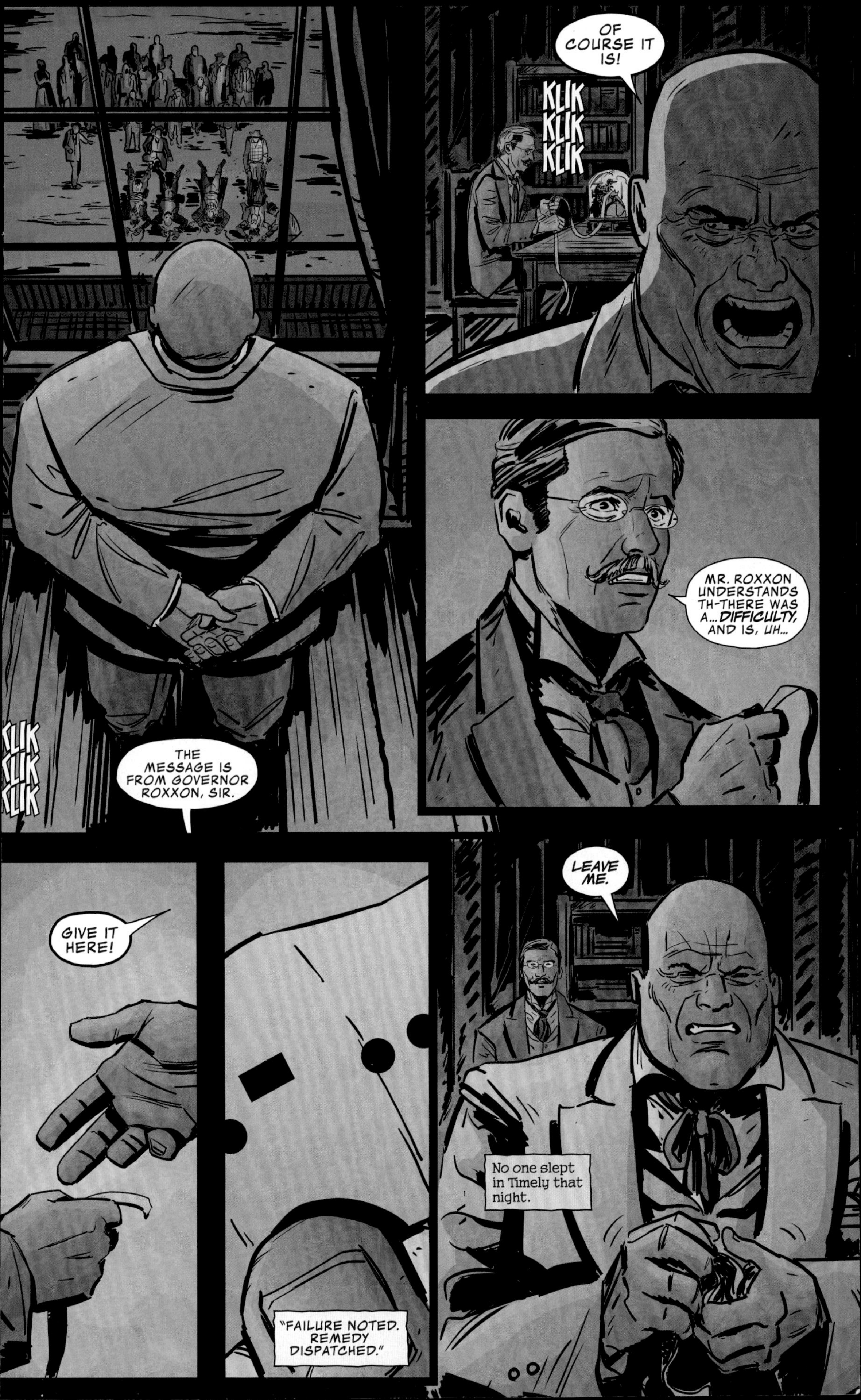

KLIK KLIK KLIK
THE MESSAGE IS FROM GOVERNOR ROXXON, SIR.
OF COURSE IT IS!
KLIK KLIK KLIK
MR. ROXXON UNDERSTANDS TH-THERE WAS A...DIFFICULTY, AND IS, UH...
GIVE IT HERE!
"FAILURE NOTED. REMEDY DISPATCHED."
LEAVE ME.
No one slept in Timely that night.

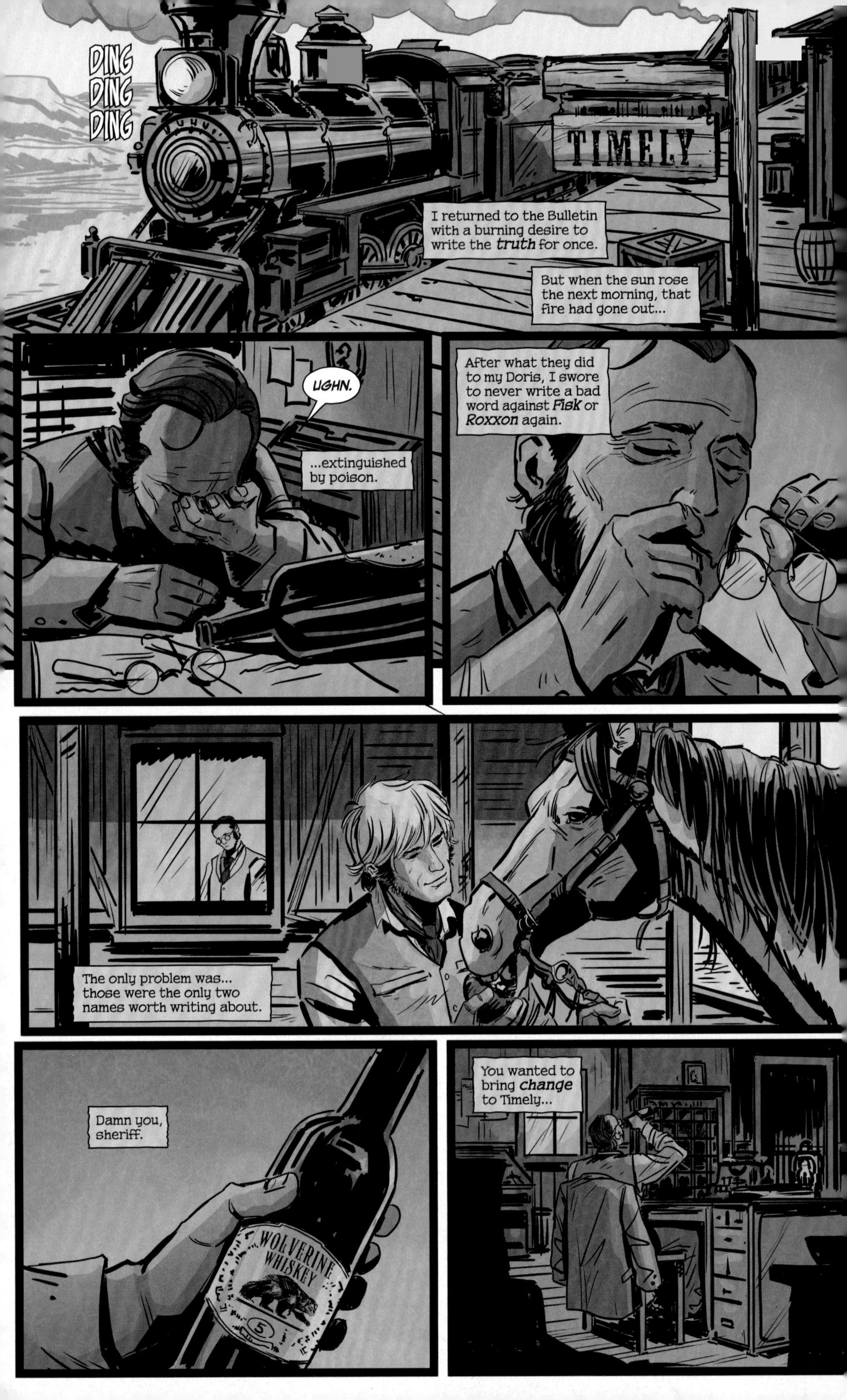
DING
DING
DING
TIMELY
I returned to the Bulletin with a burning desire to write the *truth* for once.
But when the sun rose the next morning, that fire had gone out...
UGHN.
...extinguished by poison.
After what they did to my Doris, I swore to never write a bad word against *Fisk* or *Roxxon* again.
The only problem was... those were the only two names worth writing about.
Damn you, sheriff.
WOLVERINE WHISKEY
5
You wanted to bring *change* to Timely...

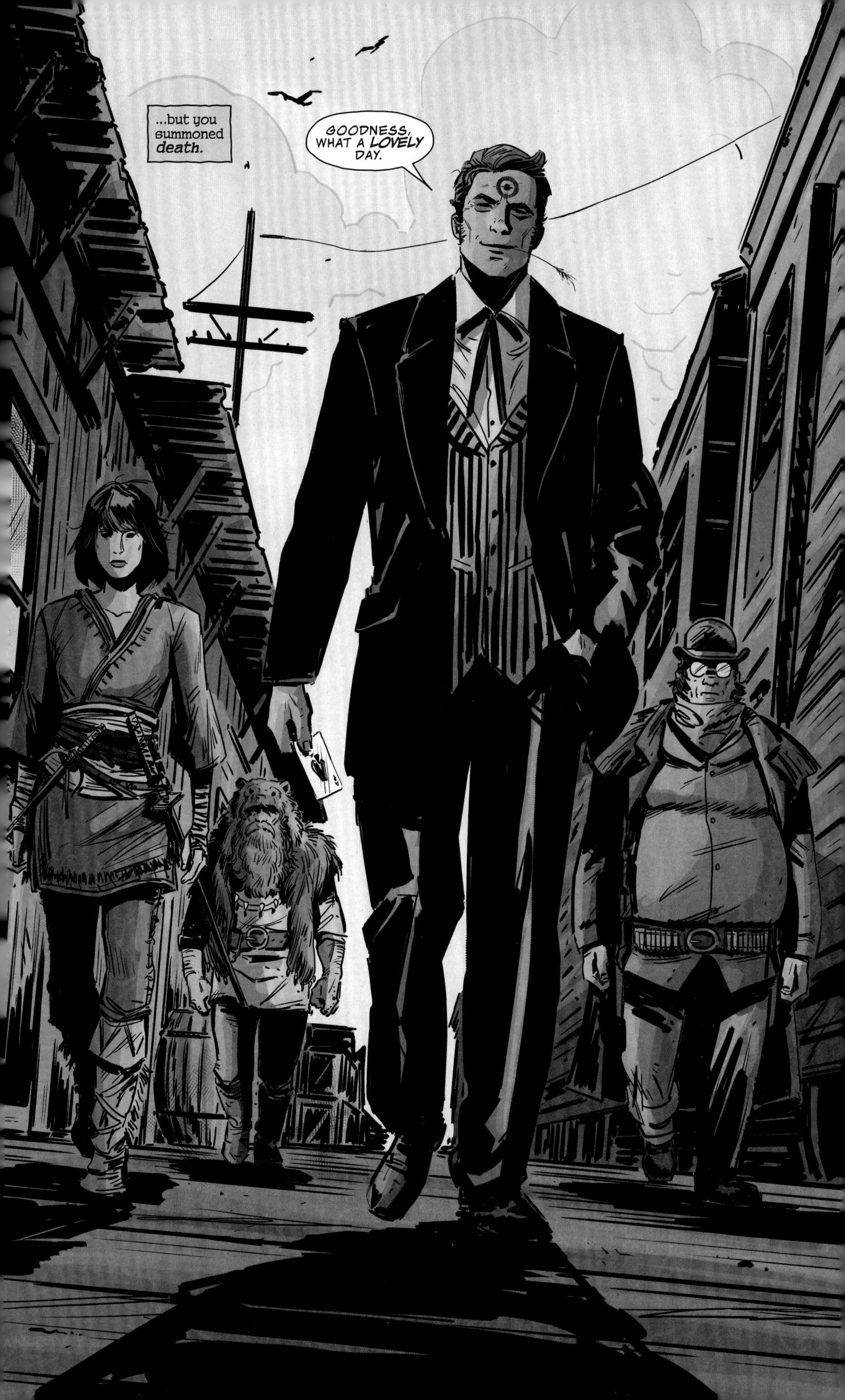
...but you summoned *death.*
GOODNESS, WHAT A **LOVELY** DAY.

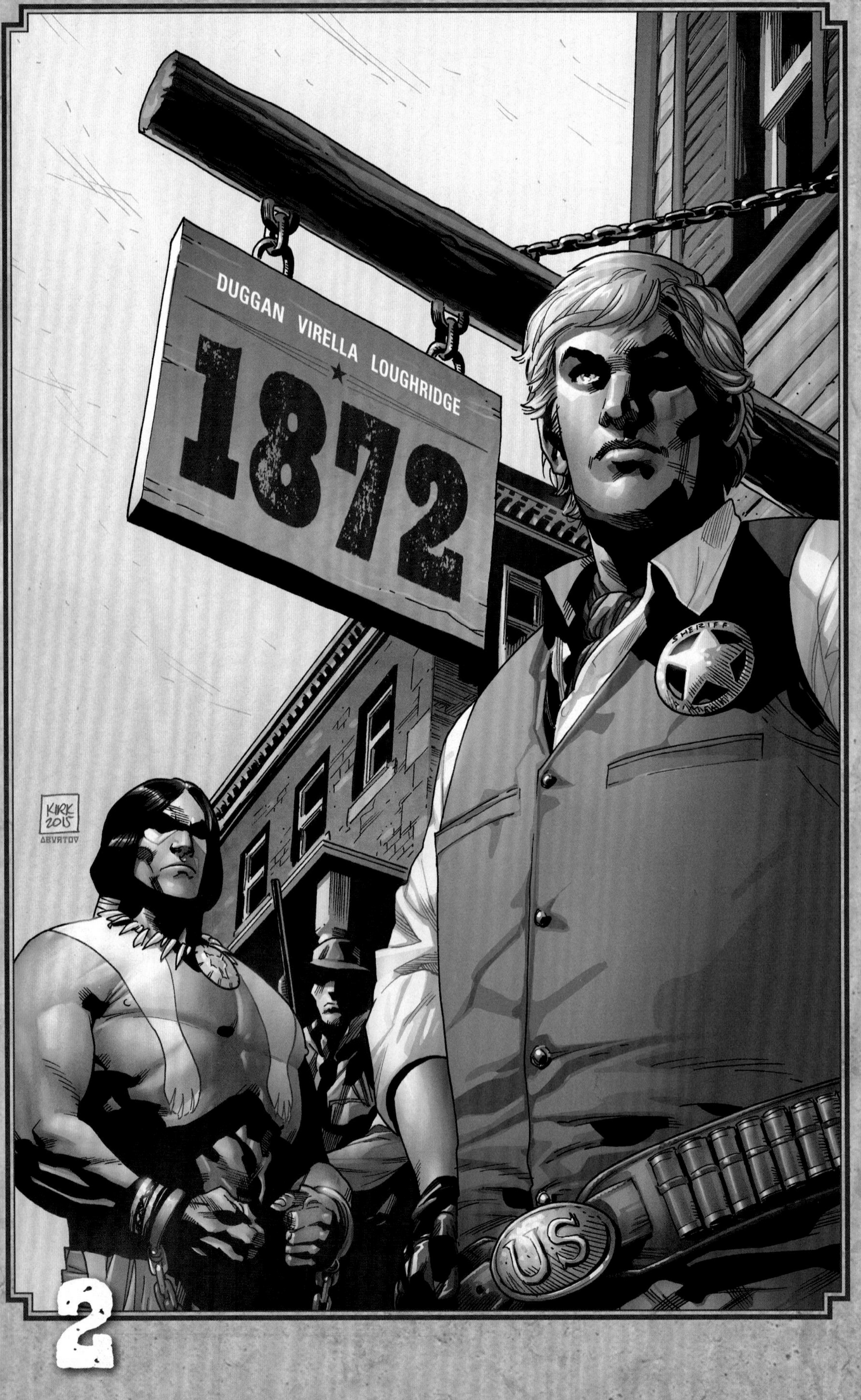
DUGGAN VIRELLA LOUGHRIDGE
1872
SHERIFF
US
KIRK 2015
2

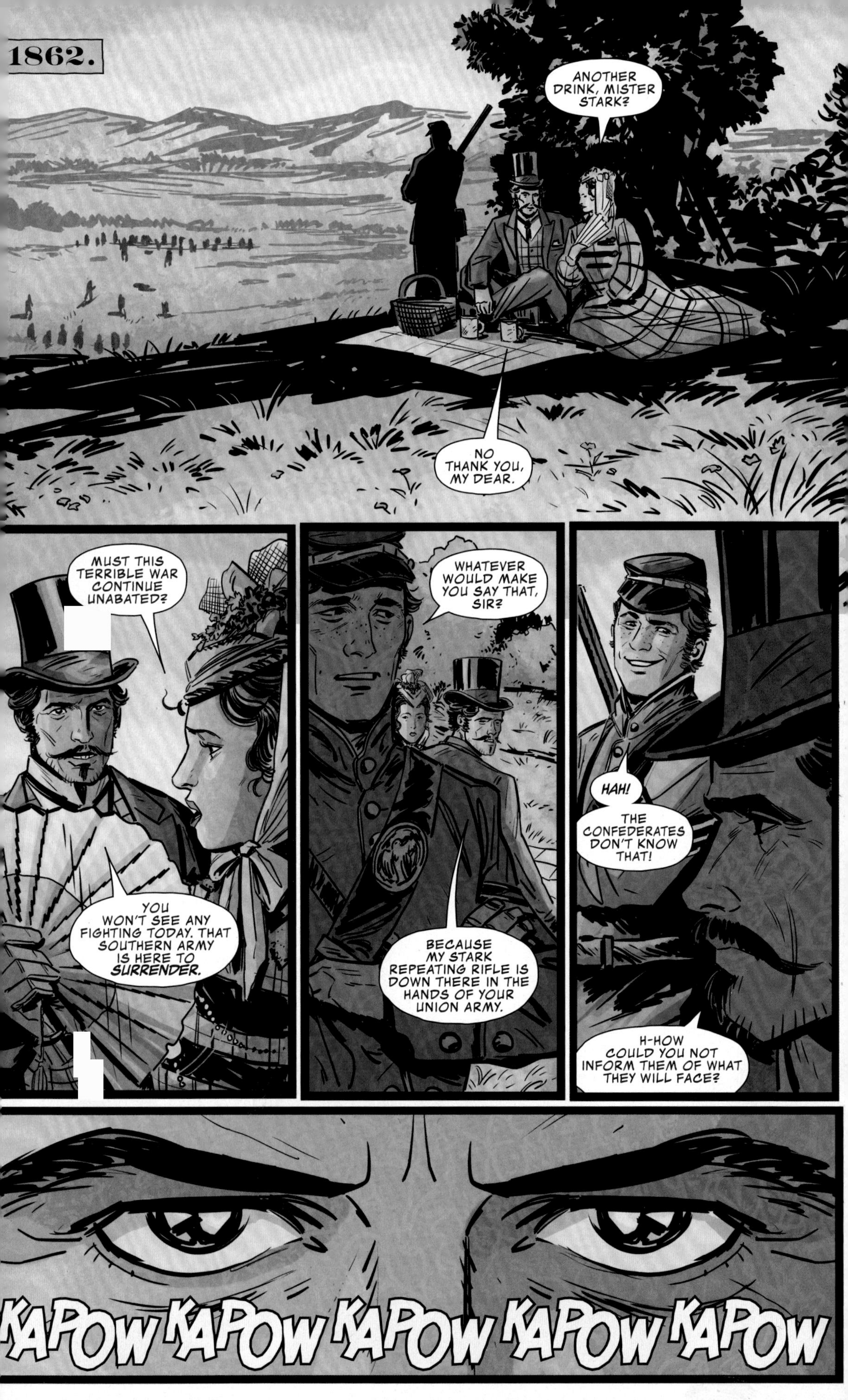
1862.
ANOTHER DRINK, MISTER STARK?
NO THANK YOU, MY DEAR.
MUST THIS TERRIBLE WAR CONTINUE UNABATED?
YOU WON'T SEE ANY FIGHTING TODAY. THAT SOUTHERN ARMY IS HERE TO SURRENDER.
WHATEVER WOULD MAKE YOU SAY THAT, SIR?
BECAUSE MY STARK REPEATING RIFLE IS DOWN THERE IN THE HANDS OF YOUR UNION ARMY.
HAH!
THE CONFEDERATES DON'T KNOW THAT!
H-HOW COULD YOU NOT INFORM THEM OF WHAT THEY WILL FACE?
KAPOW KAPOW KAPOW KAPOW KAPOW

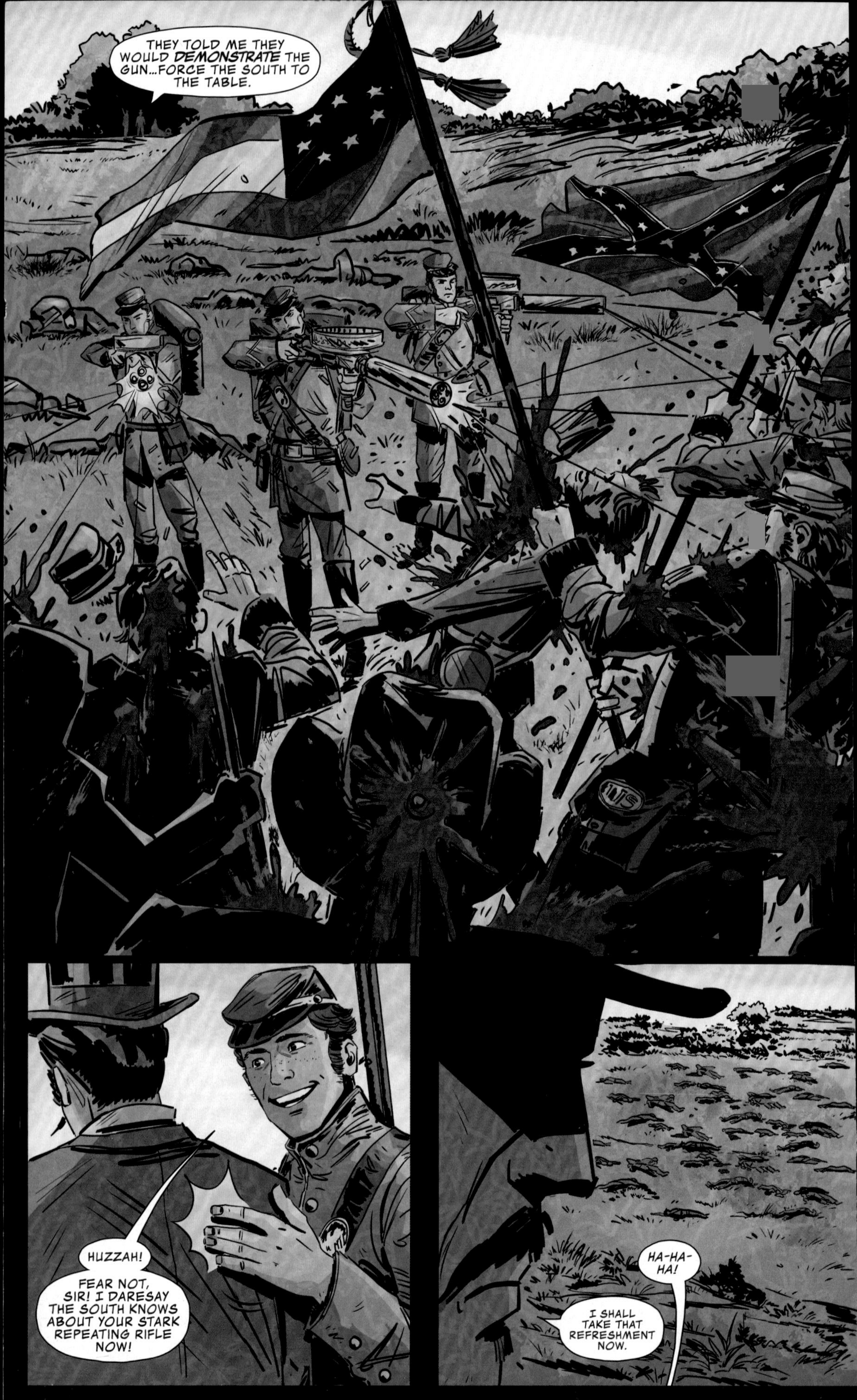
THEY TOLD ME THEY WOULD DEMONSTRATE THE GUN...FORCE THE SOUTH TO THE TABLE.
HUZZAH!
FEAR NOT, SIR! I DARESAY THE SOUTH KNOWS ABOUT YOUR STARK REPEATING RIFLE NOW!
HA-HA-HA!
I SHALL TAKE THAT REFRESHMENT NOW.

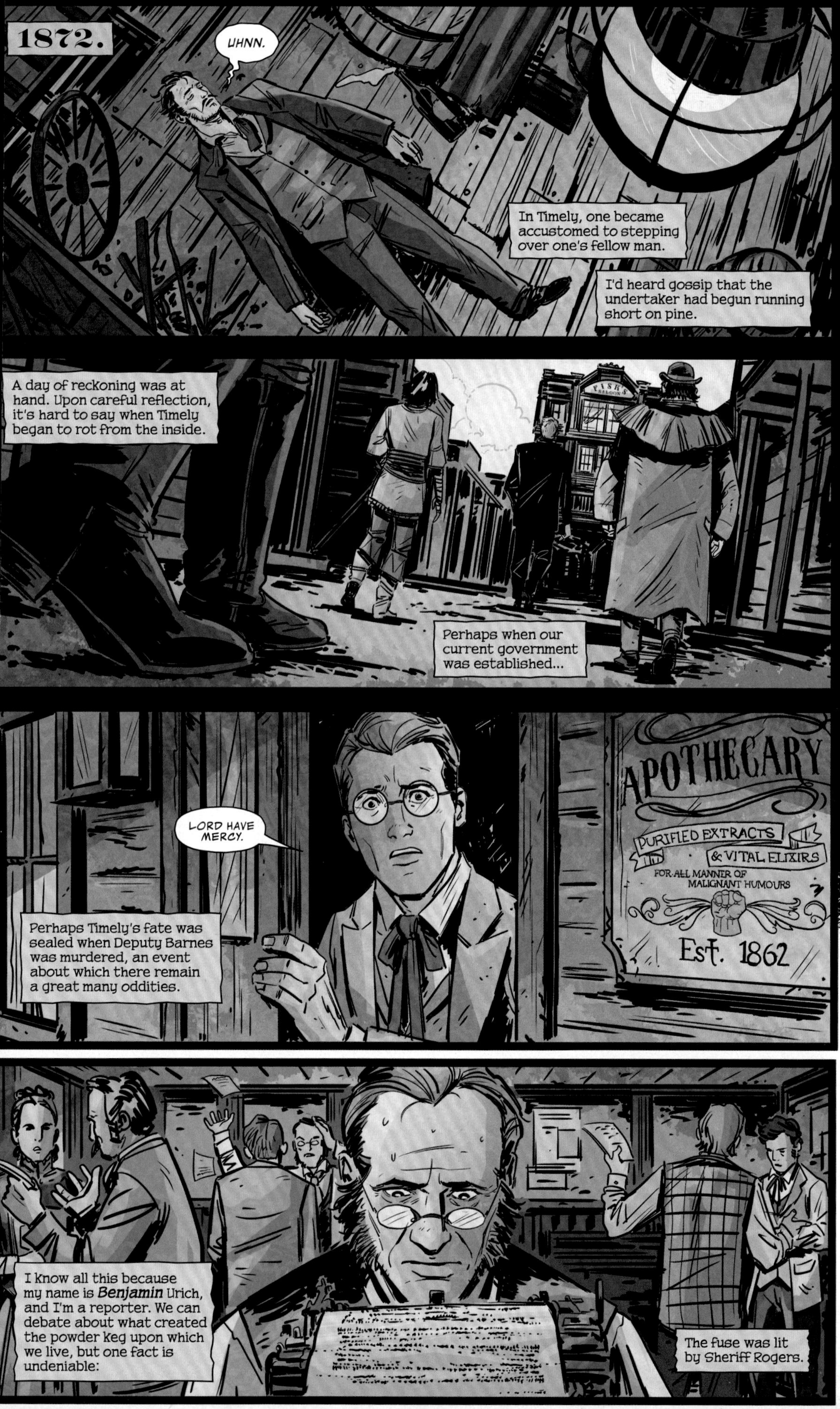
1872.
UHNN.
In Timely, one became accustomed to stepping over one's fellow man.
I'd heard gossip that the undertaker had begun running short on pine.
A day of reckoning was at hand. Upon careful reflection, it's hard to say when Timely began to rot from the inside.
FISK'S SALOON
Perhaps when our current government was established...
APOTHECARY
PURIFIED EXTRACTS
& VITAL ELIXIRS
FOR ALL MANNER OF MALIGNANT HUMOURS
Est. 1862
LORD HAVE MERCY.
Perhaps Timely's fate was sealed when Deputy Barnes was murdered, an event about which there remain a great many oddities.
I know all this because my name is *Benjamin* Urich, and I'm a reporter. We can debate about what created the powder keg upon which we live, but one fact is undeniable:
The fuse was lit by Sheriff Rogers.

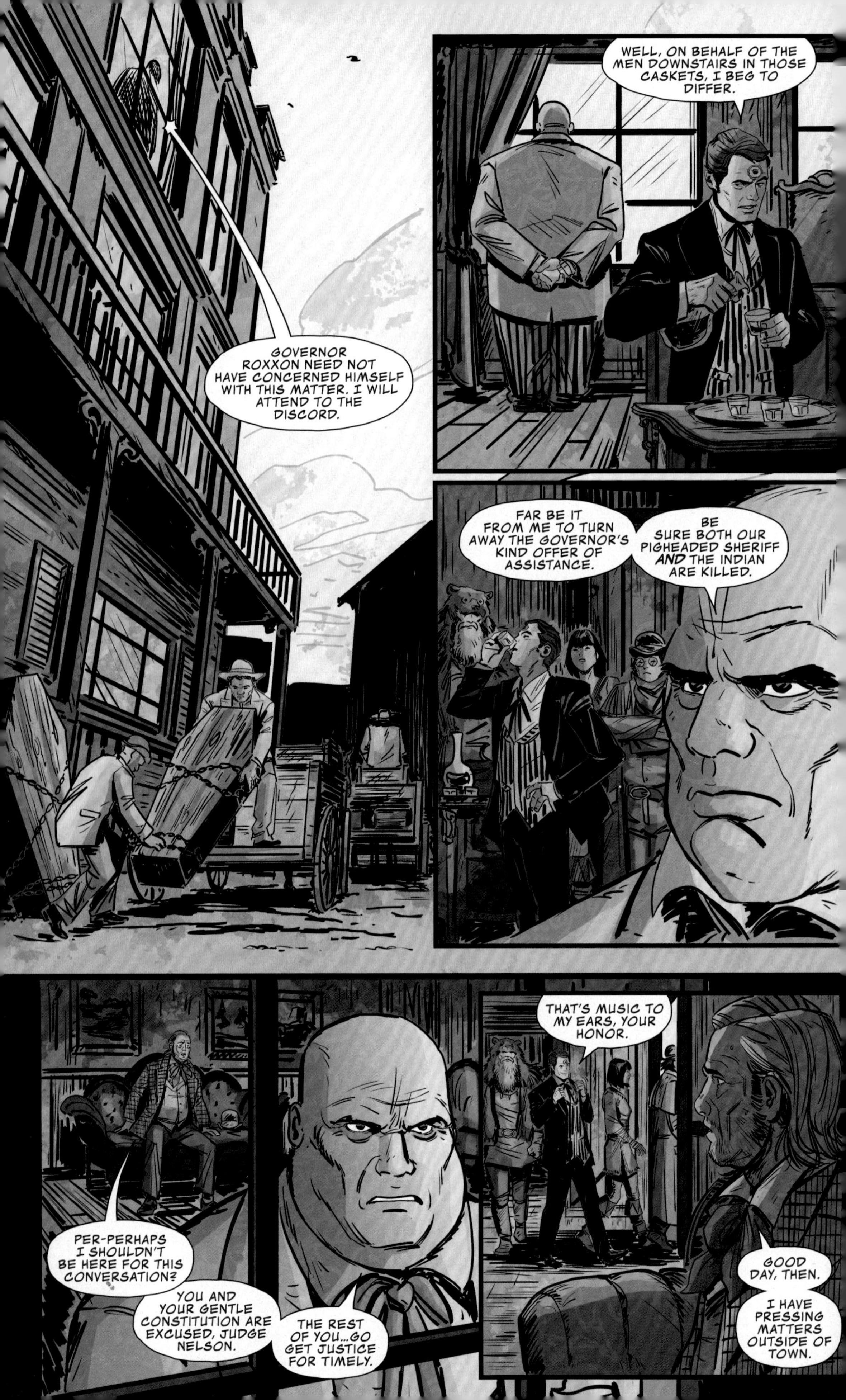
GOVERNOR ROXXON NEED NOT HAVE CONCERNED HIMSELF WITH THIS MATTER. I WILL ATTEND TO THE DISCORD.
WELL, ON BEHALF OF THE MEN DOWNSTAIRS IN THOSE CASKETS, I BEG TO DIFFER.
FAR BE IT FROM ME TO TURN AWAY THE GOVERNOR'S KIND OFFER OF ASSISTANCE.
BE SURE BOTH OUR PIGHEADED SHERIFF *AND* THE INDIAN ARE KILLED.
PER-PERHAPS I SHOULDN'T BE HERE FOR THIS CONVERSATION?
YOU AND YOUR GENTLE CONSTITUTION ARE EXCUSED, JUDGE NELSON.
THE REST OF YOU...GO GET JUSTICE FOR TIMELY.
THAT'S MUSIC TO MY EARS, YOUR HONOR.
GOOD DAY, THEN.
I HAVE PRESSING MATTERS OUTSIDE OF TOWN.

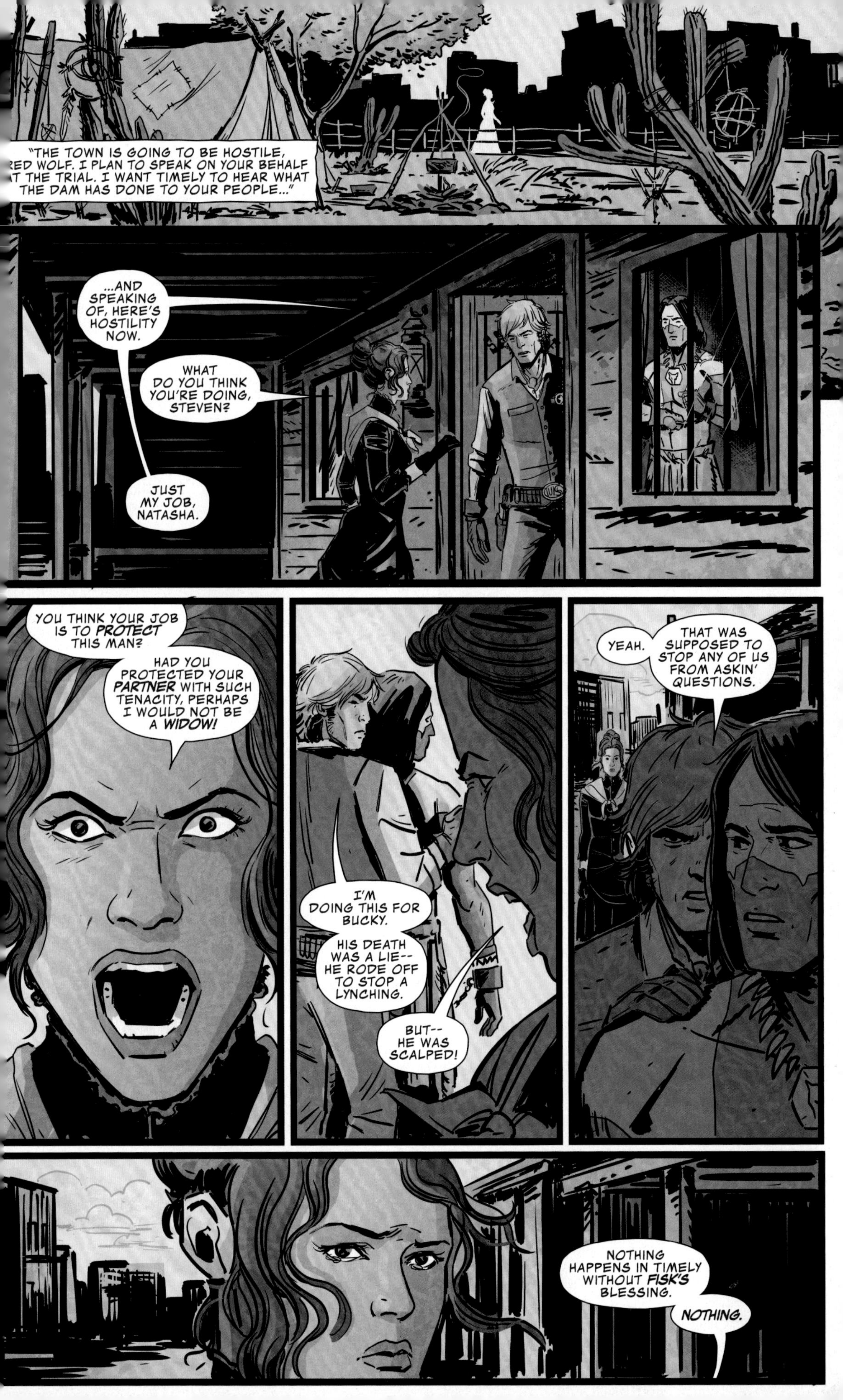
"THE TOWN IS GOING TO BE HOSTILE, RED WOLF. I PLAN TO SPEAK ON YOUR BEHALF AT THE TRIAL. I WANT TIMELY TO HEAR WHAT THE DAM HAS DONE TO YOUR PEOPLE..."
...AND SPEAKING OF, HERE'S HOSTILITY NOW.
WHAT DO YOU THINK YOU'RE DOING, STEVEN?
JUST MY JOB, NATASHA.
YOU THINK YOUR JOB IS TO PROTECT THIS MAN?
HAD YOU PROTECTED YOUR PARTNER WITH SUCH TENACITY, PERHAPS I WOULD NOT BE A WIDOW!
I'M DOING THIS FOR BUCKY.
HIS DEATH WAS A LIE-- HE RODE OFF TO STOP A LYNCHING.
BUT-- HE WAS SCALPED!
YEAH.
THAT WAS SUPPOSED TO STOP ANY OF US FROM ASKIN' QUESTIONS.
NOTHING HAPPENS IN TIMELY WITHOUT FISK'S BLESSING.
NOTHING.

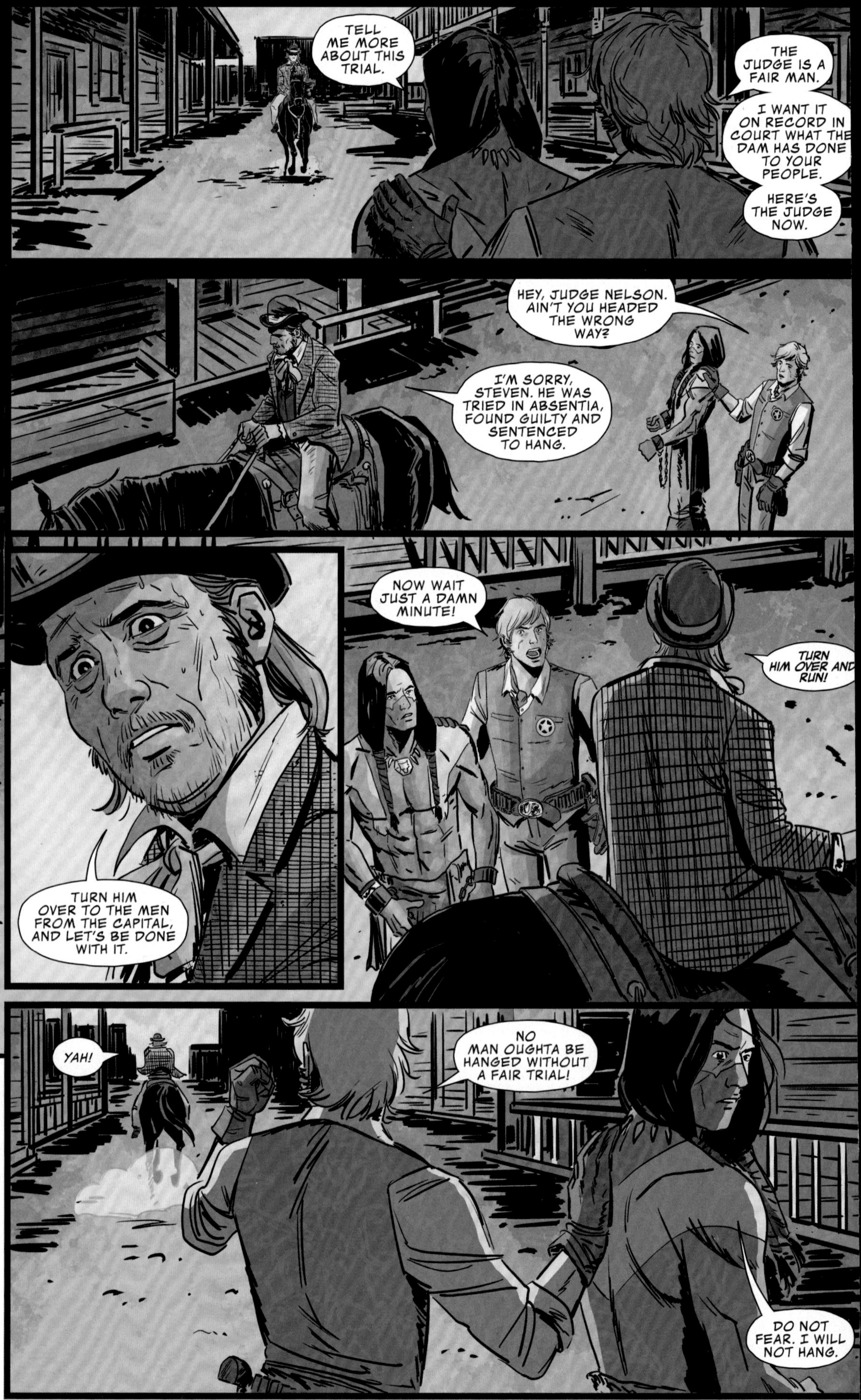
TELL ME MORE ABOUT THIS TRIAL.
THE JUDGE IS A FAIR MAN.
I WANT IT ON RECORD IN COURT WHAT THE DAM HAS DONE TO YOUR PEOPLE.
HERE'S THE JUDGE NOW.
HEY, JUDGE NELSON. AIN'T YOU HEADED THE WRONG WAY?
I'M SORRY, STEVEN. HE WAS TRIED IN ABSENTIA, FOUND GUILTY AND SENTENCED TO HANG.
TURN HIM OVER TO THE MEN FROM THE CAPITAL, AND LET'S BE DONE WITH IT.
NOW WAIT JUST A DAMN MINUTE!
TURN HIM OVER AND RUN!
YAH!
NO MAN OUGHTA BE HANGED WITHOUT A FAIR TRIAL!
DO NOT FEAR. I WILL NOT HANG.

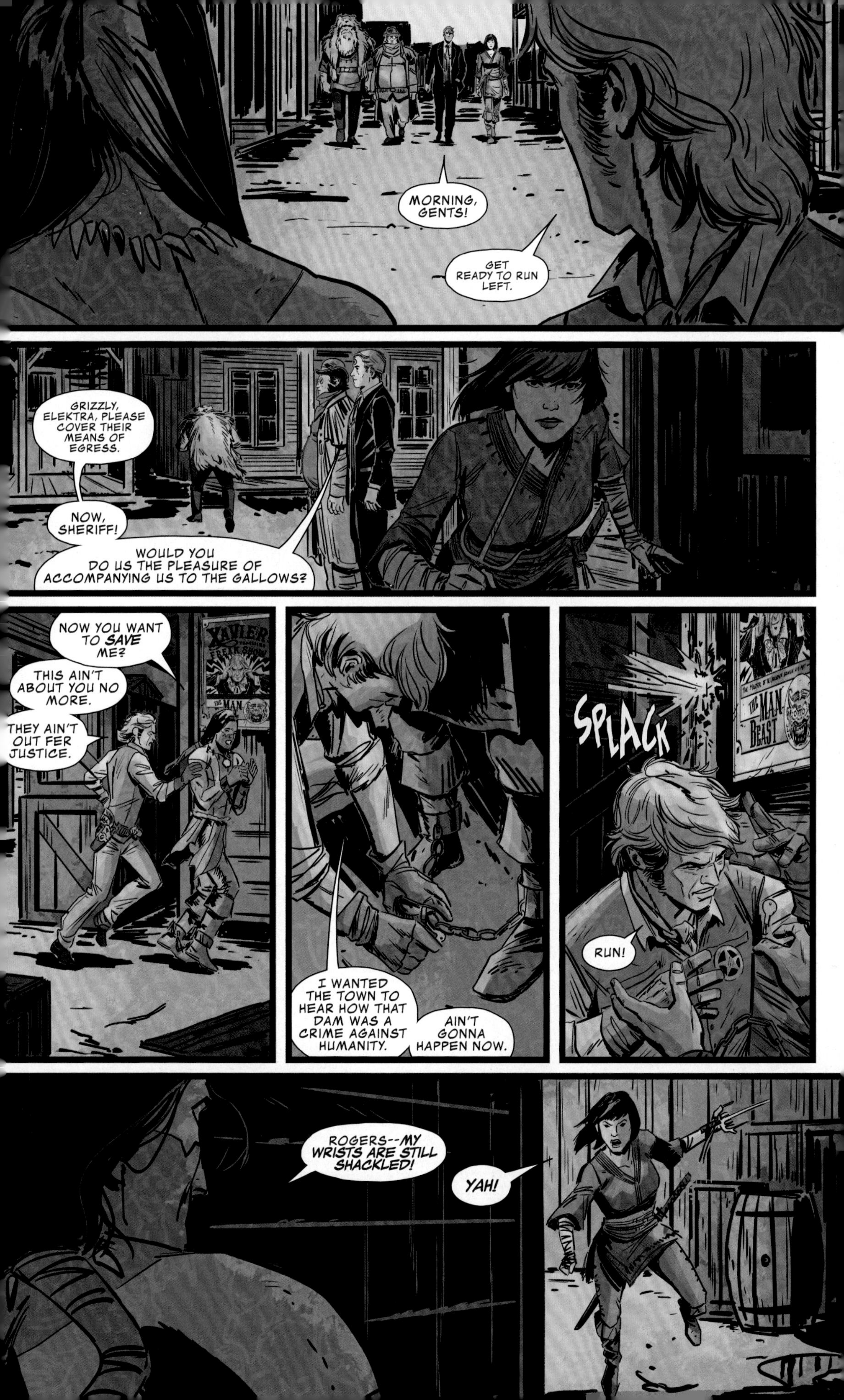
MORNING, GENTS!
GET READY TO RUN LEFT.
GRIZZLY, ELEKTRA, PLEASE COVER THEIR MEANS OF EGRESS.
NOW, SHERIFF!
WOULD YOU DO US THE PLEASURE OF ACCOMPANYING US TO THE GALLOWS?
NOW YOU WANT TO SAVE ME?
THIS AIN'T ABOUT YOU NO MORE.
THEY AIN'T OUT FER JUSTICE.
XAVIER
FREAK SHOW
I WANTED THE TOWN TO HEAR HOW THAT DAM WAS A CRIME AGAINST HUMANITY.
AIN'T GONNA HAPPEN NOW.
SPLACK
THE MAN-BEAST
RUN!
ROGERS--MY WRISTS ARE STILL SHACKLED!
YAH!

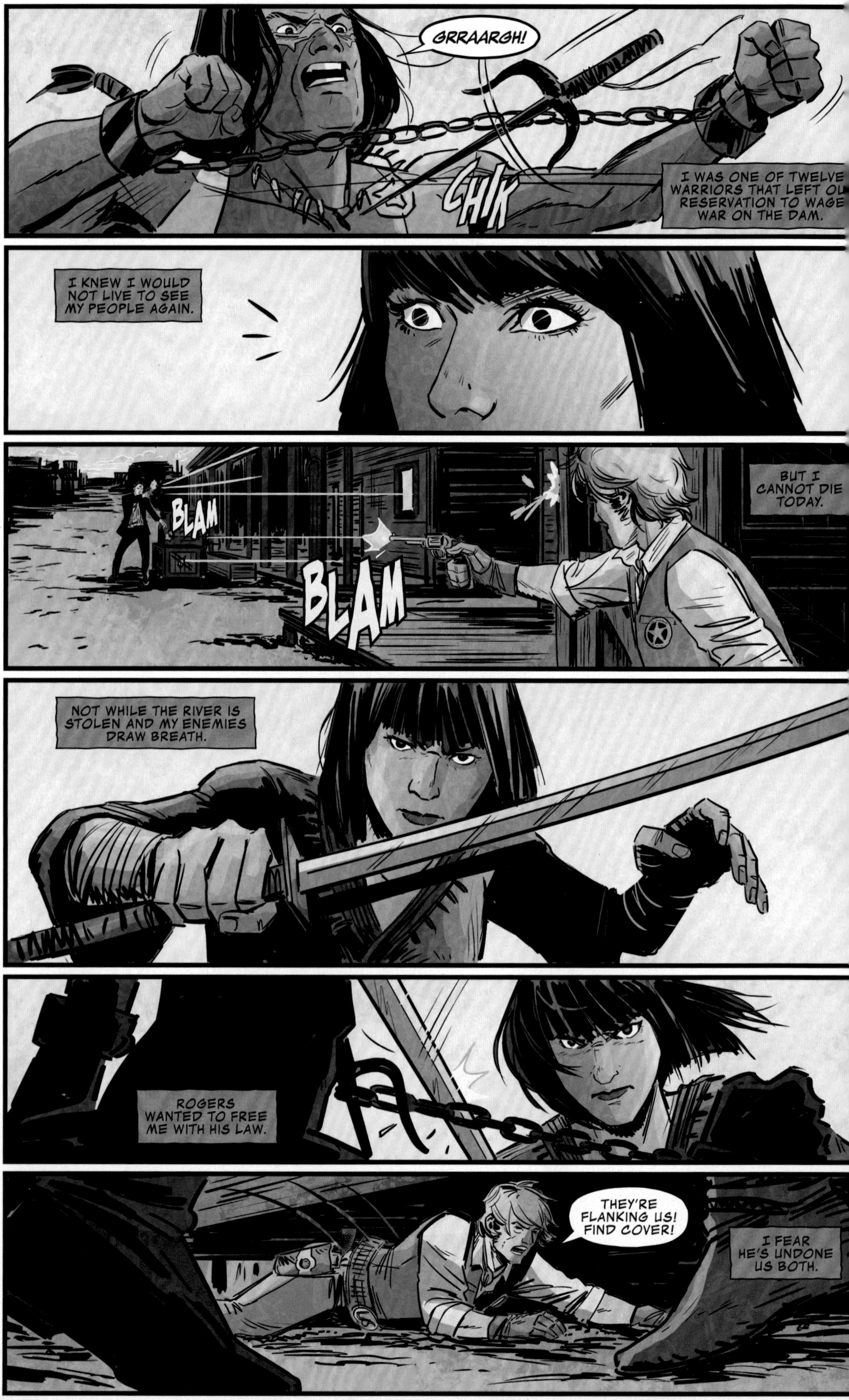
GRRAARGH!
CHIK
I WAS ONE OF TWELVE WARRIORS THAT LEFT OU RESERVATION TO WAGE WAR ON THE DAM.
I KNEW I WOULD NOT LIVE TO SEE MY PEOPLE AGAIN.
BUT I CANNOT DIE TODAY.
BLAM
BLAM
NOT WHILE THE RIVER IS STOLEN AND MY ENEMIES DRAW BREATH.
ROGERS WANTED TO FREE ME WITH HIS LAW.
THEY'RE FLANKING US! FIND COVER!
I FEAR HE'S UNDONE US BOTH.

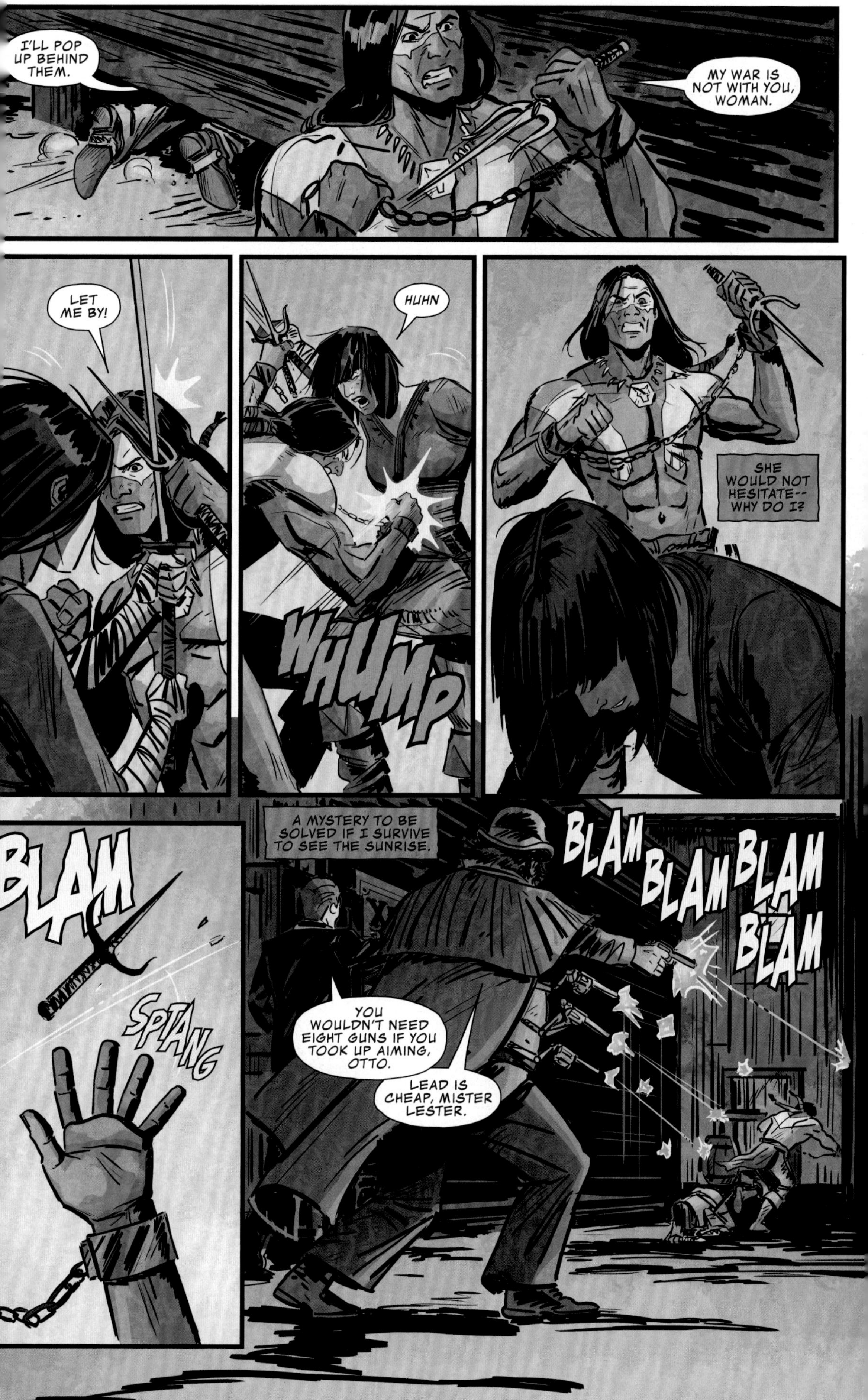
I'LL POP UP BEHIND THEM.
MY WAR IS NOT WITH YOU, WOMAN.
LET ME BY!
HUHN
WHUMP
SHE WOULD NOT HESITATE-- WHY DO I?
BLAM
SPTANG
A MYSTERY TO BE SOLVED IF I SURVIVE TO SEE THE SUNRISE.
BLAM BLAM BLAM BLAM
YOU WOULDN'T NEED EIGHT GUNS IF YOU TOOK UP AIMING, OTTO.
LEAD IS CHEAP, MISTER LESTER.

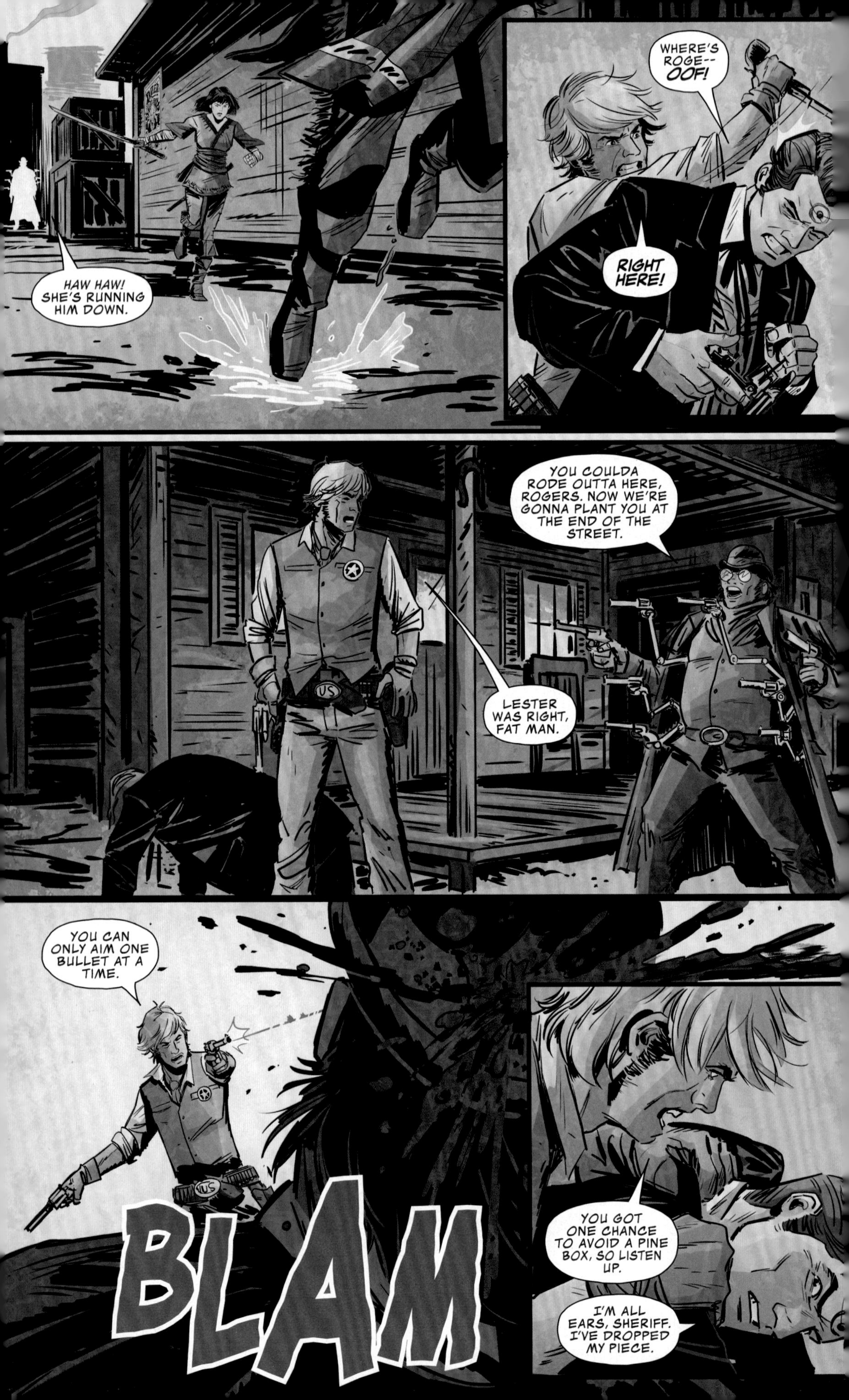
HAW HAW! SHE'S RUNNING HIM DOWN.
WHERE'S ROGE-- OOF!
RIGHT HERE!
YOU COULDA RODE OUTTA HERE, ROGERS. NOW WE'RE GONNA PLANT YOU AT THE END OF THE STREET.
LESTER WAS RIGHT, FAT MAN.
YOU CAN ONLY AIM ONE BULLET AT A TIME.
BLAM
YOU GOT ONE CHANCE TO AVOID A PINE BOX, SO LISTEN UP.
I'M ALL EARS, SHERIFF. I'VE DROPPED MY PIECE.

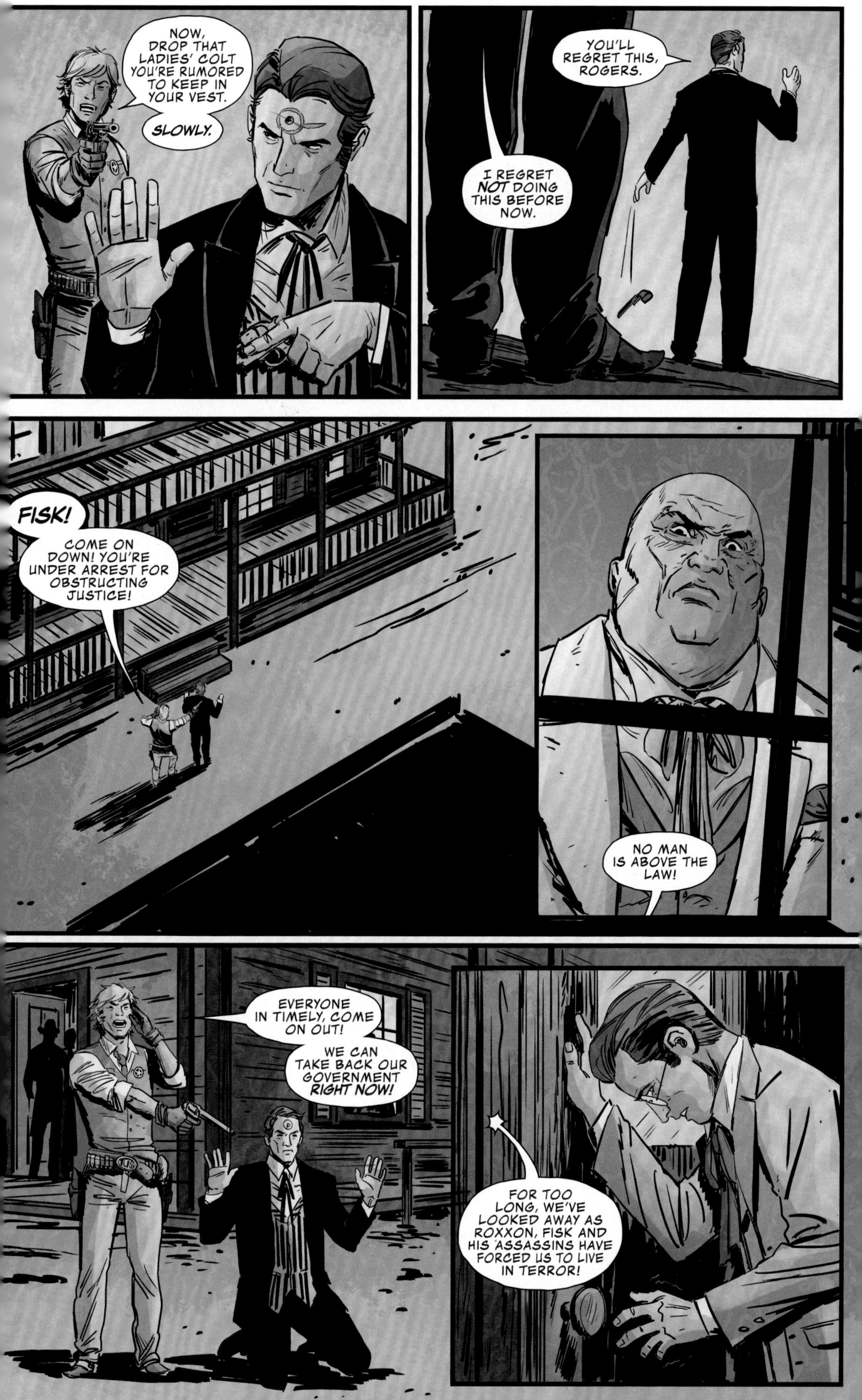

NOW, DROP THAT LADIES' COLT YOU'RE RUMORED TO KEEP IN YOUR VEST.
SLOWLY.
YOU'LL REGRET THIS, ROGERS.
I REGRET NOT DOING THIS BEFORE NOW.
FISK!
COME ON DOWN! YOU'RE UNDER ARREST FOR OBSTRUCTING JUSTICE!
NO MAN IS ABOVE THE LAW!
EVERYONE IN TIMELY, COME ON OUT!
WE CAN TAKE BACK OUR GOVERNMENT RIGHT NOW!
FOR TOO LONG, WE'VE LOOKED AWAY AS ROXXON, FISK AND HIS ASSASSINS HAVE FORCED US TO LIVE IN TERROR!

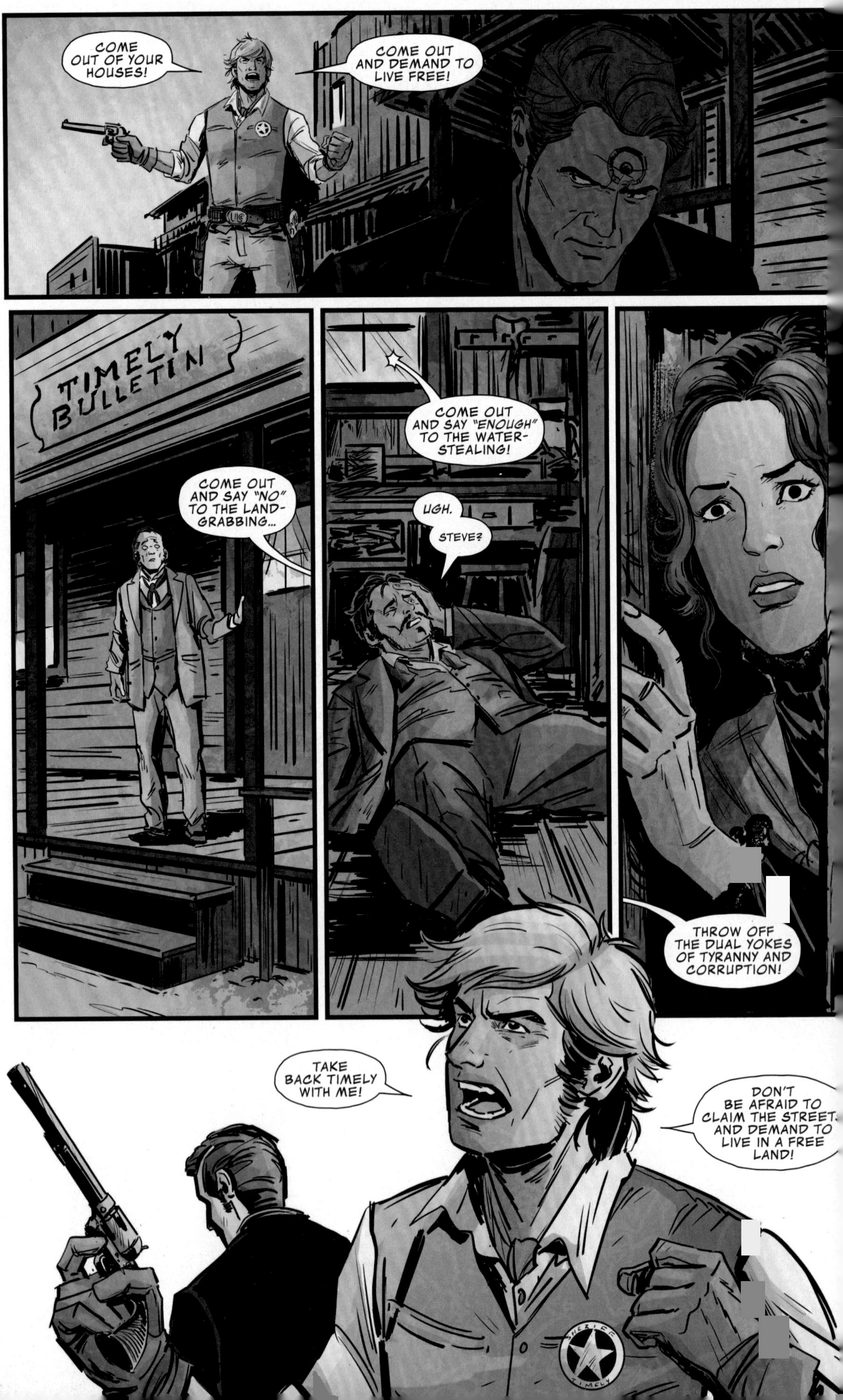
COME OUT OF YOUR HOUSES!
COME OUT AND DEMAND TO LIVE FREE!
TIMELY BULLETIN
COME OUT AND SAY "NO" TO THE LAND-GRABBING...
COME OUT AND SAY "ENOUGH" TO THE WATER-STEALING!
UGH.
STEVE?
THROW OFF THE DUAL YOKES OF TYRANNY AND CORRUPTION!
TAKE BACK TIMELY WITH ME!
DON'T BE AFRAID TO CLAIM THE STREETS AND DEMAND TO LIVE IN A FREE LAND!
SHERIFF TIMELY

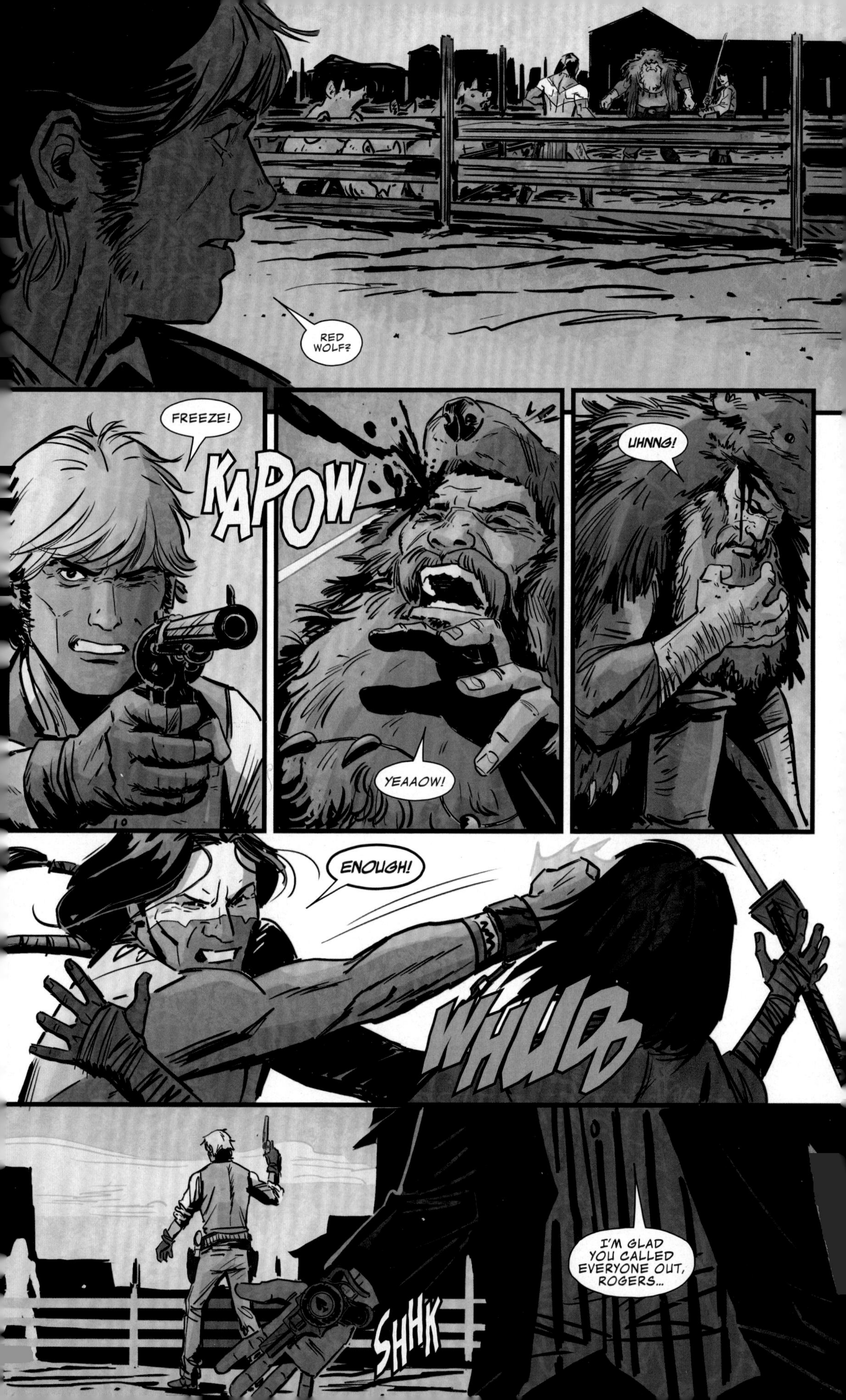
RED WOLF?
FREEZE!
KAPOW
YEAAOW!
UHNNG!
ENOUGH!
WHUD
I'M GLAD YOU CALLED EVERYONE OUT, ROGERS...
SHHK

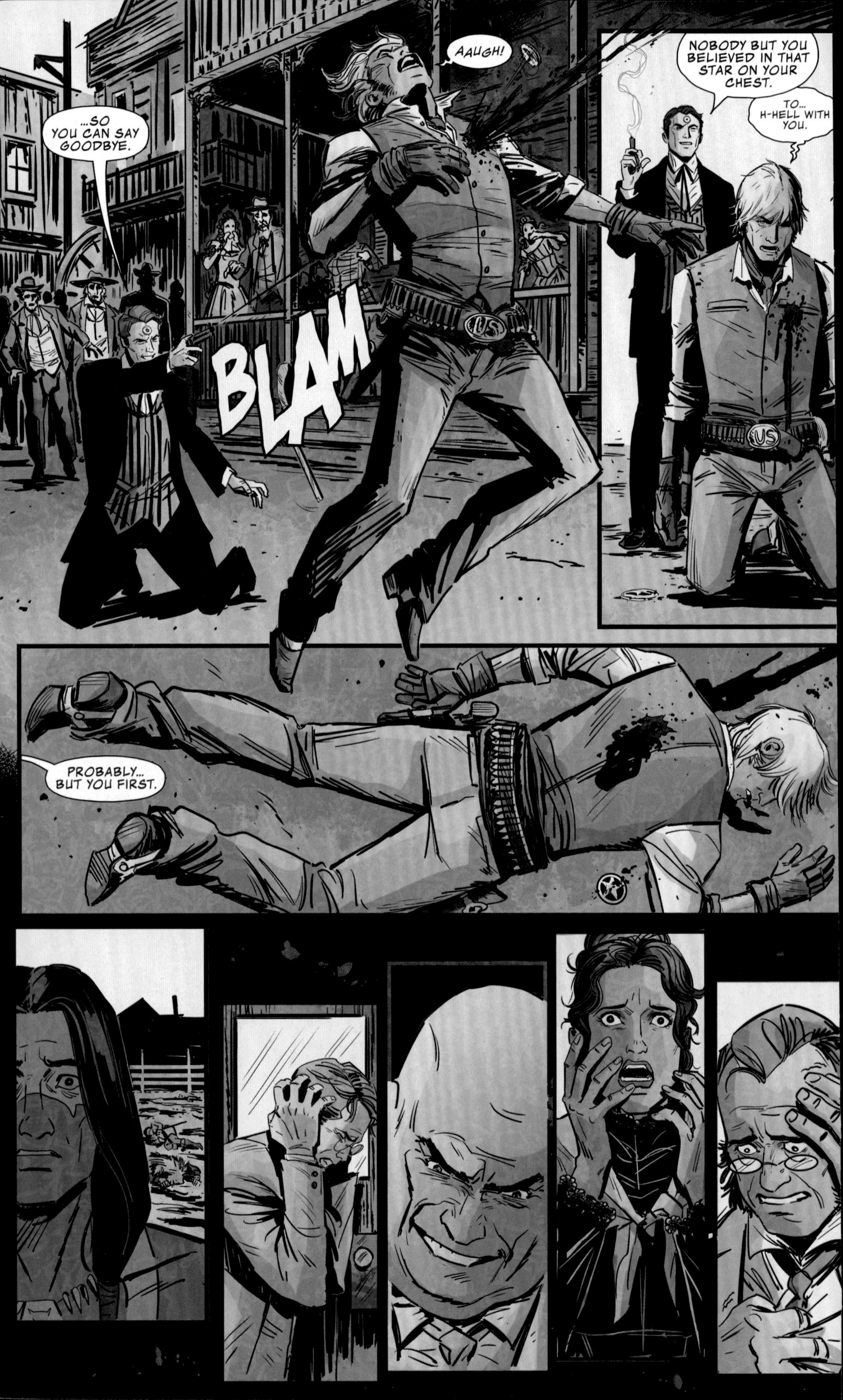
...SO YOU CAN SAY GOODBYE.
AAUGH!
BLAM
NOBODY BUT YOU BELIEVED IN THAT STAR ON YOUR CHEST.
TO... H-HELL WITH YOU.
PROBABLY... BUT YOU FIRST.

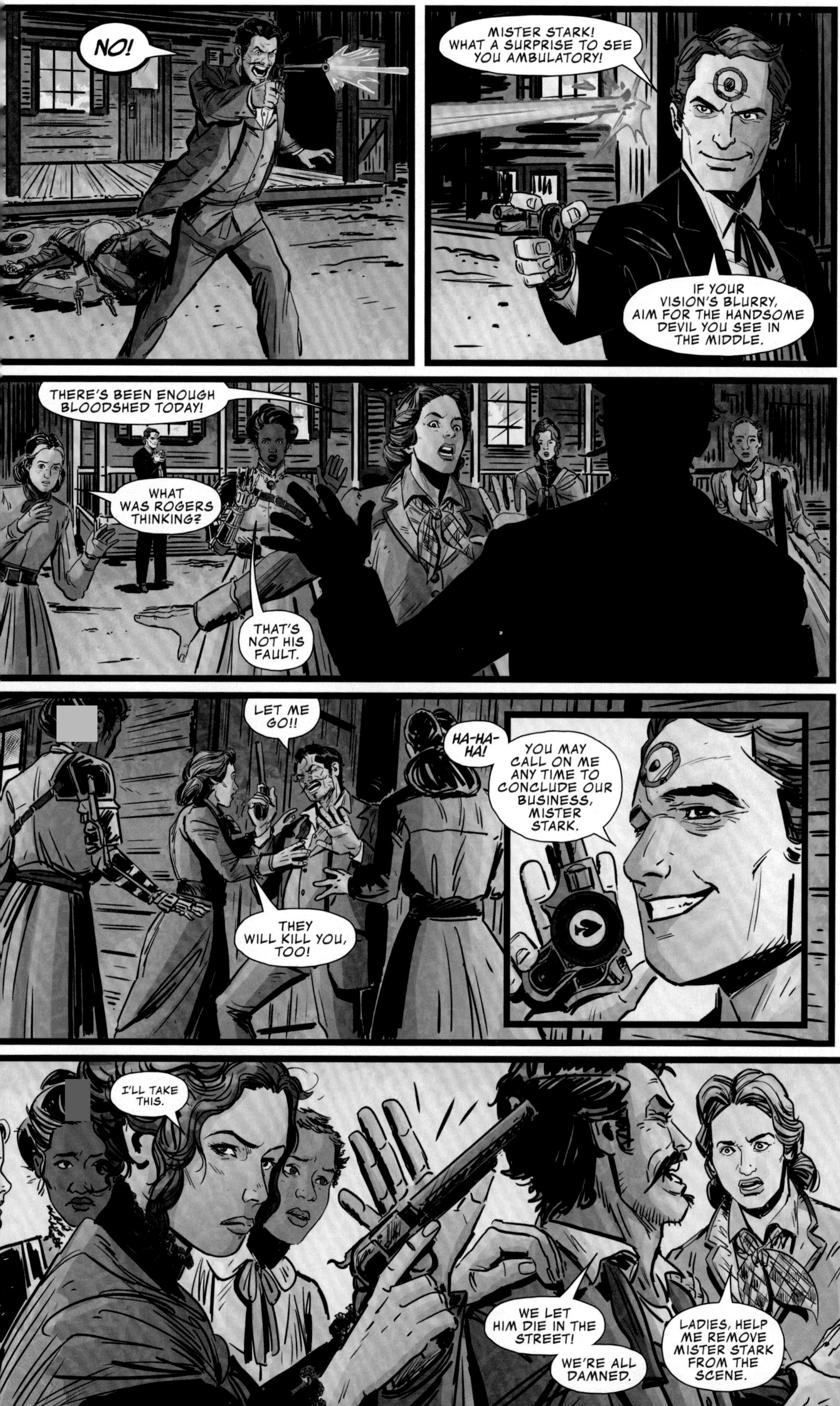
NO!
MISTER STARK! WHAT A SURPRISE TO SEE YOU AMBULATORY!
IF YOUR VISION'S BLURRY, AIM FOR THE HANDSOME DEVIL YOU SEE IN THE MIDDLE.
THERE'S BEEN ENOUGH BLOODSHED TODAY!
WHAT WAS ROGERS THINKING?
THAT'S NOT HIS FAULT.
LET ME GO!!
THEY WILL KILL YOU, TOO!
HA-HA-HA!
YOU MAY CALL ON ME ANY TIME TO CONCLUDE OUR BUSINESS, MISTER STARK.
I'LL TAKE THIS.
WE LET HIM DIE IN THE STREET!
WE'RE ALL DAMNED.
LADIES, HELP ME REMOVE MISTER STARK FROM THE SCENE.

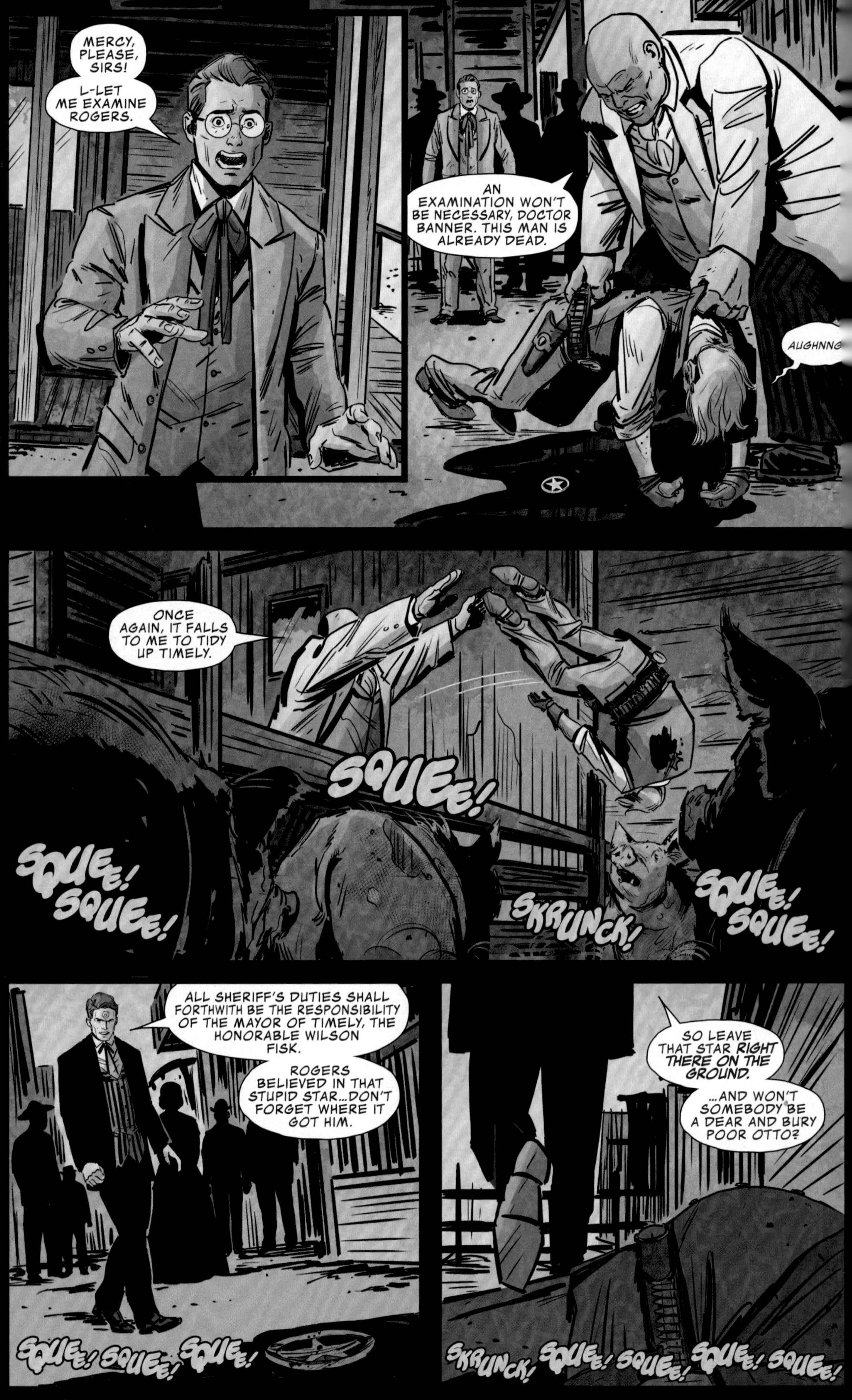
MERCY, PLEASE, SIRS!
L-LET ME EXAMINE ROGERS.
AN EXAMINATION WON'T BE NECESSARY, DOCTOR BANNER. THIS MAN IS ALREADY DEAD.
AUGHNNG
ONCE AGAIN, IT FALLS TO ME TO TIDY UP TIMELY.
SQUEE!
SQUEE! SQUEE!
SKRUNCK!
SQUEE! SQUEE!
ALL SHERIFF'S DUTIES SHALL FORTHWITH BE THE RESPONSIBILITY OF THE MAYOR OF TIMELY, THE HONORABLE WILSON FISK.
ROGERS BELIEVED IN THAT STUPID STAR...DON'T FORGET WHERE IT GOT HIM.
SQUEE! SQUEE! SQUEE!
SO LEAVE THAT STAR RIGHT THERE ON THE GROUND.
...AND WON'T SOMEBODY BE A DEAR AND BURY POOR OTTO?
SKRUNCK! SQUEE! SQUEE! SQUEE! SQUEE!

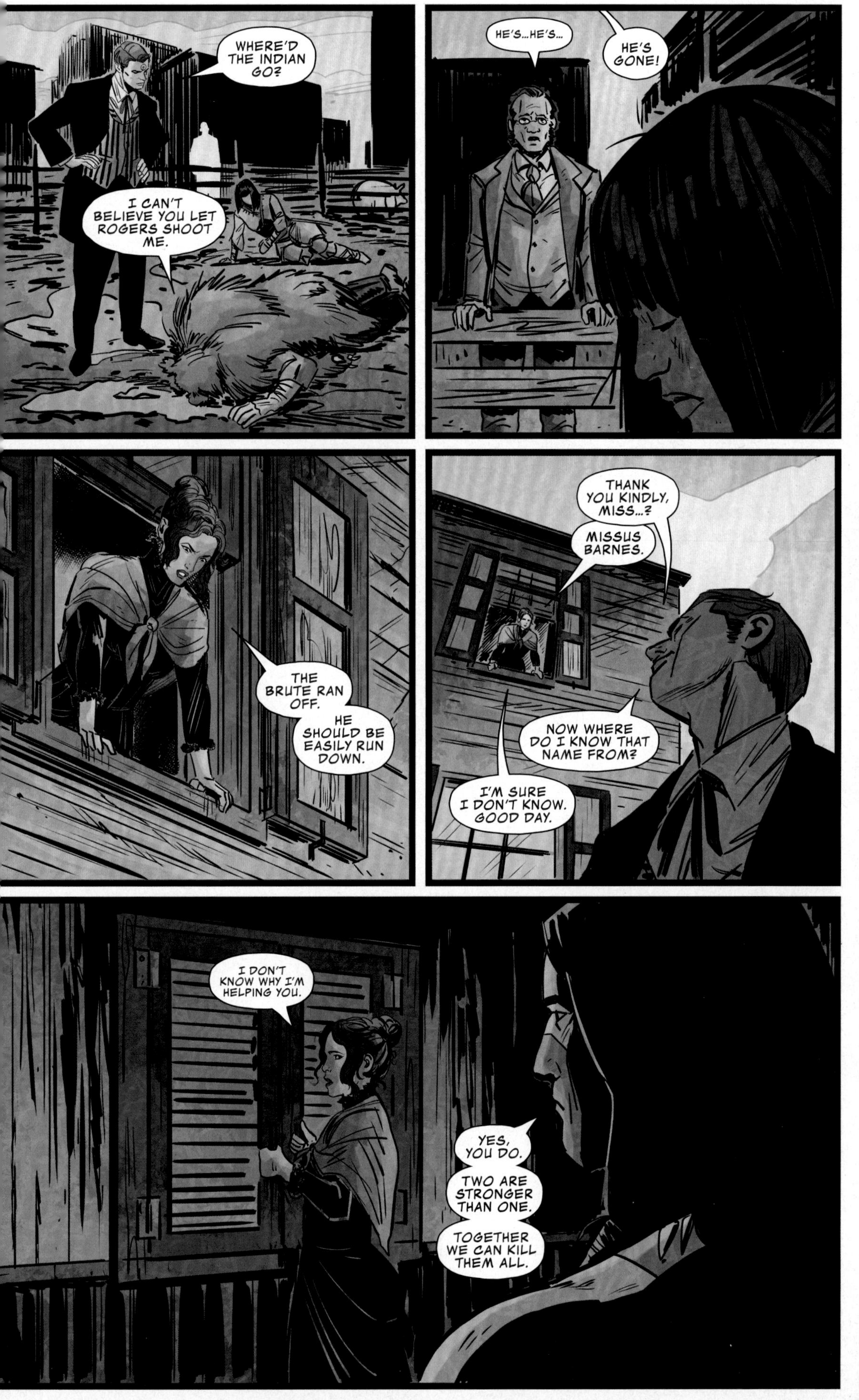
WHERE'D THE INDIAN GO?
I CAN'T BELIEVE YOU LET ROGERS SHOOT ME.
HE'S...HE'S...
HE'S GONE!
THE BRUTE RAN OFF.
HE SHOULD BE EASILY RUN DOWN.
THANK YOU KINDLY, MISS...?
MISSUS BARNES.
NOW WHERE DO I KNOW THAT NAME FROM?
I'M SURE I DON'T KNOW. GOOD DAY.
I DON'T KNOW WHY I'M HELPING YOU.
YES, YOU DO.
TWO ARE STRONGER THAN ONE.
TOGETHER WE CAN KILL THEM ALL.

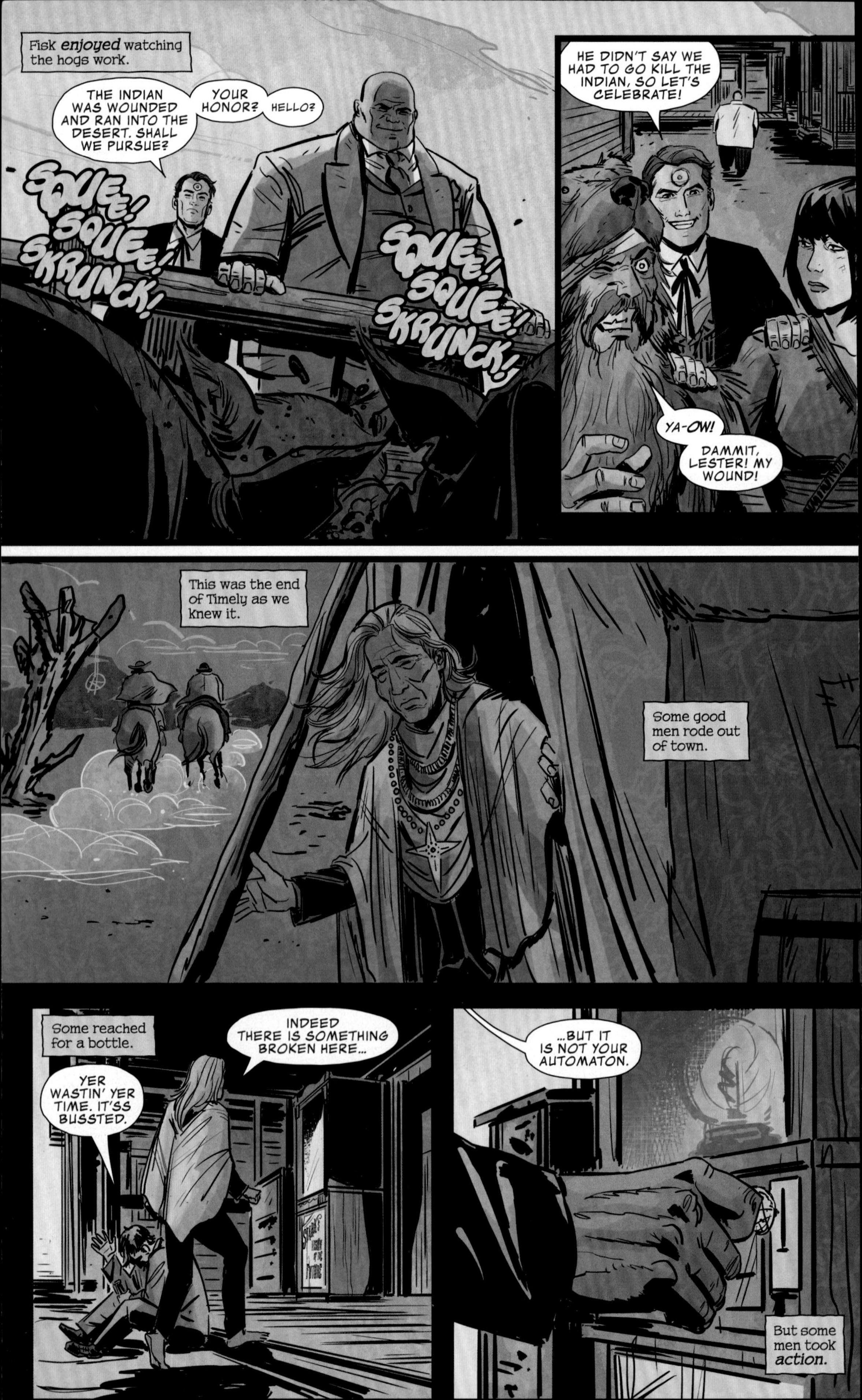
Fisk enjoyed watching the hogs work.
THE INDIAN WAS WOUNDED AND RAN INTO THE DESERT. SHALL WE PURSUE?
YOUR HONOR?
HELLO?
SQUEE! SQUEE! SKRUNCK!
SQUEE! SQUEE! SKRUNCK!
HE DIDN'T SAY WE HAD TO GO KILL THE INDIAN, SO LET'S CELEBRATE!
YA-OW!
DAMMIT, LESTER! MY WOUND!
This was the end of Timely as we knew it.
Some good men rode out of town.
Some reached for a bottle.
INDEED THERE IS SOMETHING BROKEN HERE...
YER WASTIN' YER TIME. IT'SS BUSSTED.
...BUT IT IS NOT YOUR AUTOMATON.
But some men took action.

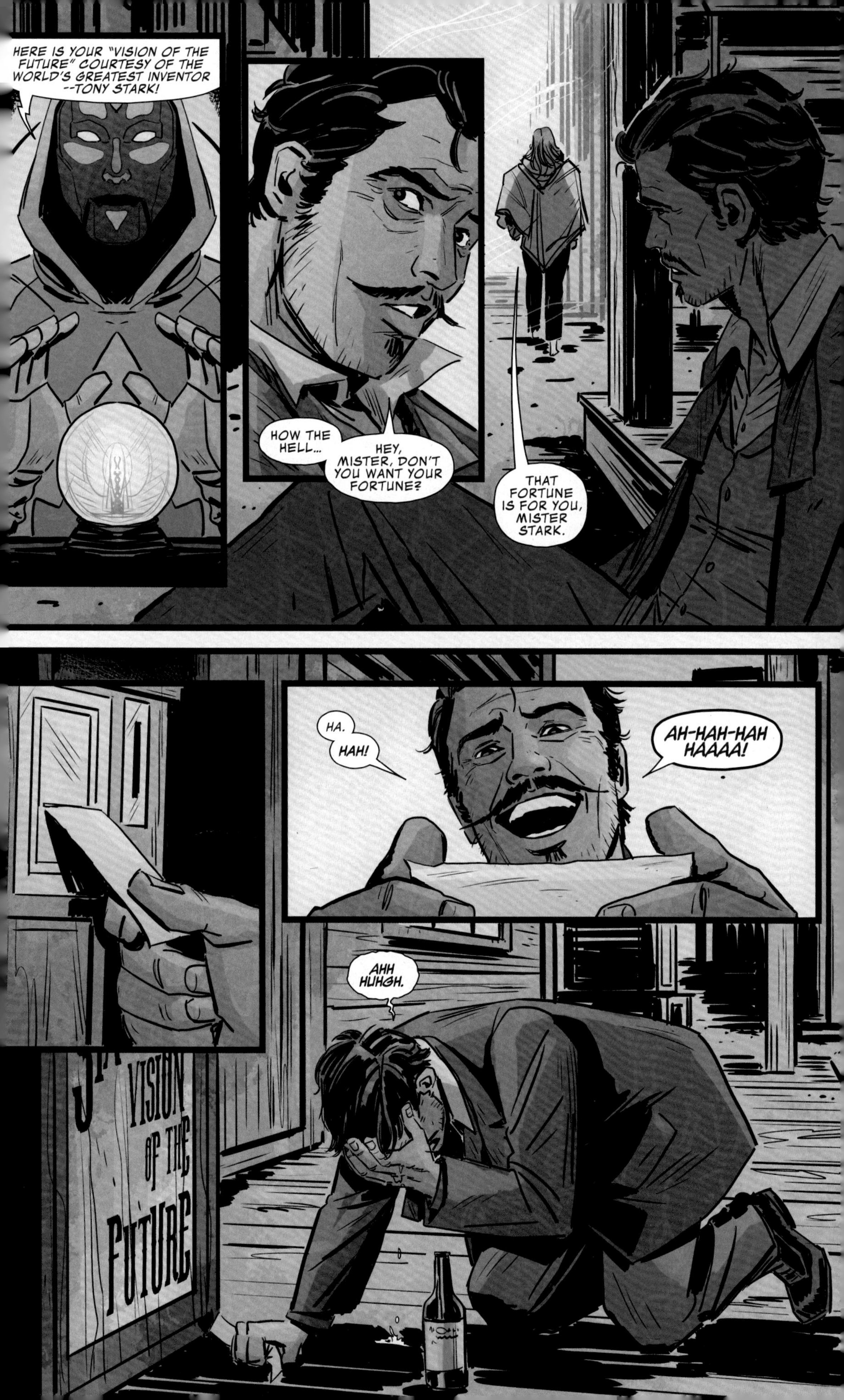

HERE IS YOUR "VISION OF THE FUTURE" COURTESY OF THE WORLD'S GREATEST INVENTOR --TONY STARK!
HOW THE HELL...
HEY, MISTER, DON'T YOU WANT YOUR FORTUNE?
THAT FORTUNE IS FOR YOU, MISTER STARK.
HA.
HAH!
AH-HAH-HAH HAAAA!
AHH HUHGH.
VISION OF THE FUTURE

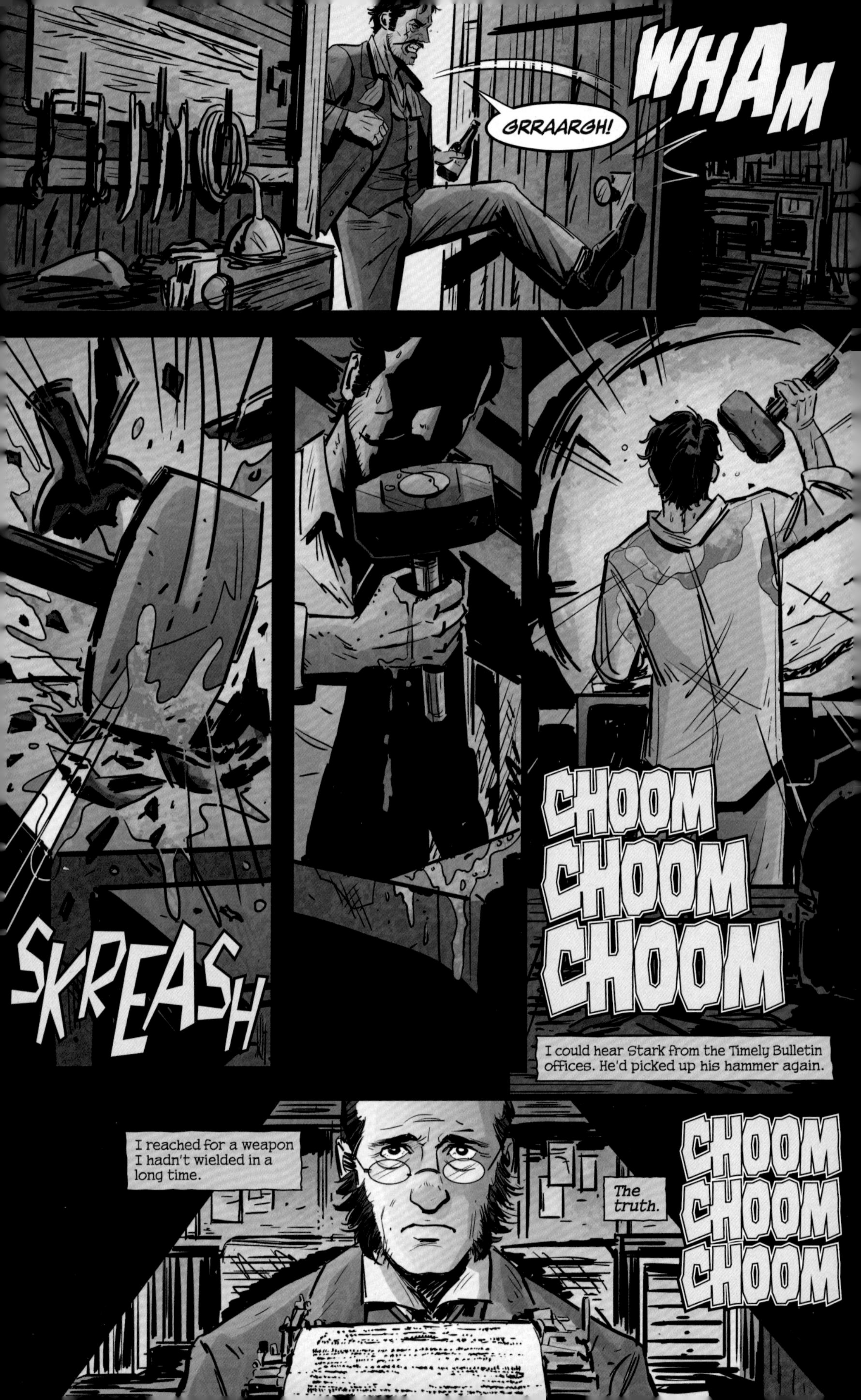

GRRAARGH!
WHAM
SKREASH
CHOOM CHOOM CHOOM
I could hear Stark from the Timely Bulletin offices. He'd picked up his hammer again.
I reached for a weapon I hadn't wielded in a long time.
The truth.
CHOOM CHOOM CHOOM

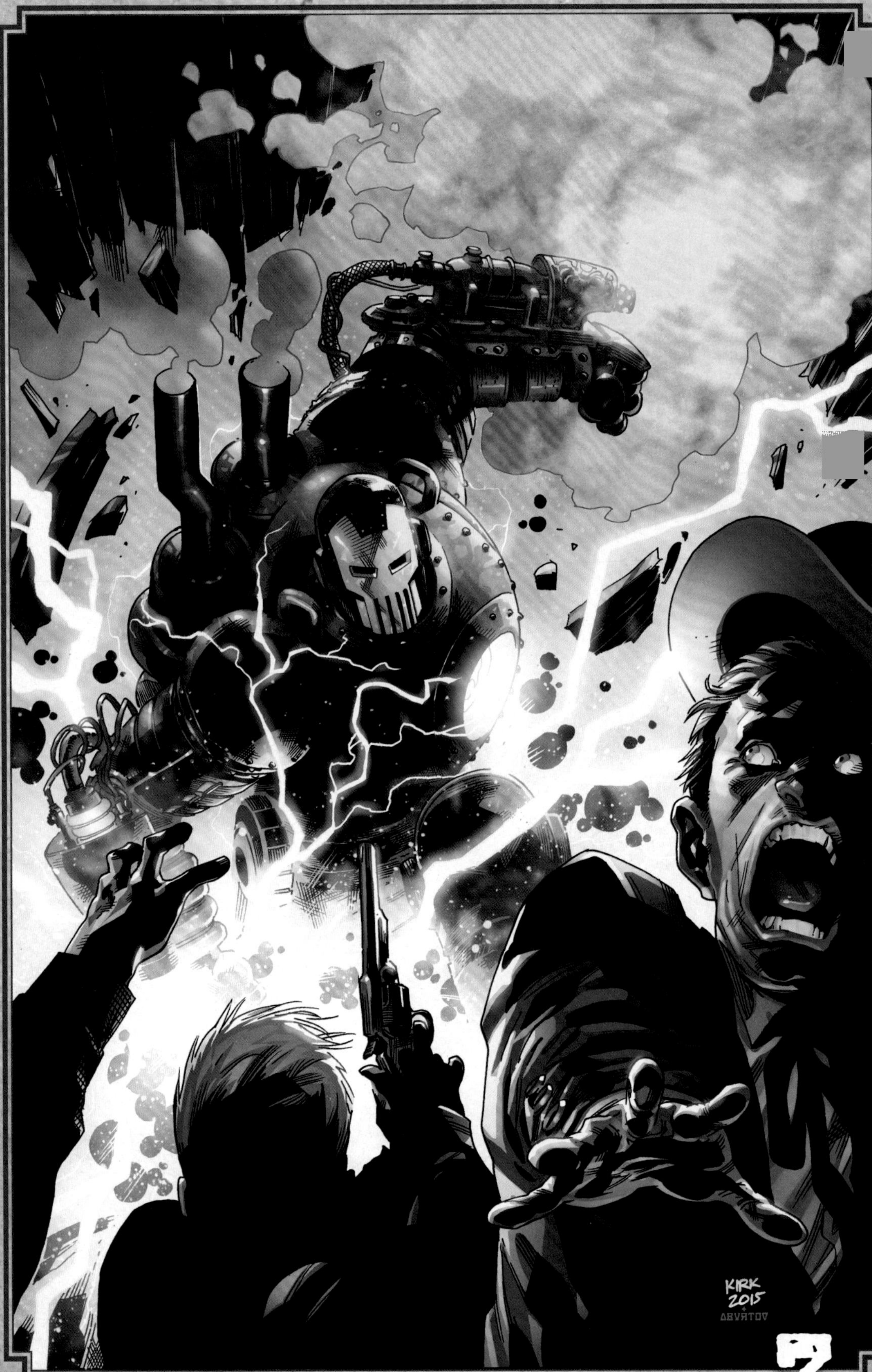
KIRK
2015

3

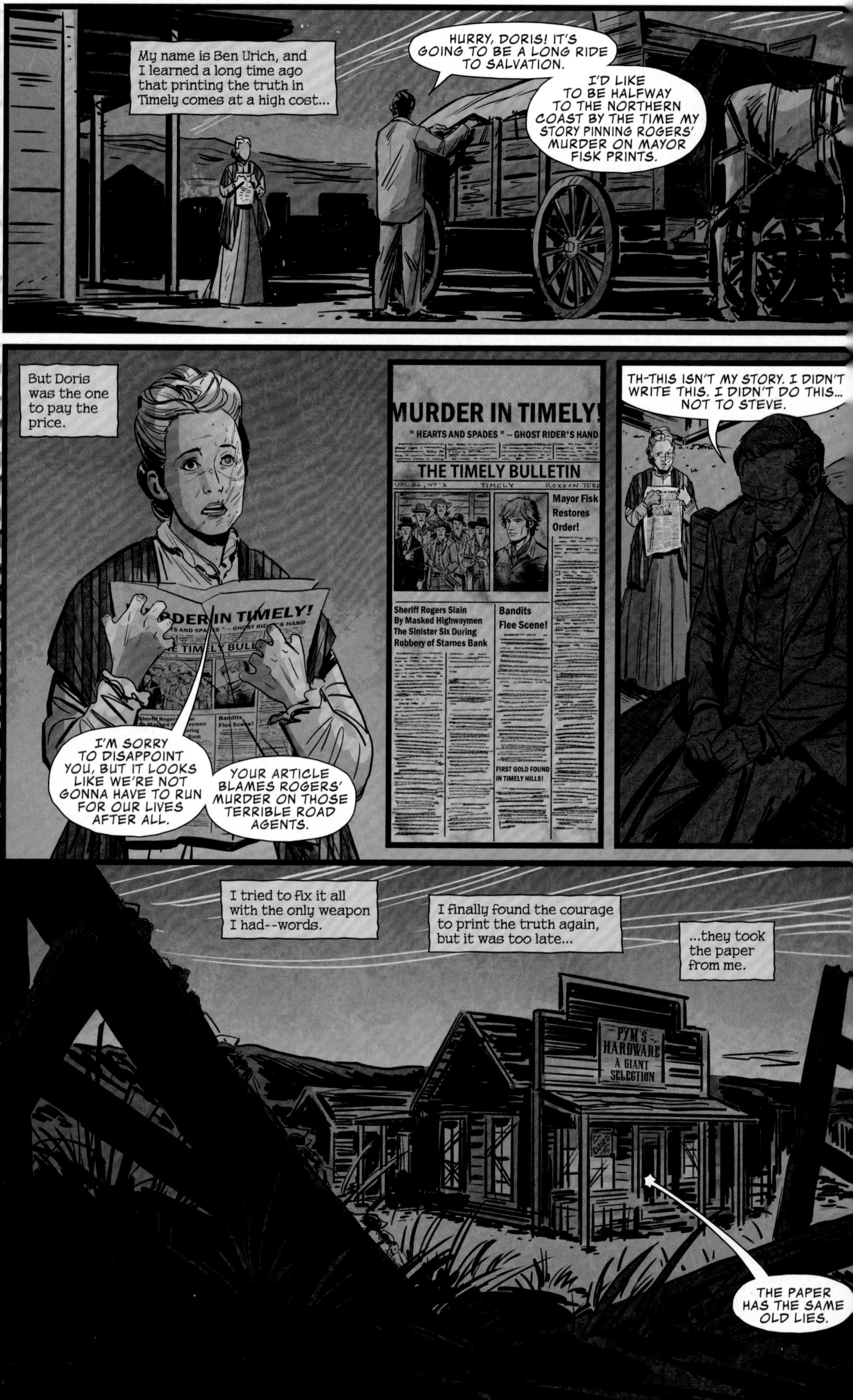

My name is Ben Urich, and I learned a long time ago that printing the truth in Timely comes at a high cost...
HURRY, DORIS! IT'S GOING TO BE A LONG RIDE TO SALVATION.
I'D LIKE TO BE HALFWAY TO THE NORTHERN COAST BY THE TIME MY STORY PINNING ROGERS' MURDER ON MAYOR FISK PRINTS.
But Doris was the one to pay the price.
I'M SORRY TO DISAPPOINT YOU, BUT IT LOOKS LIKE WE'RE NOT GONNA HAVE TO RUN FOR OUR LIVES AFTER ALL.
YOUR ARTICLE BLAMES ROGERS' MURDER ON THOSE TERRIBLE ROAD AGENTS.
MURDER IN TIMELY!
" HEARTS AND SPADES " -- GHOST RIDER'S HAND
THE TIMELY BULLETIN
Mayor Fisk Restores Order!
Sheriff Rogers Slain By Masked Highwaymen The Sinister Six During Robbery of Starnes Bank
Bandits Flee Scene!
FIRST GOLD FOUND IN TIMELY HILLS!
TH-THIS ISN'T MY STORY. I DIDN'T WRITE THIS. I DIDN'T DO THIS... NOT TO STEVE.
I tried to fix it all with the only weapon I had--words.
I finally found the courage to print the truth again, but it was too late...
...they took the paper from me.
PYM'S HARDWARE A GIANT SELECTION
THE PAPER HAS THE SAME OLD LIES.

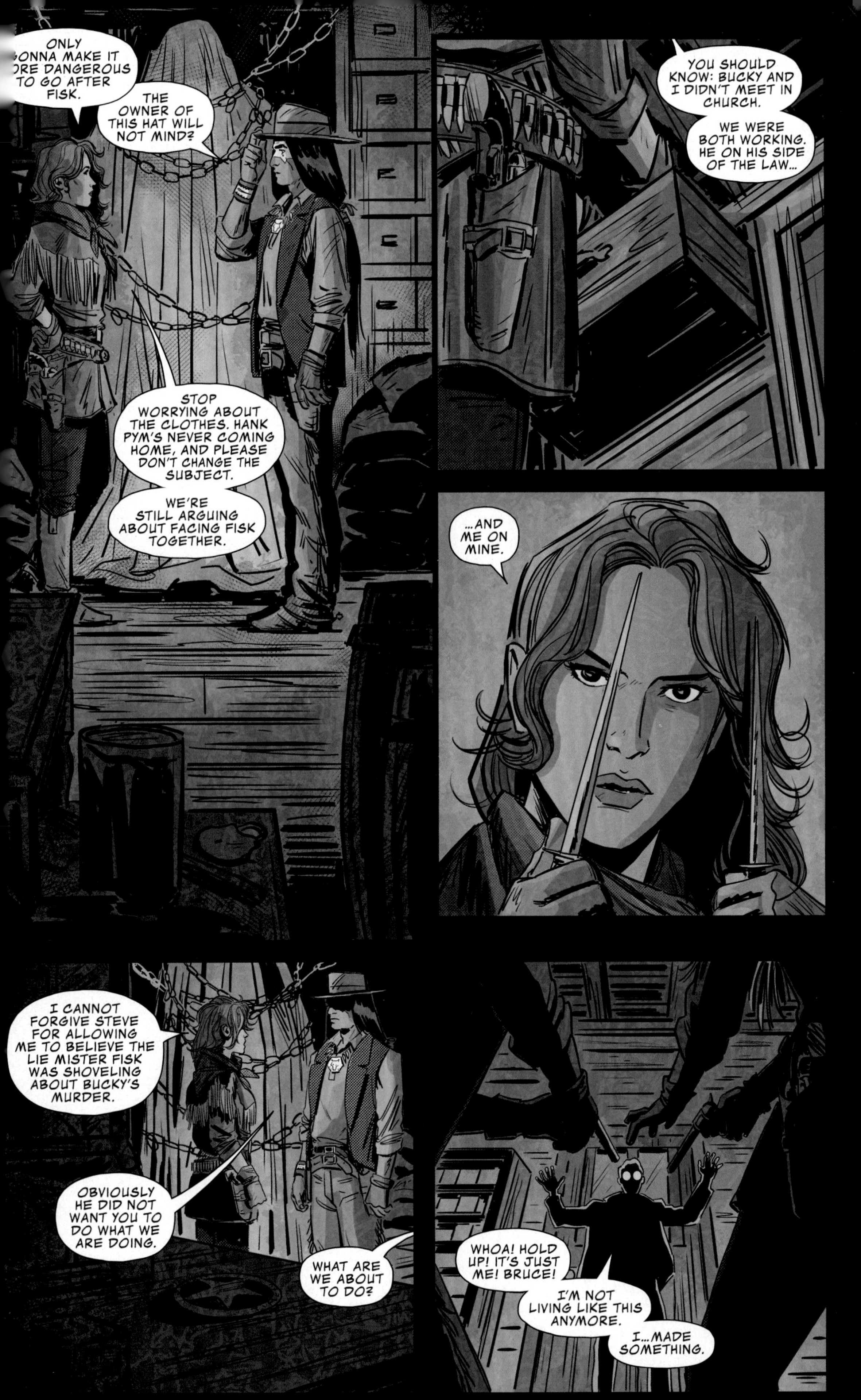
ONLY GONNA MAKE IT MORE DANGEROUS TO GO AFTER FISK.
THE OWNER OF THIS HAT WILL NOT MIND?
STOP WORRYING ABOUT THE CLOTHES. HANK PYM'S NEVER COMING HOME, AND PLEASE DON'T CHANGE THE SUBJECT.
WE'RE STILL ARGUING ABOUT FACING FISK TOGETHER.
YOU SHOULD KNOW: BUCKY AND I DIDN'T MEET IN CHURCH.
WE WERE BOTH WORKING. HE ON HIS SIDE OF THE LAW...
...AND ME ON MINE.
I CANNOT FORGIVE STEVE FOR ALLOWING ME TO BELIEVE THE LIE MISTER FISK WAS SHOVELING ABOUT BUCKY'S MURDER.
OBVIOUSLY HE DID NOT WANT YOU TO DO WHAT WE ARE DOING.
WHAT ARE WE ABOUT TO DO?
WHOA! HOLD UP! IT'S JUST ME! BRUCE!
I'M NOT LIVING LIKE THIS ANYMORE.
I...MADE SOMETHING.

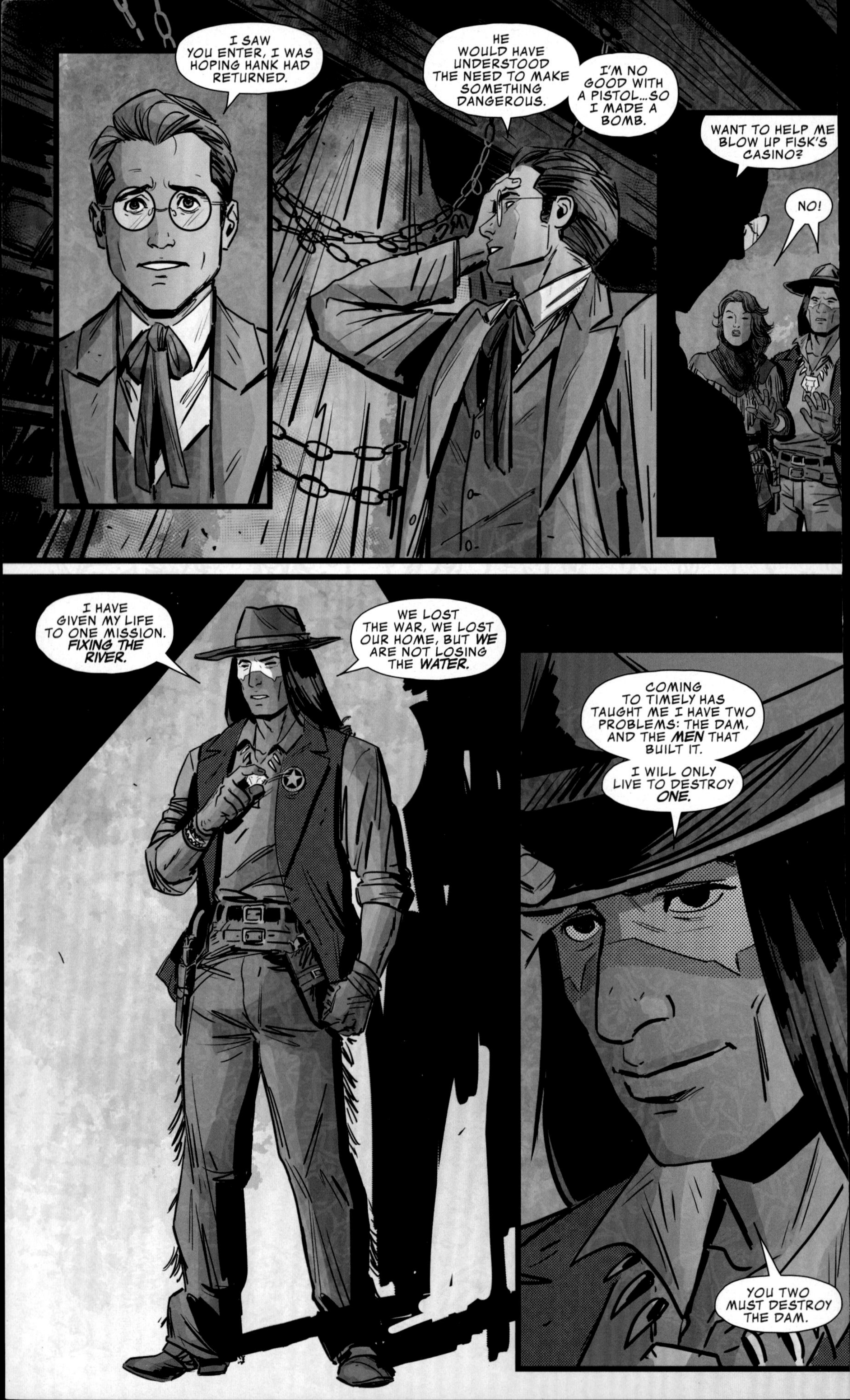
I SAW YOU ENTER, I WAS HOPING HANK HAD RETURNED.
HE WOULD HAVE UNDERSTOOD THE NEED TO MAKE SOMETHING DANGEROUS.
I'M NO GOOD WITH A PISTOL...SO I MADE A BOMB.
WANT TO HELP ME BLOW UP FISK'S CASINO?
NO!
I HAVE GIVEN MY LIFE TO ONE MISSION. FIXING THE RIVER.
WE LOST THE WAR, WE LOST OUR HOME, BUT WE ARE NOT LOSING THE WATER.
COMING TO TIMELY HAS TAUGHT ME I HAVE TWO PROBLEMS: THE DAM, AND THE MEN THAT BUILT IT.
I WILL ONLY LIVE TO DESTROY ONE.
YOU TWO MUST DESTROY THE DAM.

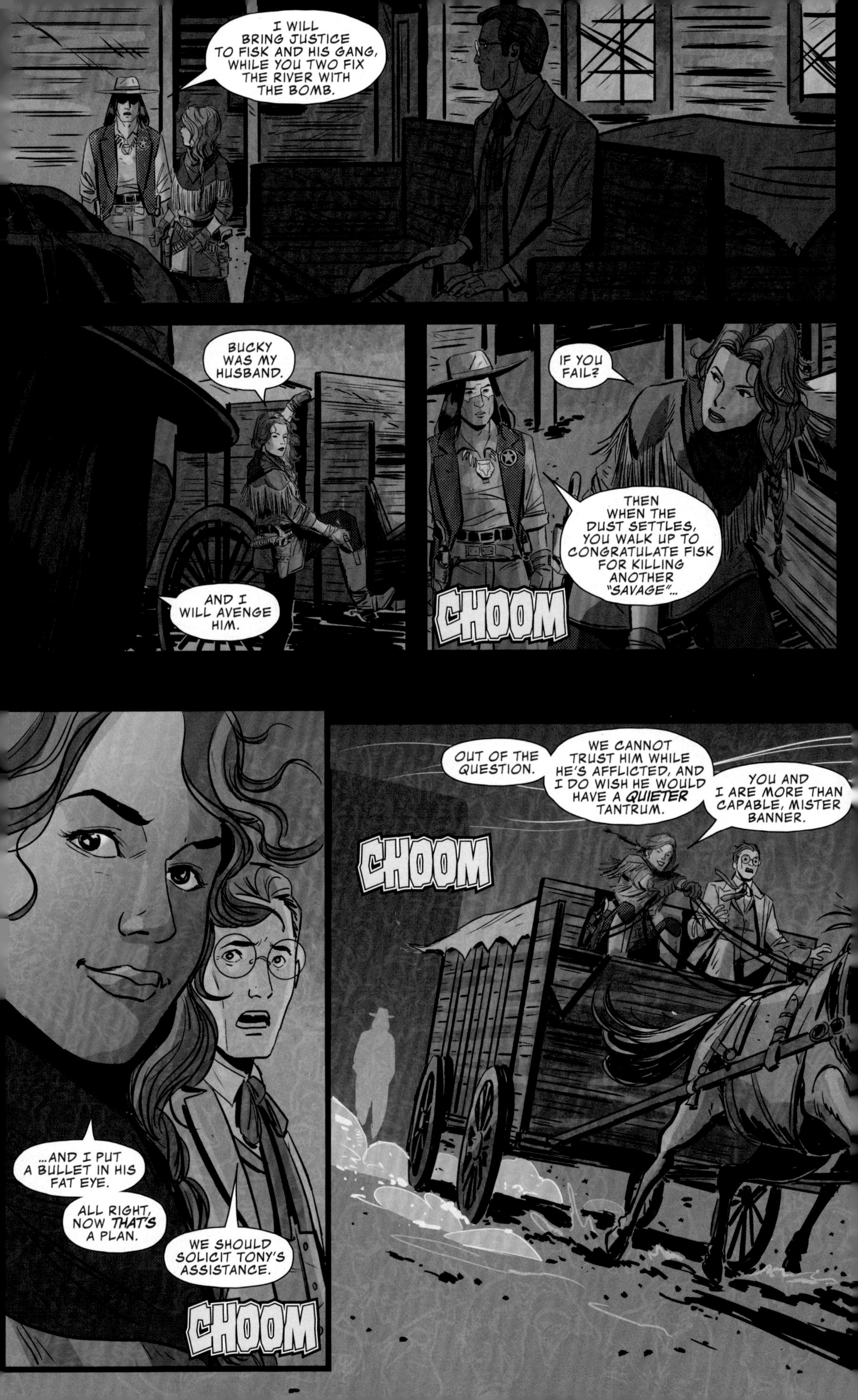
I WILL BRING JUSTICE TO FISK AND HIS GANG, WHILE YOU TWO FIX THE RIVER WITH THE BOMB.
BUCKY WAS MY HUSBAND.
AND I WILL AVENGE HIM.
IF YOU FAIL?
THEN WHEN THE DUST SETTLES, YOU WALK UP TO CONGRATULATE FISK FOR KILLING ANOTHER "SAVAGE"...
CHOOM
...AND I PUT A BULLET IN HIS FAT EYE.
ALL RIGHT, NOW THAT'S A PLAN.
WE SHOULD SOLICIT TONY'S ASSISTANCE.
CHOOM
OUT OF THE QUESTION.
WE CANNOT TRUST HIM WHILE HE'S AFFLICTED, AND I DO WISH HE WOULD HAVE A QUIETER TANTRUM.
YOU AND I ARE MORE THAN CAPABLE, MISTER BANNER.
CHOOM

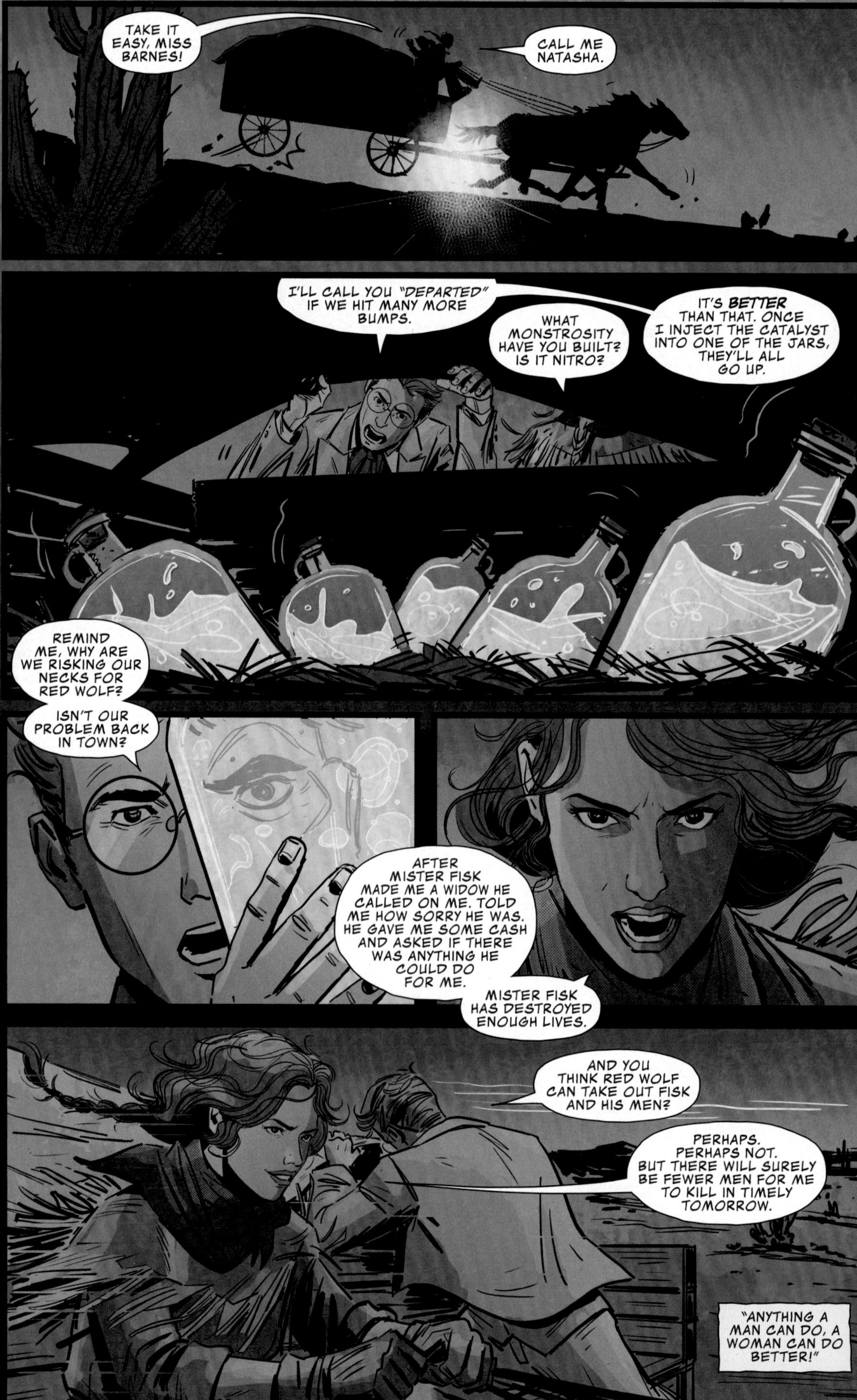
TAKE IT EASY, MISS BARNES!
CALL ME NATASHA.
I'LL CALL YOU "DEPARTED" IF WE HIT MANY MORE BUMPS.
WHAT MONSTROSITY HAVE YOU BUILT? IS IT NITRO?
IT'S BETTER THAN THAT. ONCE I INJECT THE CATALYST INTO ONE OF THE JARS, THEY'LL ALL GO UP.
REMIND ME, WHY ARE WE RISKING OUR NECKS FOR RED WOLF?
ISN'T OUR PROBLEM BACK IN TOWN?
AFTER MISTER FISK MADE ME A WIDOW HE CALLED ON ME. TOLD ME HOW SORRY HE WAS. HE GAVE ME SOME CASH AND ASKED IF THERE WAS ANYTHING HE COULD DO FOR ME.
MISTER FISK HAS DESTROYED ENOUGH LIVES.
AND YOU THINK RED WOLF CAN TAKE OUT FISK AND HIS MEN?
PERHAPS. PERHAPS NOT. BUT THERE WILL SURELY BE FEWER MEN FOR ME TO KILL IN TIMELY TOMORROW.
"ANYTHING A MAN CAN DO, A WOMAN CAN DO BETTER!"

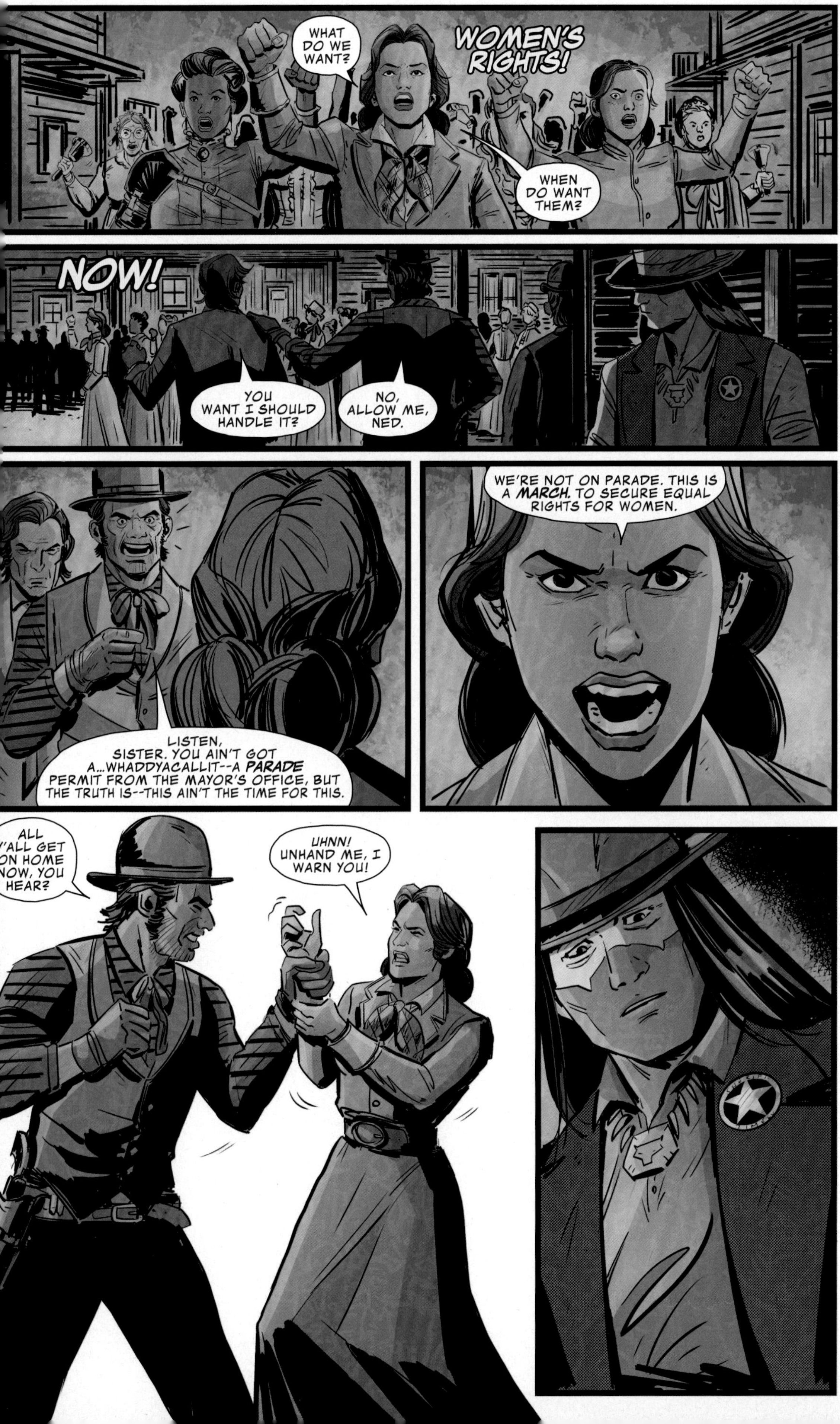
WHAT DO WE WANT?
WOMEN'S RIGHTS!
WHEN DO WANT THEM?
NOW!
YOU WANT I SHOULD HANDLE IT?
NO, ALLOW ME, NED.
LISTEN, SISTER. YOU AIN'T GOT A...WHADDYACALLIT--A PARADE PERMIT FROM THE MAYOR'S OFFICE, BUT THE TRUTH IS--THIS AIN'T THE TIME FOR THIS.
WE'RE NOT ON PARADE. THIS IS A MARCH. TO SECURE EQUAL RIGHTS FOR WOMEN.
ALL Y'ALL GET ON HOME NOW, YOU HEAR?
UHNN! UNHAND ME, I WARN YOU!

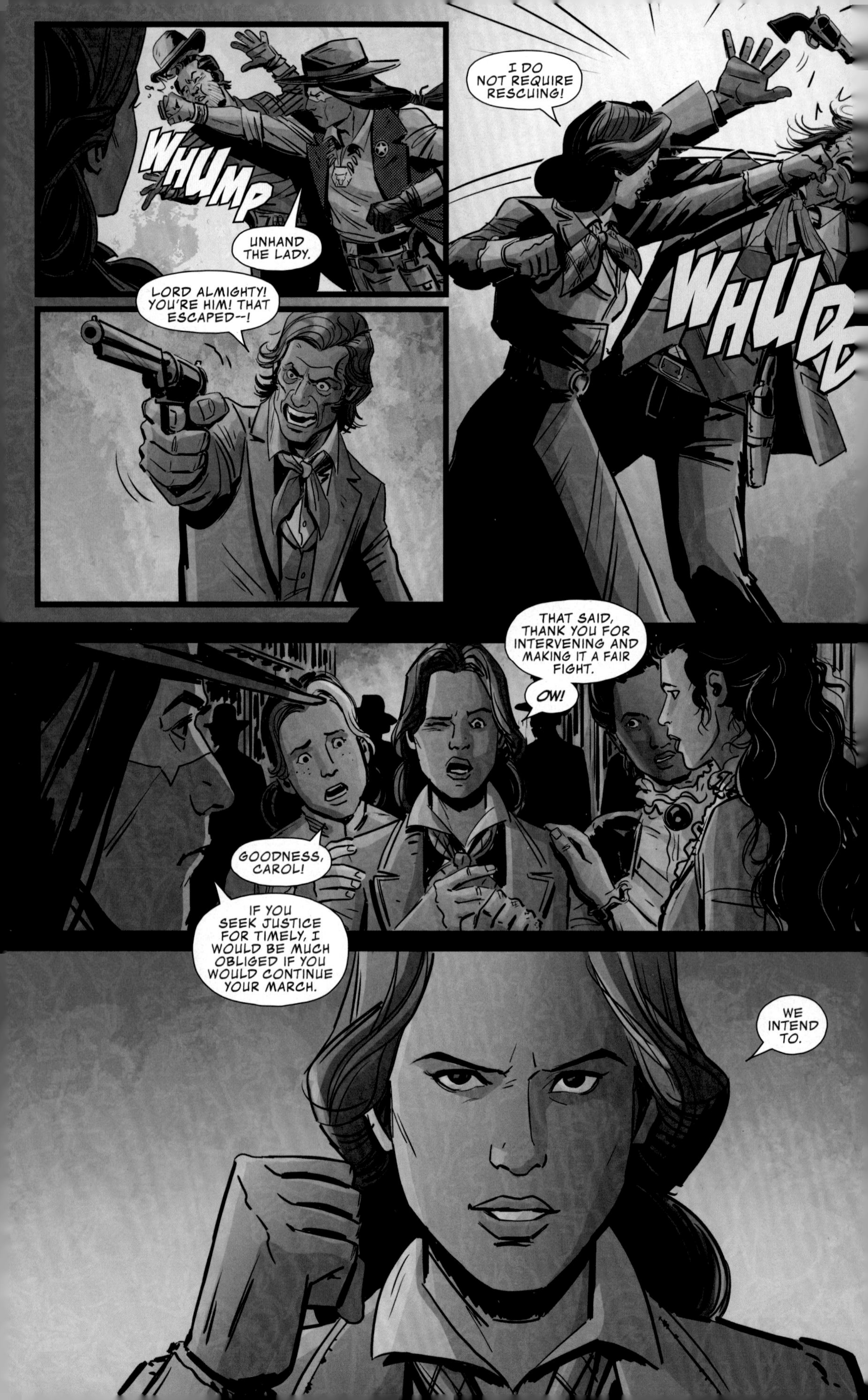
WHUMP
UNHAND THE LADY.
LORD ALMIGHTY! YOU'RE HIM! THAT ESCAPED--!
I DO NOT REQUIRE RESCUING!
WHUD
THAT SAID, THANK YOU FOR INTERVENING AND MAKING IT A FAIR FIGHT.
OW!
GOODNESS, CAROL!
IF YOU SEEK JUSTICE FOR TIMELY, I WOULD BE MUCH OBLIGED IF YOU WOULD CONTINUE YOUR MARCH.
WE INTEND TO.

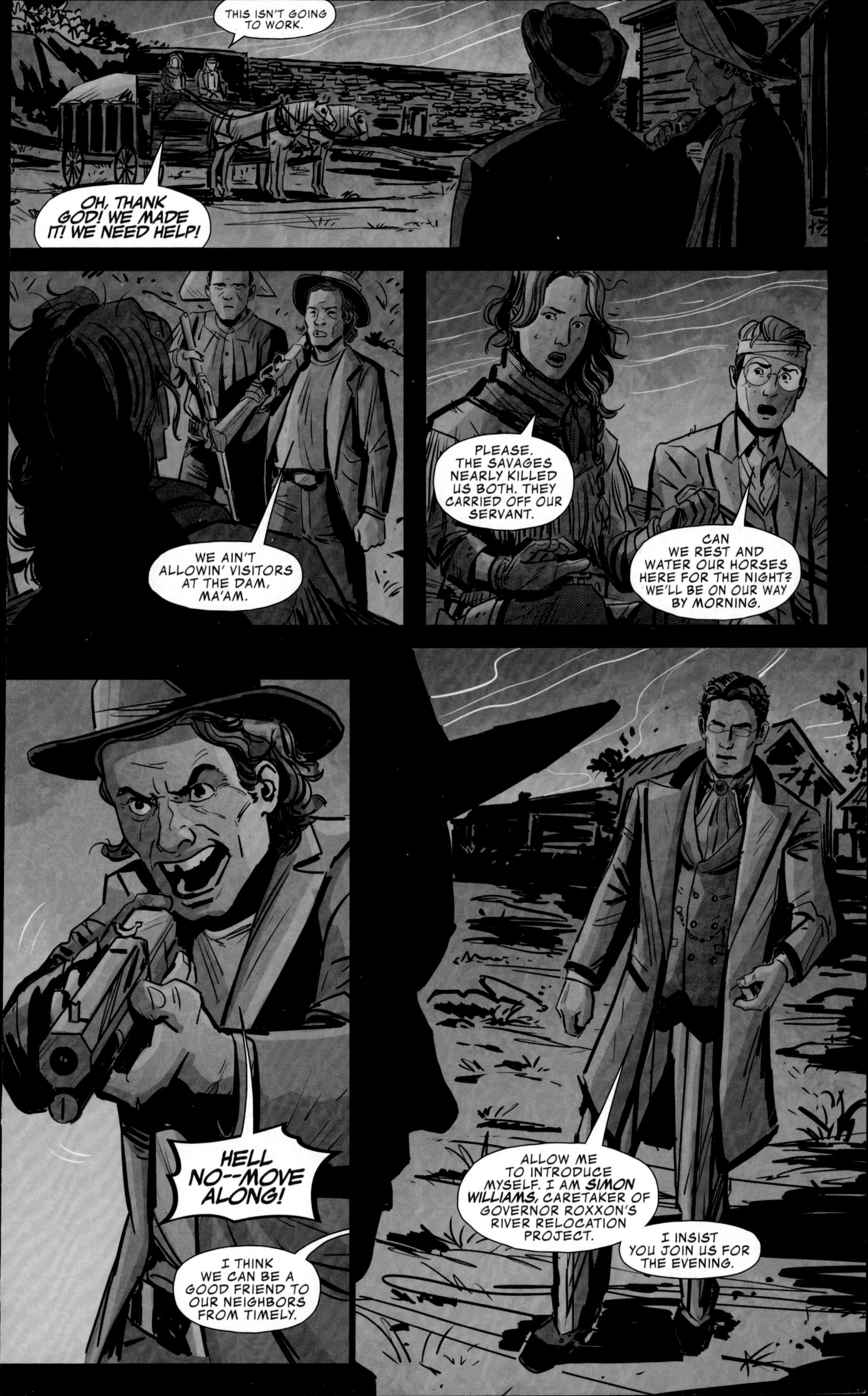
THIS ISN'T GOING TO WORK.
OH, THANK GOD! WE MADE IT! WE NEED HELP!
WE AIN'T ALLOWIN' VISITORS AT THE DAM, MA'AM.
PLEASE. THE SAVAGES NEARLY KILLED US BOTH. THEY CARRIED OFF OUR SERVANT.
CAN WE REST AND WATER OUR HORSES HERE FOR THE NIGHT? WE'LL BE ON OUR WAY BY MORNING.
HELL NO--MOVE ALONG!
I THINK WE CAN BE A GOOD FRIEND TO OUR NEIGHBORS FROM TIMELY.
ALLOW ME TO INTRODUCE MYSELF. I AM SIMON WILLIAMS, CARETAKER OF GOVERNOR ROXXON'S RIVER RELOCATION PROJECT.
I INSIST YOU JOIN US FOR THE EVENING.

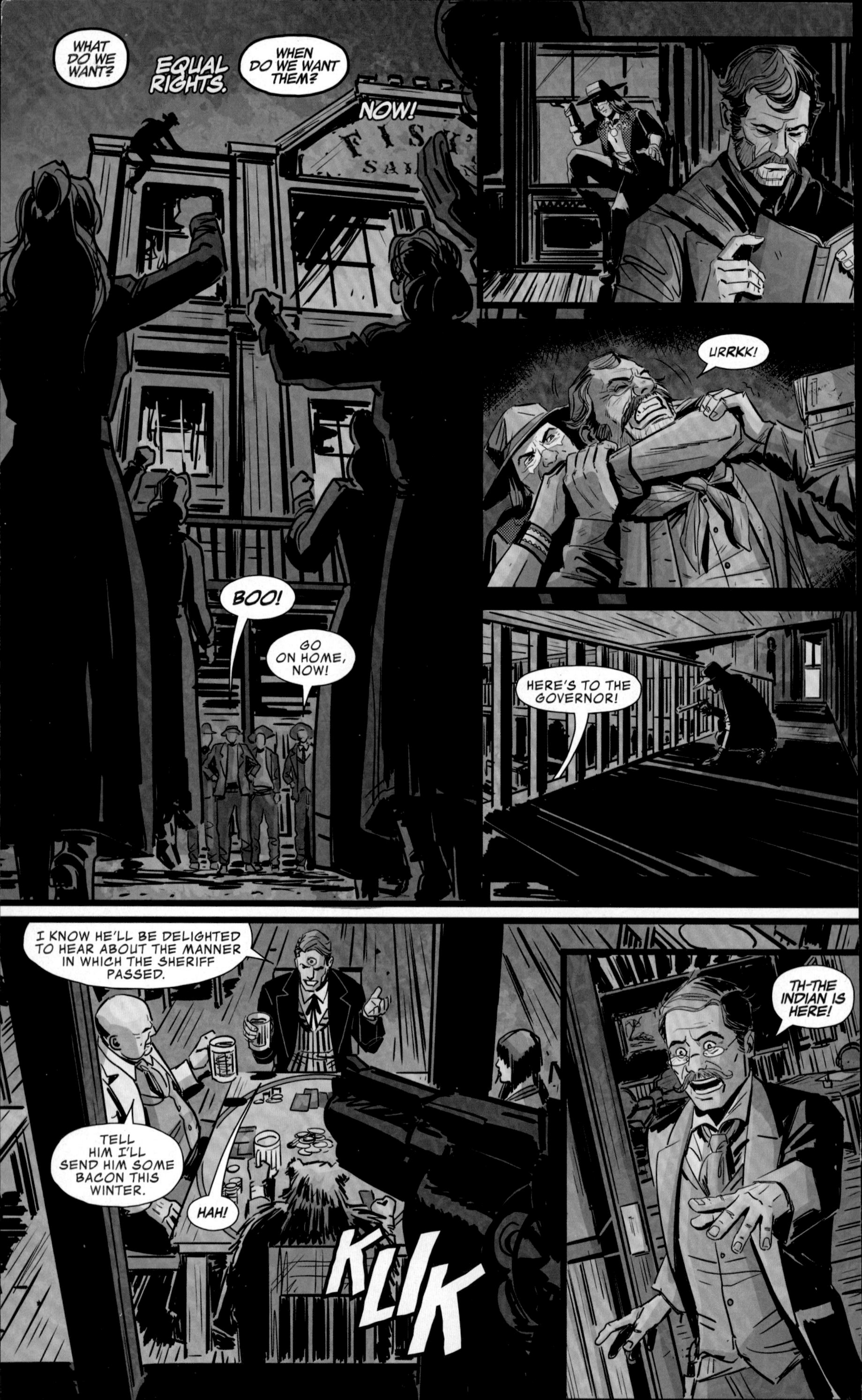
WHAT DO WE WANT?
EQUAL RIGHTS.
WHEN DO WE WANT THEM?
NOW!
BOO!
GO ON HOME, NOW!
URRKK!
HERE'S TO THE GOVERNOR!
I KNOW HE'LL BE DELIGHTED TO HEAR ABOUT THE MANNER IN WHICH THE SHERIFF PASSED.
TELL HIM I'LL SEND HIM SOME BACON THIS WINTER.
HAH!
KLIK
TH-THE INDIAN IS HERE!

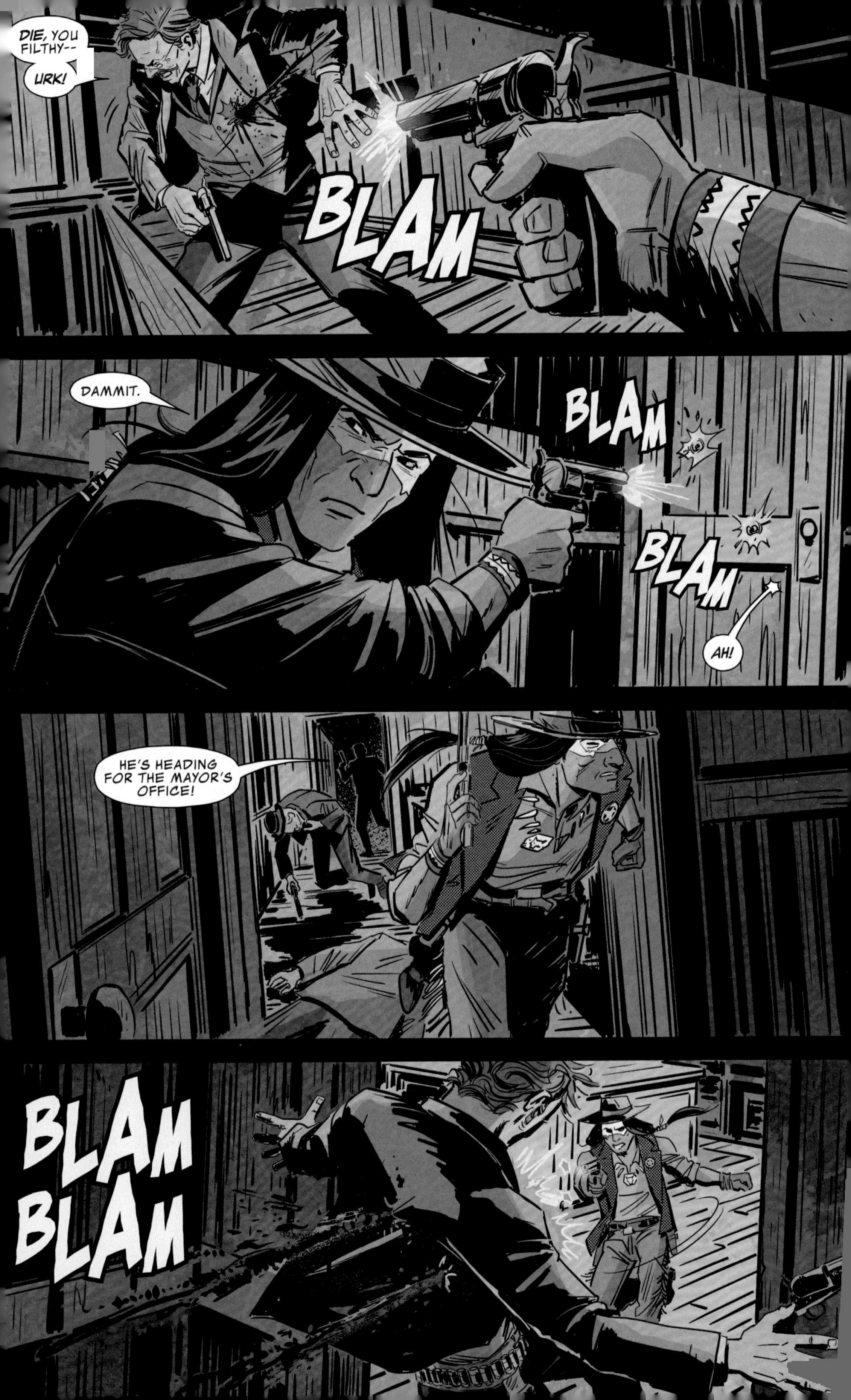
DIE, YOU FILTHY--
URK!
BLAM
DAMMIT.
BLAM
BLAM
AH!
HE'S HEADING FOR THE MAYOR'S OFFICE!
BLAM
BLAM

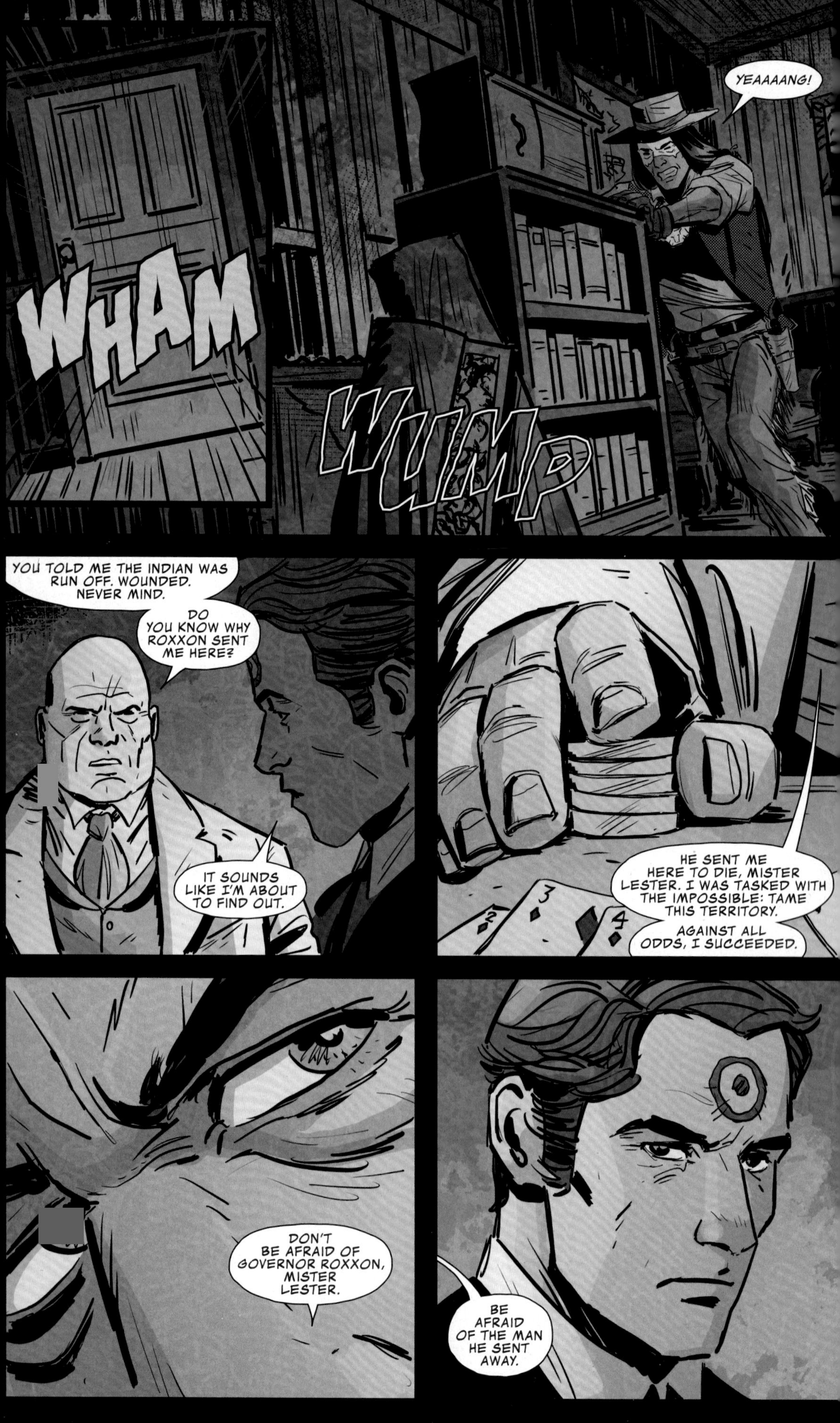
WHAM
WUMP
YEAAAANG!
YOU TOLD ME THE INDIAN WAS RUN OFF. WOUNDED. NEVER MIND.
DO YOU KNOW WHY ROXXON SENT ME HERE?
IT SOUNDS LIKE I'M ABOUT TO FIND OUT.
HE SENT ME HERE TO DIE, MISTER LESTER. I WAS TASKED WITH THE IMPOSSIBLE: TAME THIS TERRITORY.
AGAINST ALL ODDS, I SUCCEEDED.
DON'T BE AFRAID OF GOVERNOR ROXXON, MISTER LESTER.
BE AFRAID OF THE MAN HE SENT AWAY.

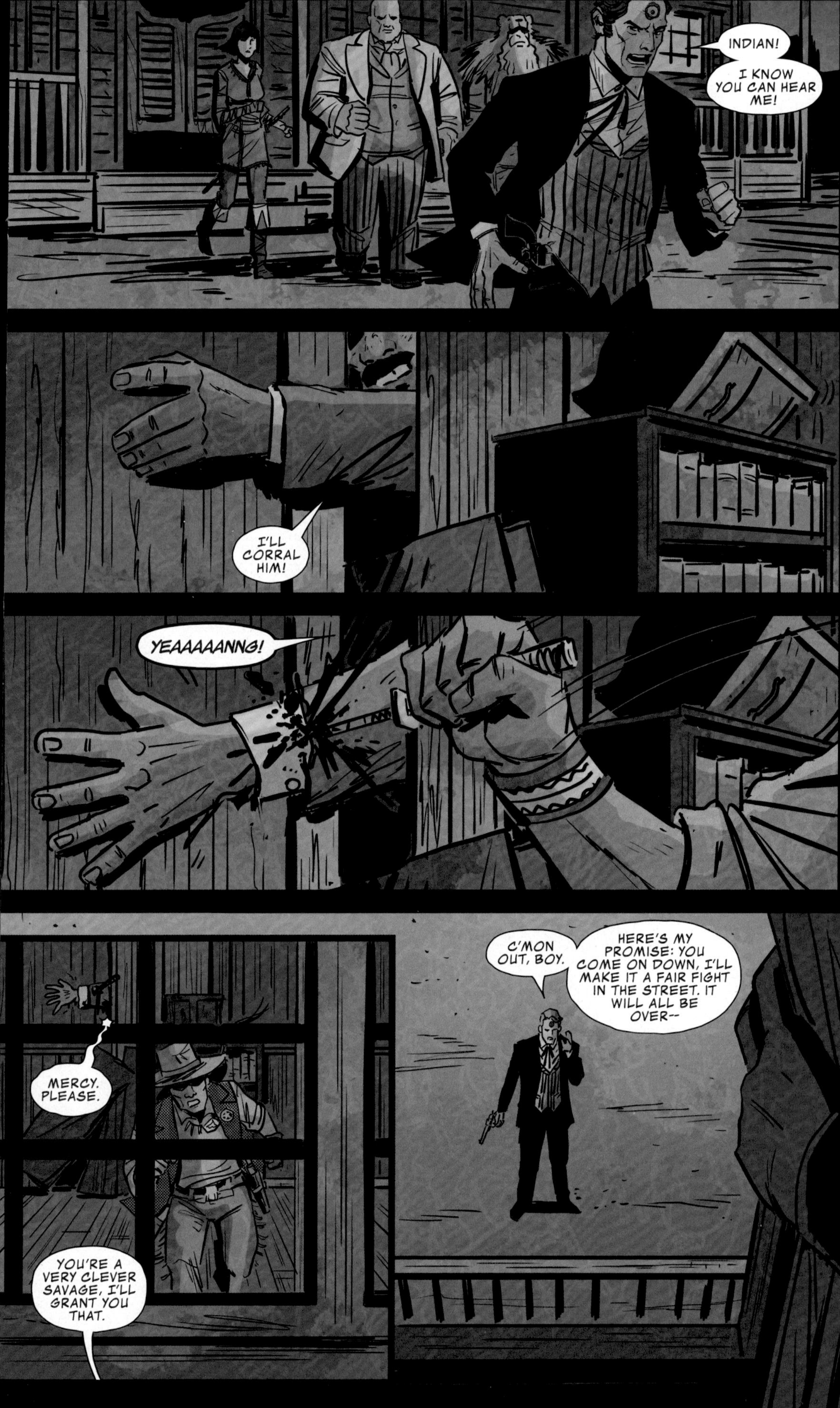
INDIAN!
I KNOW YOU CAN HEAR ME!
I'LL CORRAL HIM!
YEAAAAANNG!
MERCY. PLEASE.
YOU'RE A VERY CLEVER SAVAGE, I'LL GRANT YOU THAT.
C'MON OUT, BOY.
HERE'S MY PROMISE: YOU COME ON DOWN, I'LL MAKE IT A FAIR FIGHT IN THE STREET. IT WILL ALL BE OVER--

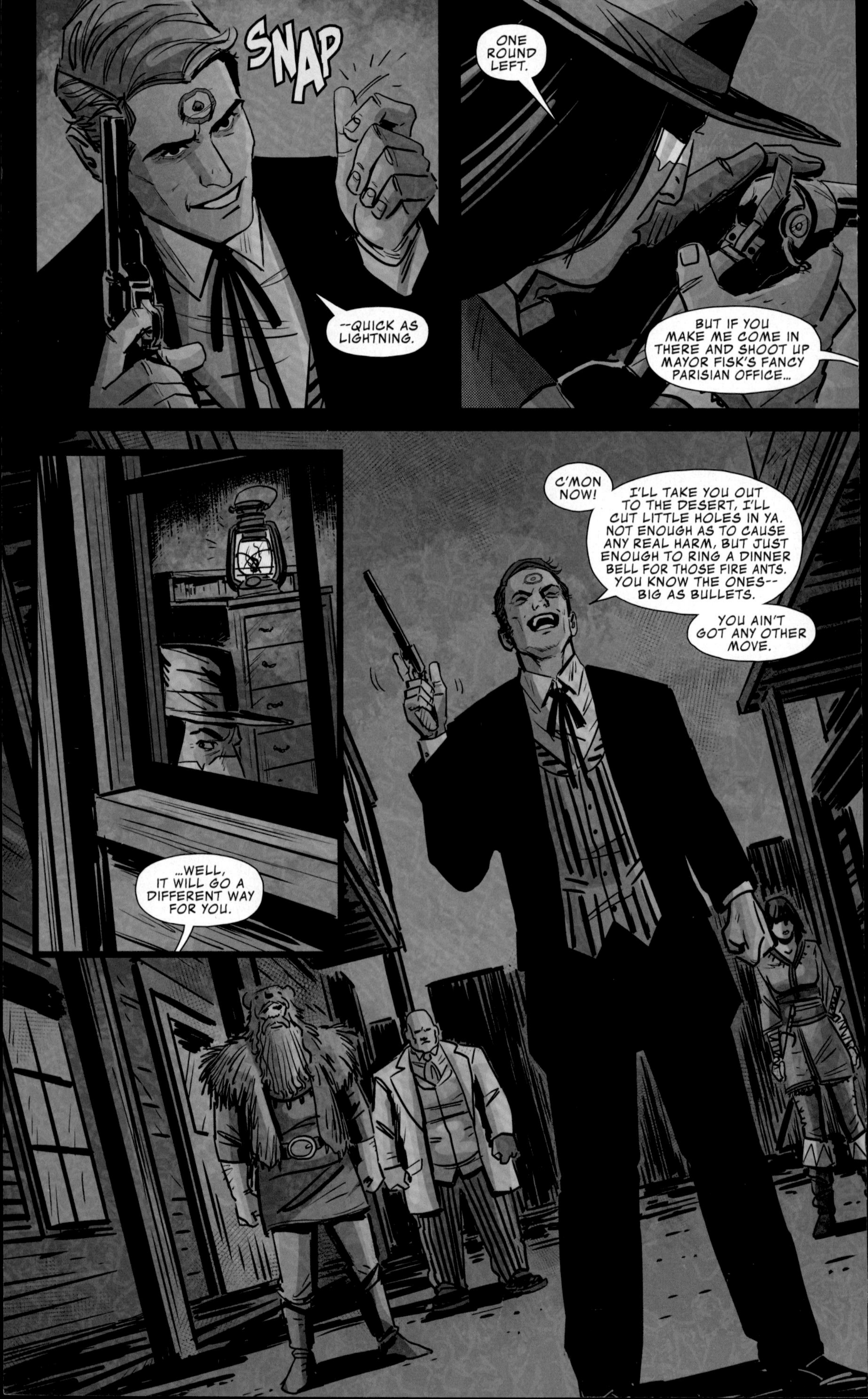
SNAP
--QUICK AS LIGHTNING.
ONE ROUND LEFT.
BUT IF YOU MAKE ME COME IN THERE AND SHOOT UP MAYOR FISK'S FANCY PARISIAN OFFICE...
...WELL, IT WILL GO A DIFFERENT WAY FOR YOU.
C'MON NOW!
I'LL TAKE YOU OUT TO THE DESERT, I'LL CUT LITTLE HOLES IN YA. NOT ENOUGH AS TO CAUSE ANY REAL HARM, BUT JUST ENOUGH TO RING A DINNER BELL FOR THOSE FIRE ANTS. YOU KNOW THE ONES--BIG AS BULLETS.
YOU AIN'T GOT ANY OTHER MOVE.

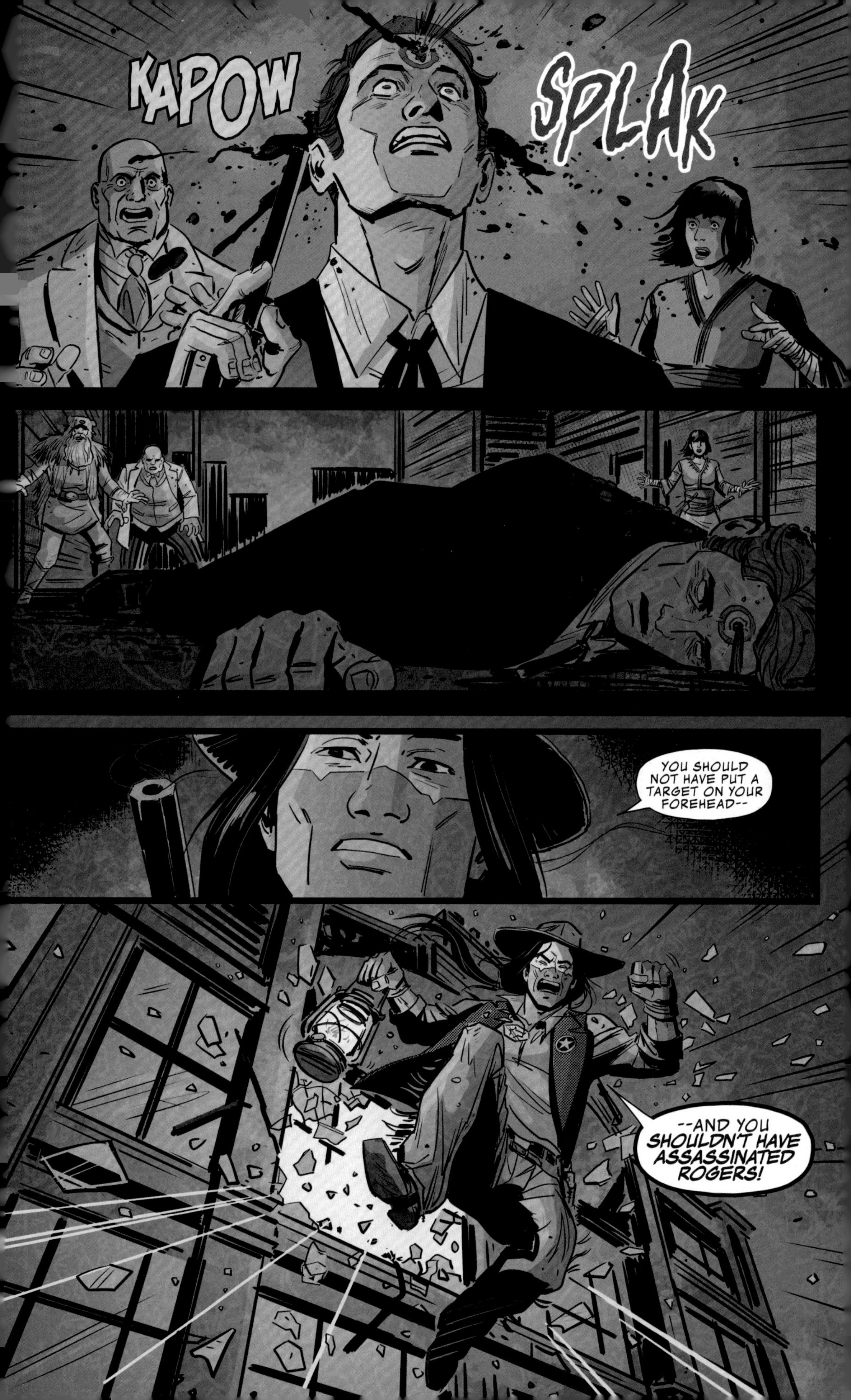
KAPOW
SPLAK
YOU SHOULD NOT HAVE PUT A TARGET ON YOUR FOREHEAD--
--AND YOU SHOULDN'T HAVE ASSASSINATED ROGERS!

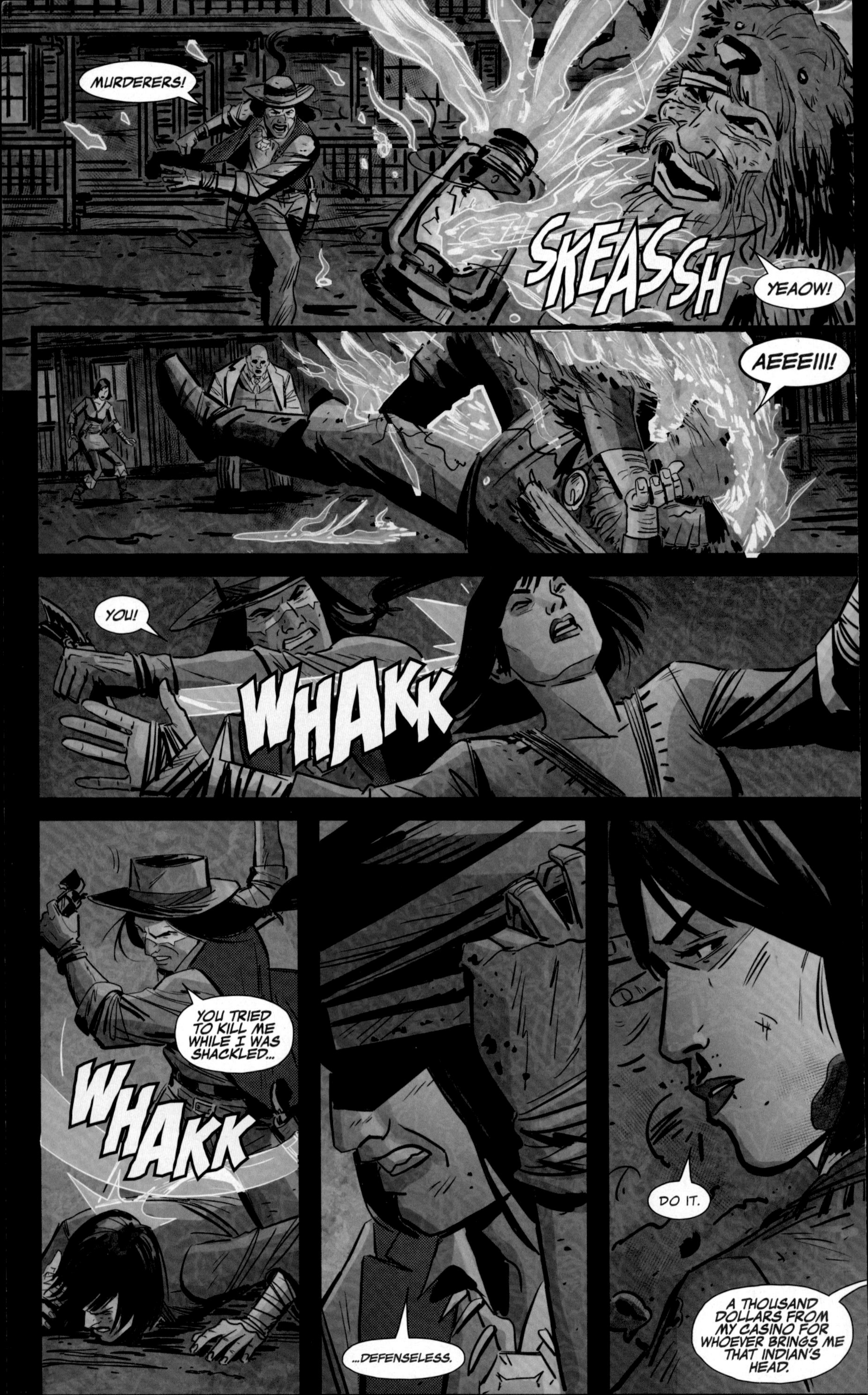
MURDERERS!
SKEASSH
YEAOW!
AEEEIII!
YOU!
WHAKK
YOU TRIED TO KILL ME WHILE I WAS SHACKLED...
WHAKK
...DEFENSELESS.
DO IT.
A THOUSAND DOLLARS FROM MY CASINO FOR WHOEVER BRINGS ME THAT INDIAN'S HEAD.

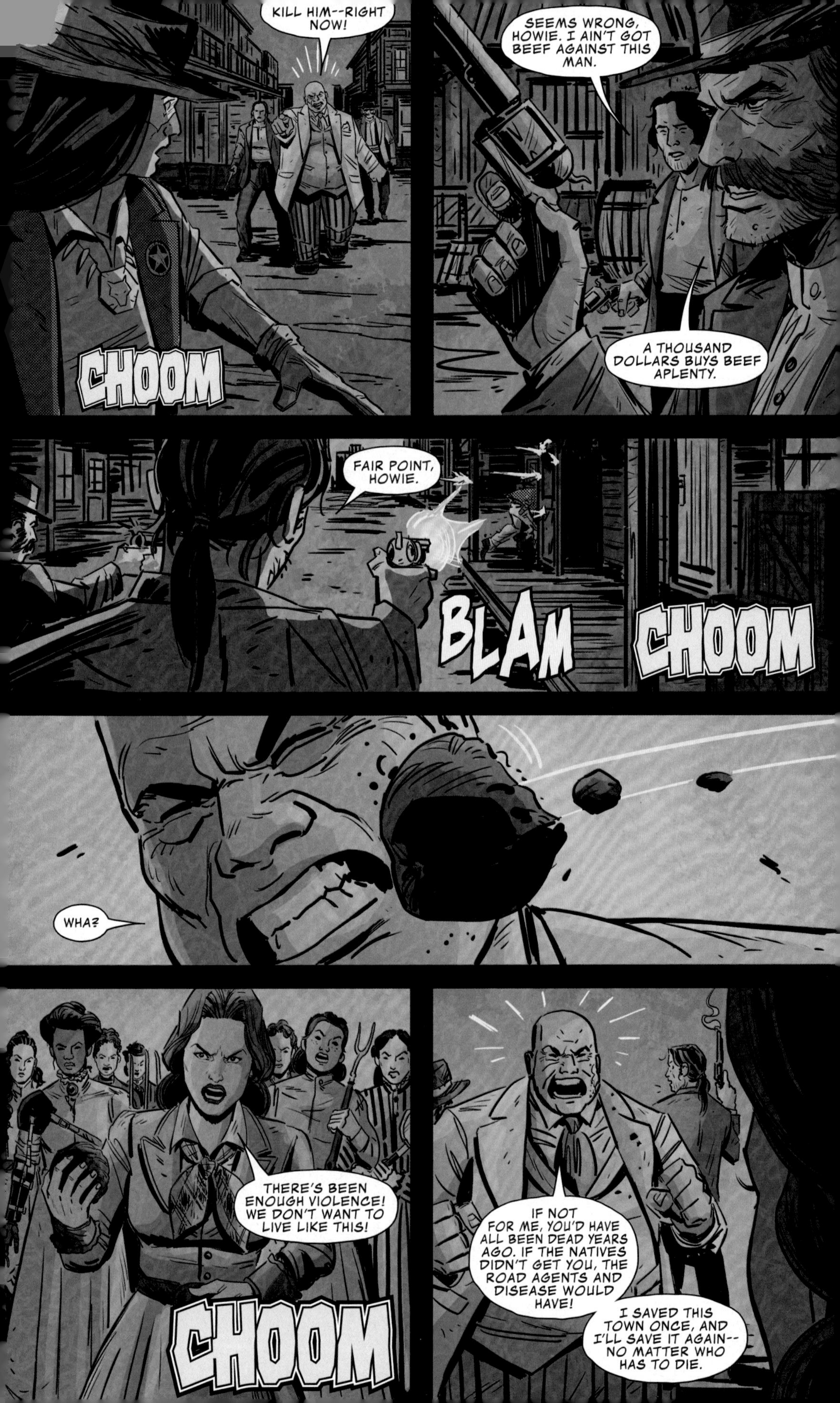
KILL HIM--RIGHT NOW!
CHOOM
SEEMS WRONG, HOWIE. I AIN'T GOT BEEF AGAINST THIS MAN.
A THOUSAND DOLLARS BUYS BEEF APLENTY.
FAIR POINT, HOWIE.
BLAM
CHOOM
WHA?
THERE'S BEEN ENOUGH VIOLENCE! WE DON'T WANT TO LIVE LIKE THIS!
CHOOM
IF NOT FOR ME, YOU'D HAVE ALL BEEN DEAD YEARS AGO. IF THE NATIVES DIDN'T GET YOU, THE ROAD AGENTS AND DISEASE WOULD HAVE!
I SAVED THIS TOWN ONCE, AND I'LL SAVE IT AGAIN-- NO MATTER WHO HAS TO DIE.

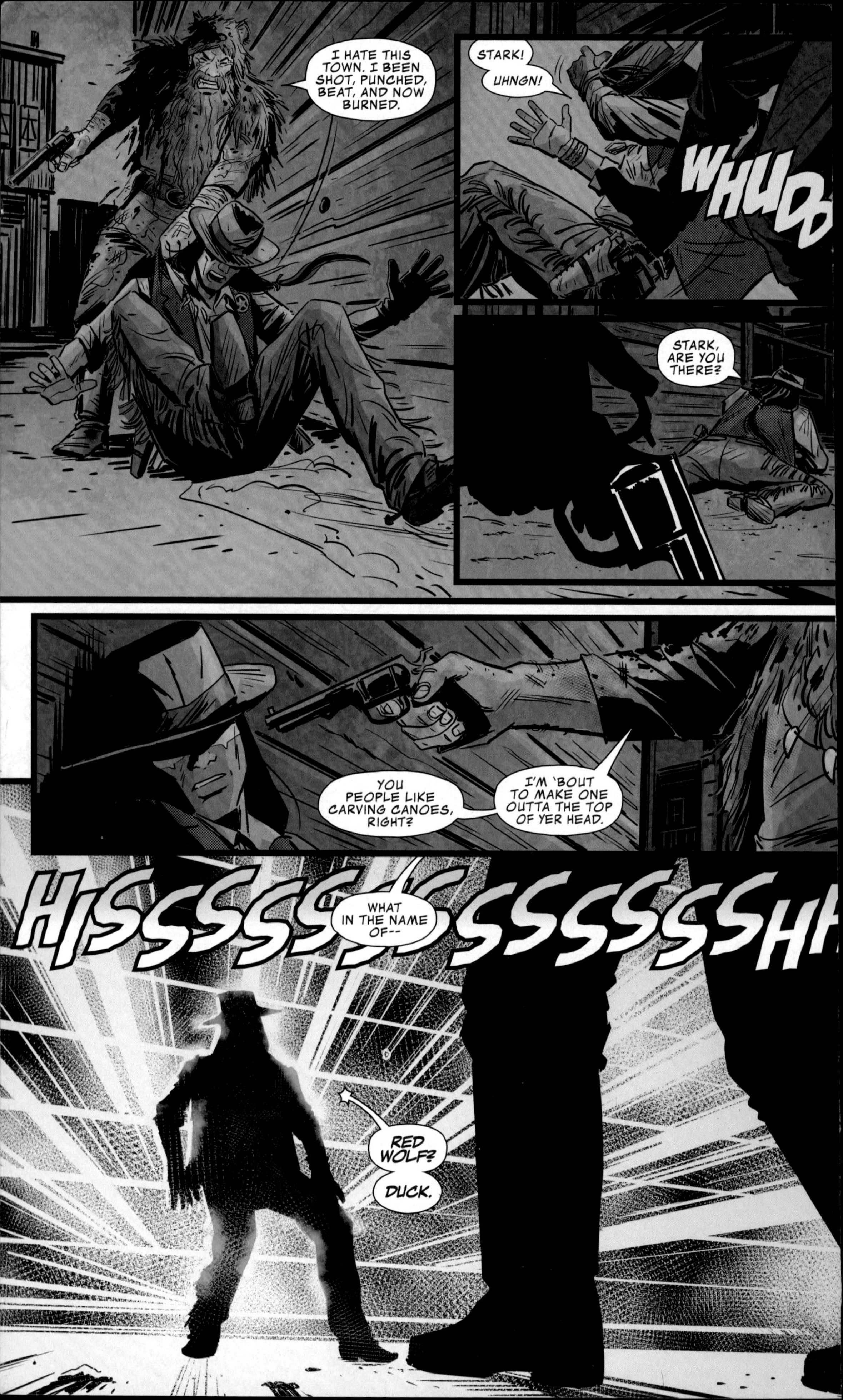
I HATE THIS TOWN. I BEEN SHOT, PUNCHED, BEAT, AND NOW BURNED.
STARK!
UHNGN!
WHUDD
STARK, ARE YOU THERE?
YOU PEOPLE LIKE CARVING CANOES, RIGHT?
I'M 'BOUT TO MAKE ONE OUTTA THE TOP OF YER HEAD.
HISSSSSSSSSSSSSSHH
WHAT IN THE NAME OF--
RED WOLF?
DUCK.

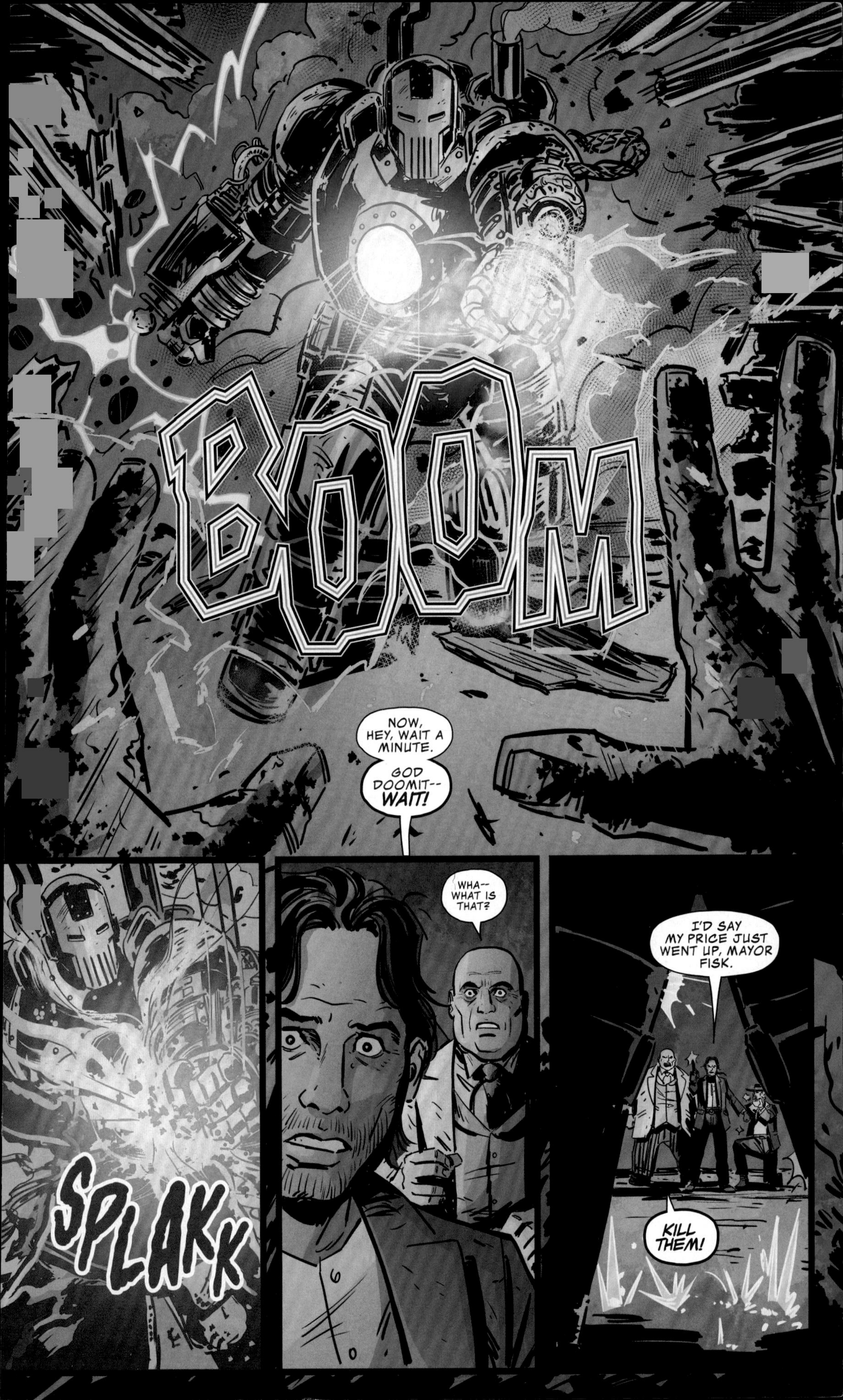
BOOM
NOW, HEY, WAIT A MINUTE.
GOD DOOMIT-- WAIT!
SPLAKK
WHA-- WHAT IS THAT?
I'D SAY MY PRICE JUST WENT UP, MAYOR FISK.
KILL THEM!

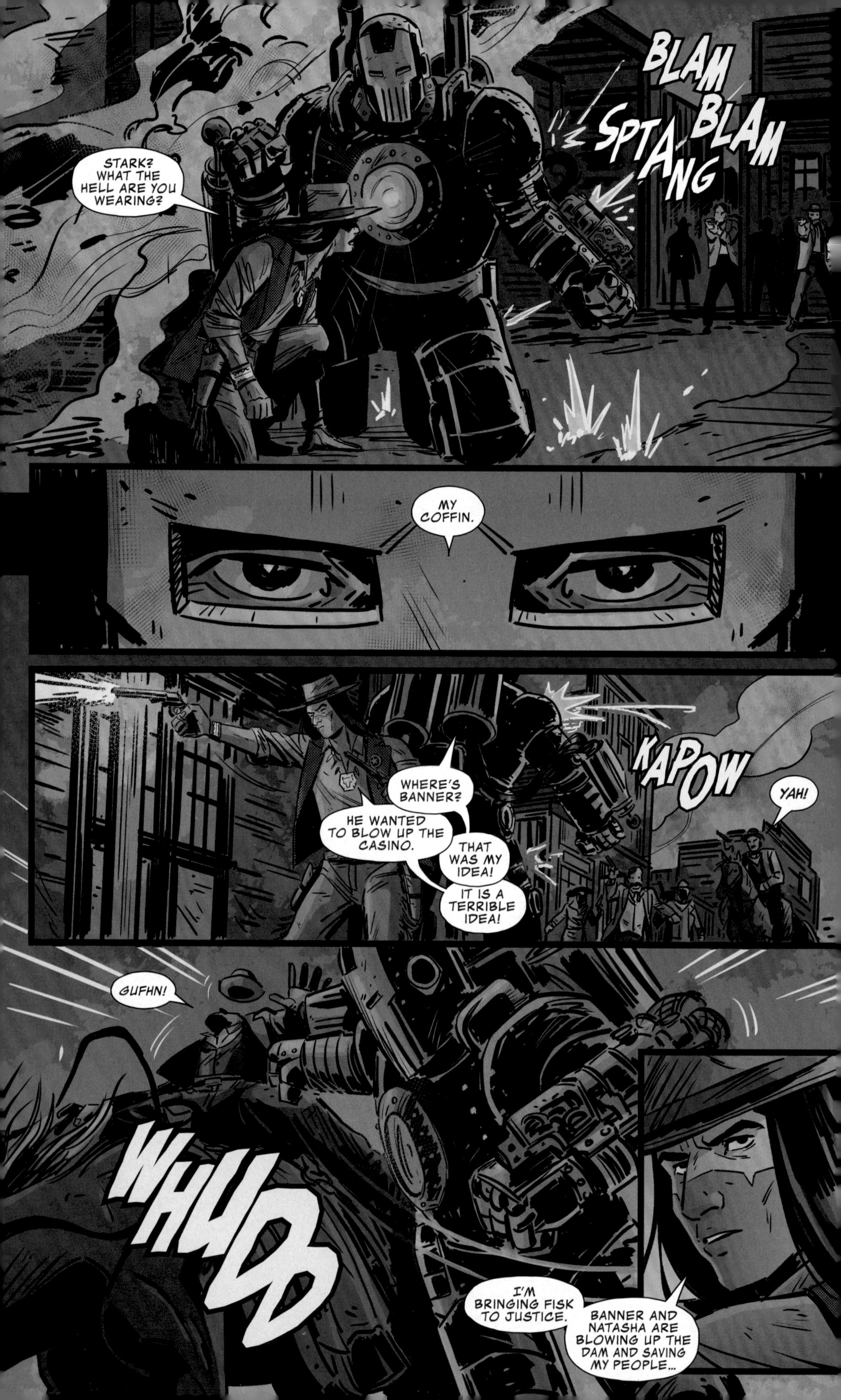
STARK? WHAT THE HELL ARE YOU WEARING?
BLAM
BLAM
BLAM
SPTANG
MY COFFIN.
WHERE'S BANNER?
HE WANTED TO BLOW UP THE CASINO.
THAT WAS MY IDEA!
IT IS A TERRIBLE IDEA!
KAPOW
YAH!
GUFHN!
WHUD
I'M BRINGING FISK TO JUSTICE.
BANNER AND NATASHA ARE BLOWING UP THE DAM AND SAVING MY PEOPLE...

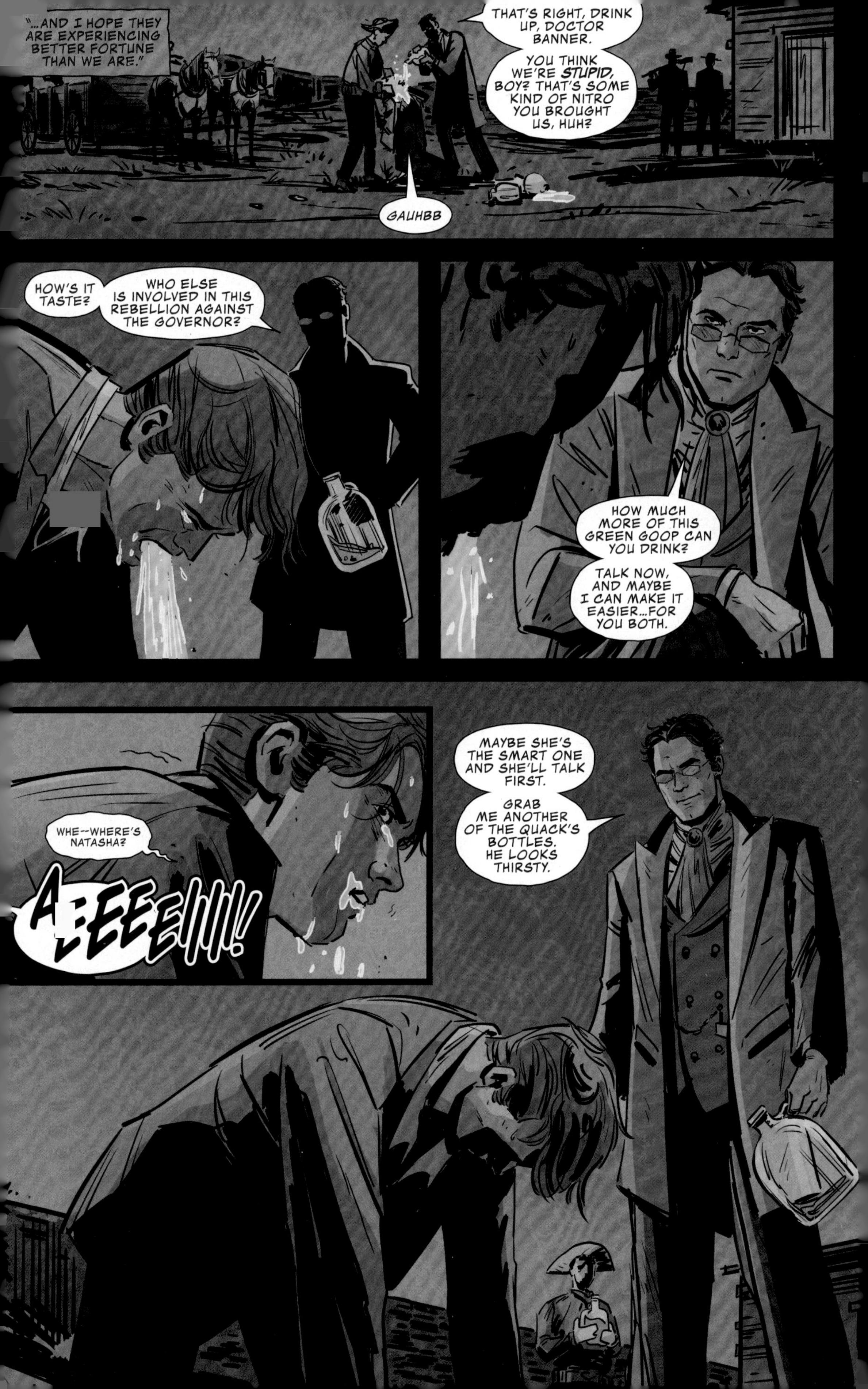
"...AND I HOPE THEY ARE EXPERIENCING BETTER FORTUNE THAN WE ARE."
THAT'S RIGHT, DRINK UP, DOCTOR BANNER.
YOU THINK WE'RE STUPID, BOY? THAT'S SOME KIND OF NITRO YOU BROUGHT US, HUH?
GAUHBB
HOW'S IT TASTE?
WHO ELSE IS INVOLVED IN THIS REBELLION AGAINST THE GOVERNOR?
HOW MUCH MORE OF THIS GREEN GOOP CAN YOU DRINK?
TALK NOW, AND MAYBE I CAN MAKE IT EASIER...FOR YOU BOTH.
WHE--WHERE'S NATASHA?
AEEEEIIIII!
MAYBE SHE'S THE SMART ONE AND SHE'LL TALK FIRST.
GRAB ME ANOTHER OF THE QUACK'S BOTTLES. HE LOOKS THIRSTY.

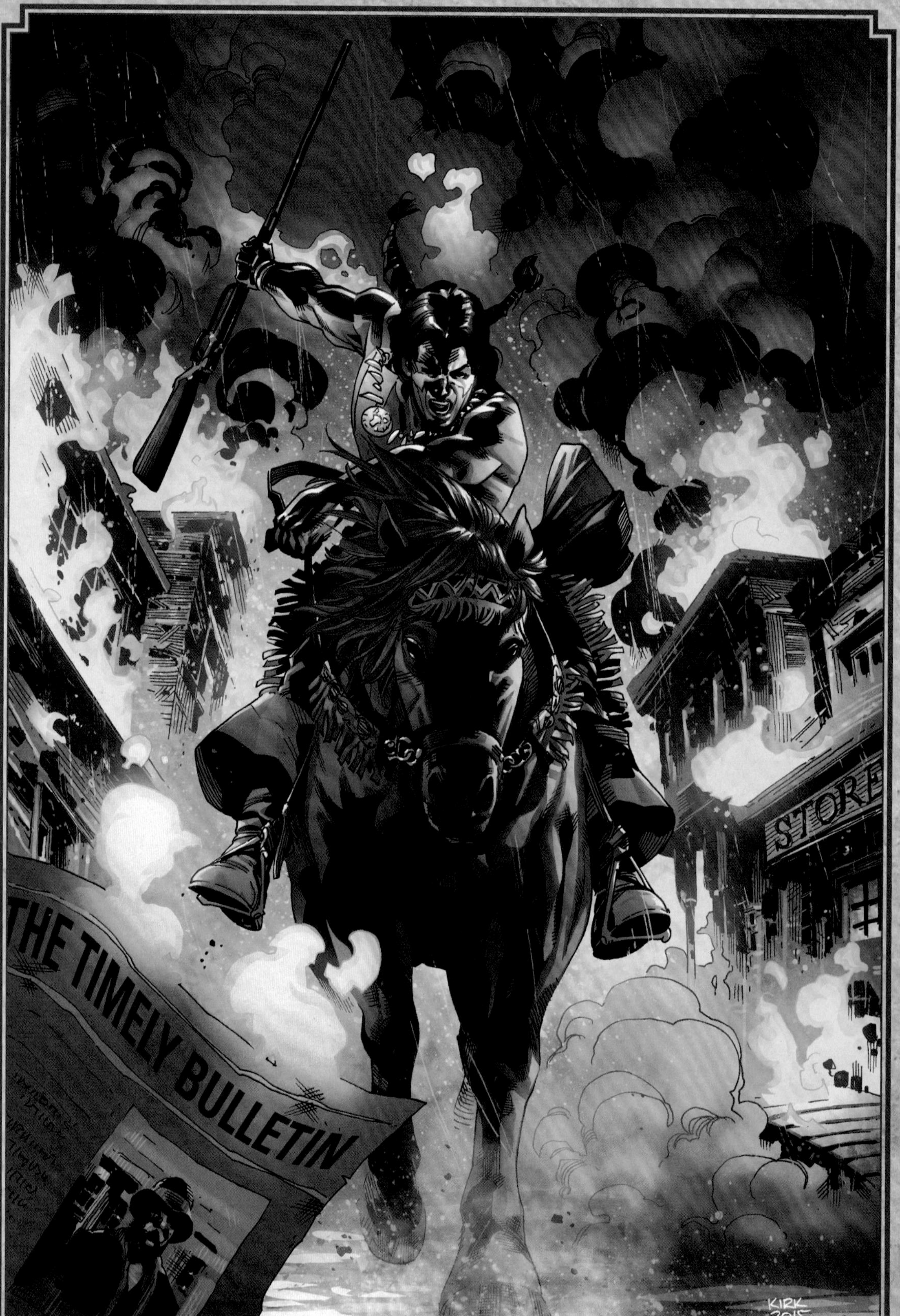
THE TIMELY BULLETIN
STORE
KIRK 2015

4

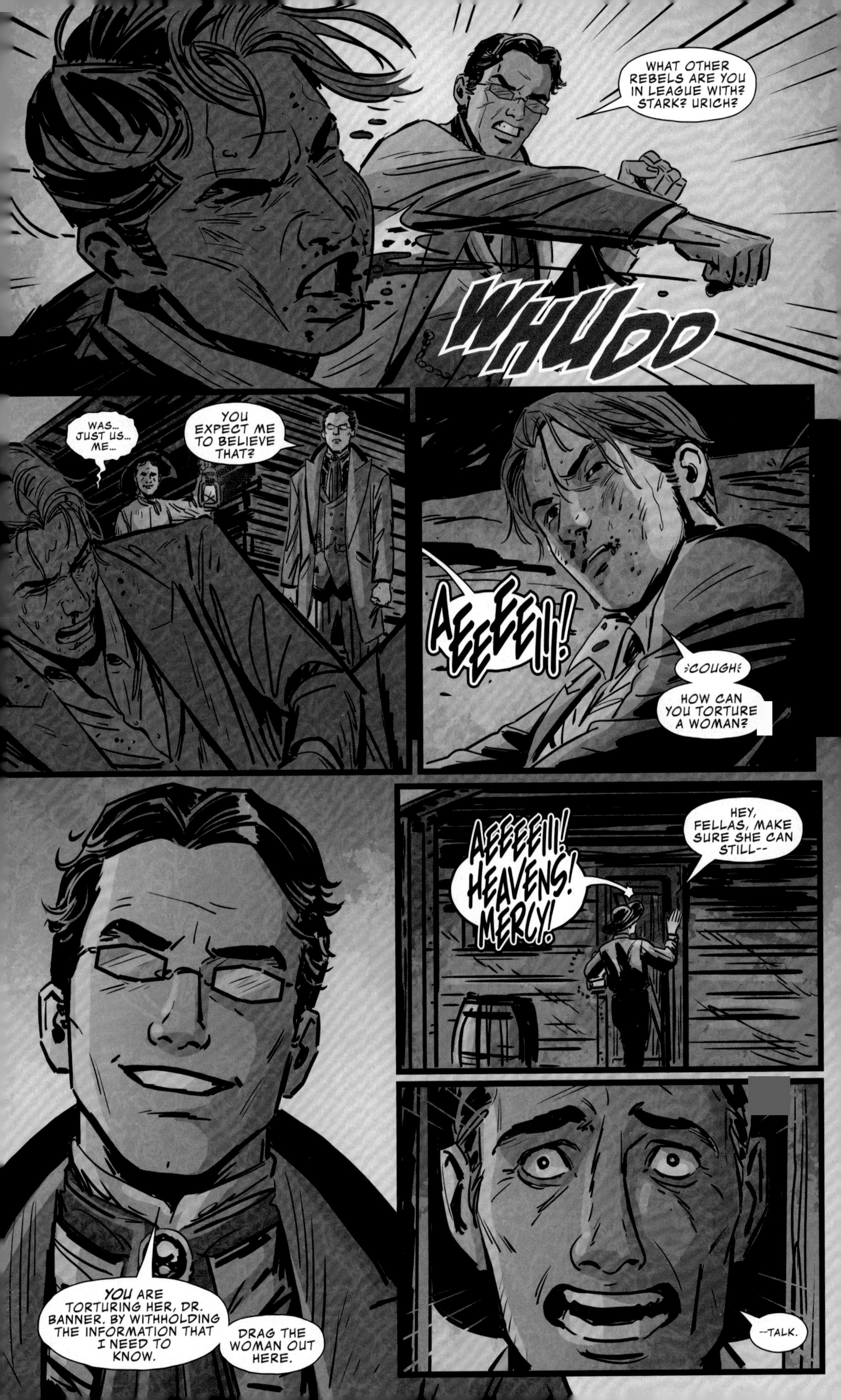
WHAT OTHER REBELS ARE YOU IN LEAGUE WITH? STARK? URICH?
WHUDD
WAS... JUST US... ME...
YOU EXPECT ME TO BELIEVE THAT?
AEEEEIII!
:COUGH:
HOW CAN YOU TORTURE A WOMAN?
YOU ARE TORTURING HER, DR. BANNER. BY WITHHOLDING THE INFORMATION THAT I NEED TO KNOW.
DRAG THE WOMAN OUT HERE.
AEEEEIII! HEAVENS! MERCY!
HEY, FELLAS, MAKE SURE SHE CAN STILL--
--TALK.

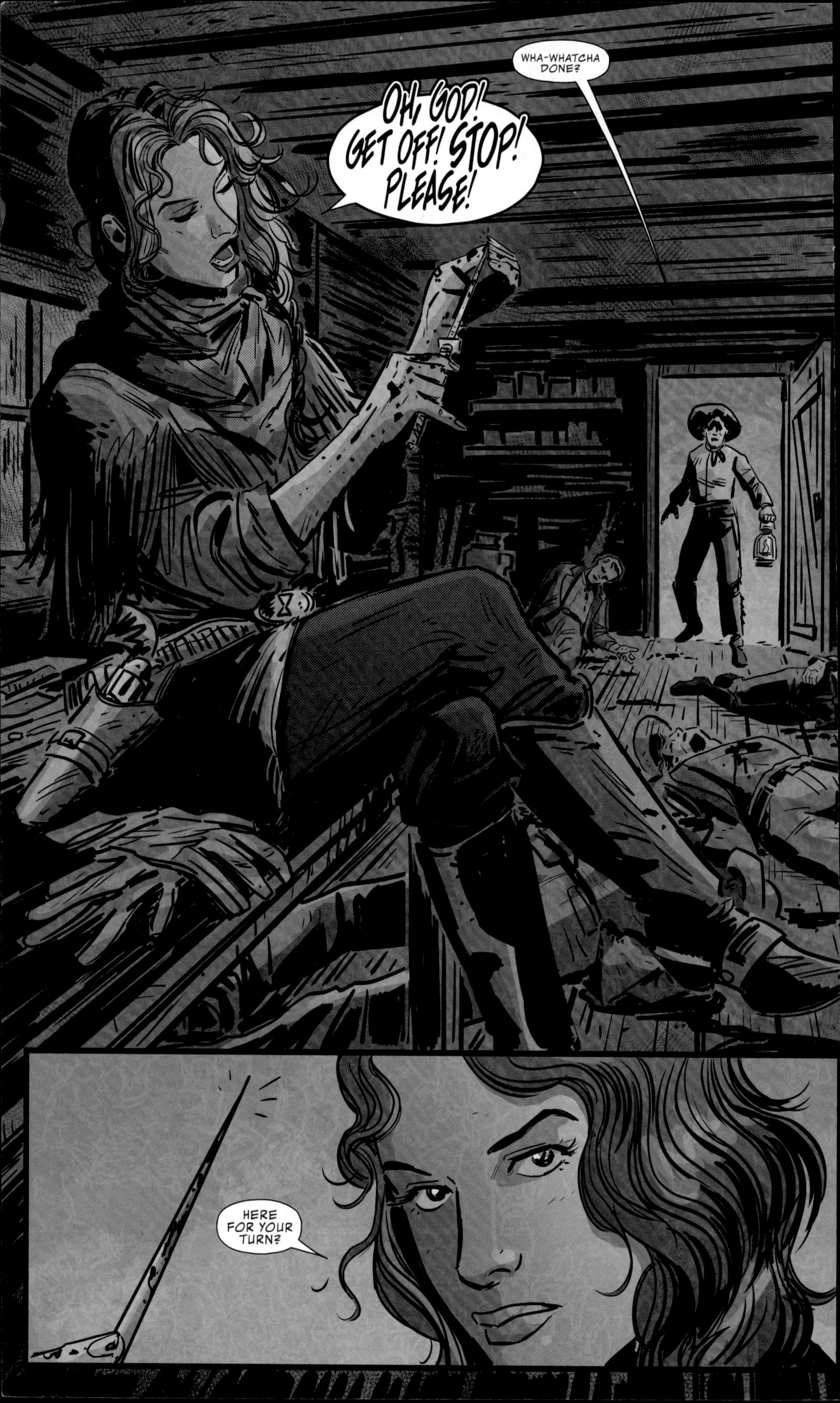

WHA-WHATCHA DONE?
OH, GOD! GET OFF! STOP! PLEASE!
HERE FOR YOUR TURN?

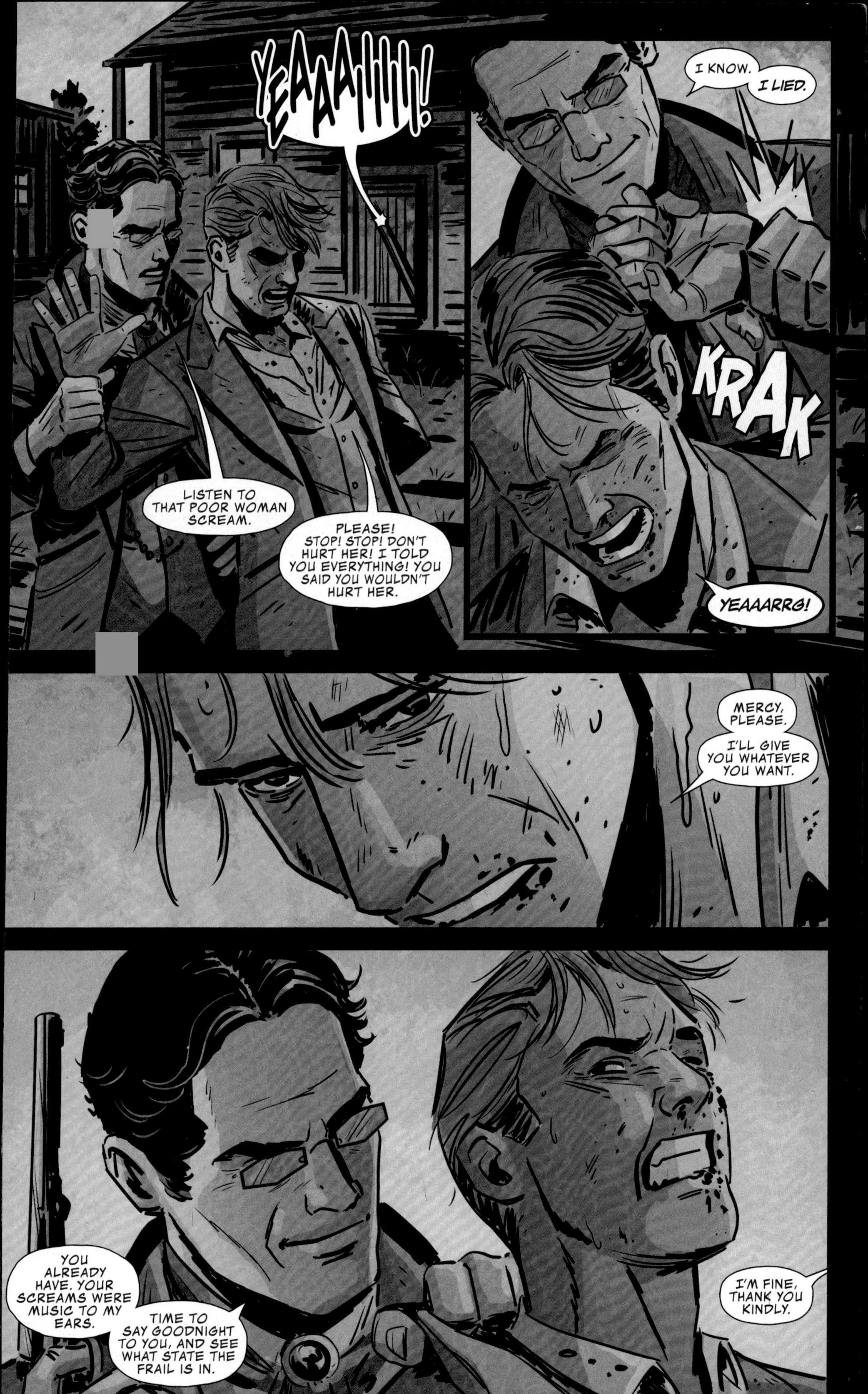
YEAAAHHHH!
LISTEN TO THAT POOR WOMAN SCREAM.
PLEASE! STOP! STOP! DON'T HURT HER! I TOLD YOU EVERYTHING! YOU SAID YOU WOULDN'T HURT HER.
I KNOW. I LIED.
KRAK
YEAAARRG!
MERCY, PLEASE.
I'LL GIVE YOU WHATEVER YOU WANT.
YOU ALREADY HAVE. YOUR SCREAMS WERE MUSIC TO MY EARS.
TIME TO SAY GOODNIGHT TO YOU, AND SEE WHAT STATE THE FRAIL IS IN.
I'M FINE, THANK YOU KINDLY.

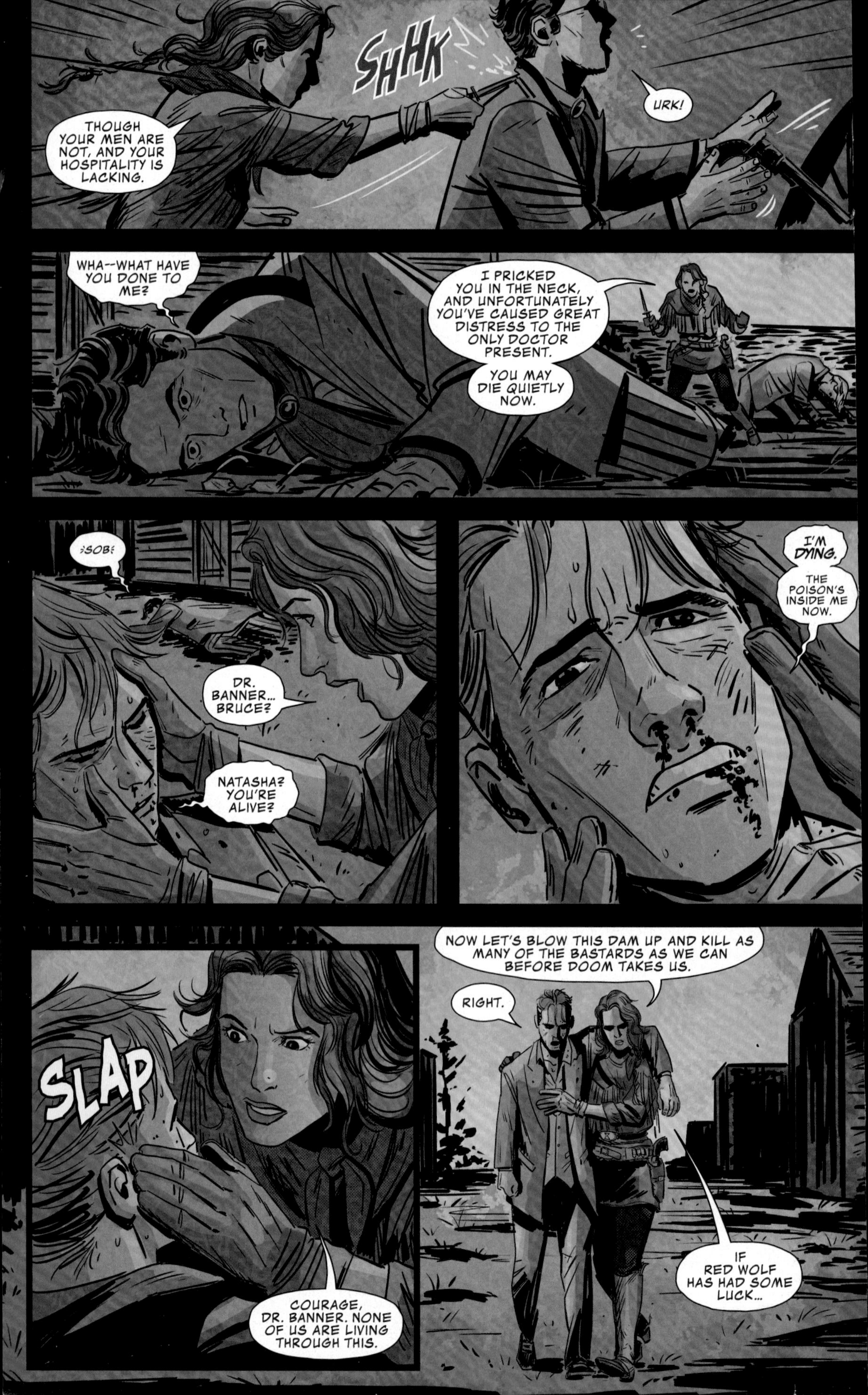
THOUGH YOUR MEN ARE NOT, AND YOUR HOSPITALITY IS LACKING.
SHHK
URK!
WHA--WHAT HAVE YOU DONE TO ME?
I PRICKED YOU IN THE NECK, AND UNFORTUNATELY YOU'VE CAUSED GREAT DISTRESS TO THE ONLY DOCTOR PRESENT.
YOU MAY DIE QUIETLY NOW.
SOB
DR. BANNER... BRUCE?
NATASHA? YOU'RE ALIVE?
I'M DYING.
THE POISON'S INSIDE ME NOW.
SLAP
COURAGE, DR. BANNER. NONE OF US ARE LIVING THROUGH THIS.
NOW LET'S BLOW THIS DAM UP AND KILL AS MANY OF THE BASTARDS AS WE CAN BEFORE DOOM TAKES US.
RIGHT.
IF RED WOLF HAS HAD SOME LUCK...

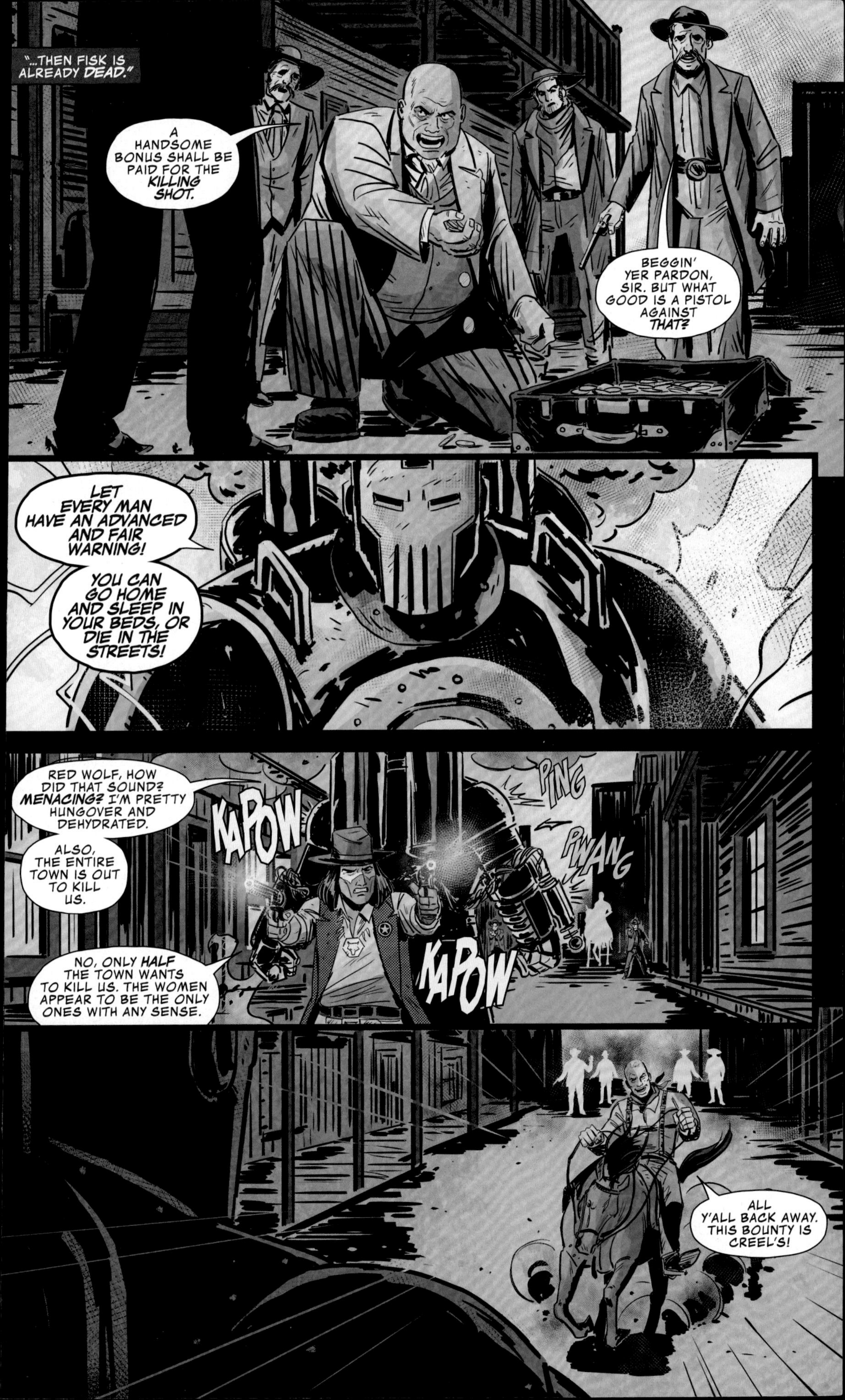
"...THEN FISK IS ALREADY DEAD."
A HANDSOME BONUS SHALL BE PAID FOR THE KILLING SHOT.
BEGGIN' YER PARDON, SIR. BUT WHAT GOOD IS A PISTOL AGAINST THAT?
LET EVERY MAN HAVE AN ADVANCED AND FAIR WARNING!
YOU CAN GO HOME AND SLEEP IN YOUR BEDS, OR DIE IN THE STREETS!
RED WOLF, HOW DID THAT SOUND? MENACING? I'M PRETTY HUNGOVER AND DEHYDRATED.
ALSO, THE ENTIRE TOWN IS OUT TO KILL US.
KAPOW
PING
PWANG
KAPOW
NO, ONLY HALF THE TOWN WANTS TO KILL US. THE WOMEN APPEAR TO BE THE ONLY ONES WITH ANY SENSE.
ALL Y'ALL BACK AWAY. THIS BOUNTY IS CREEL'S!

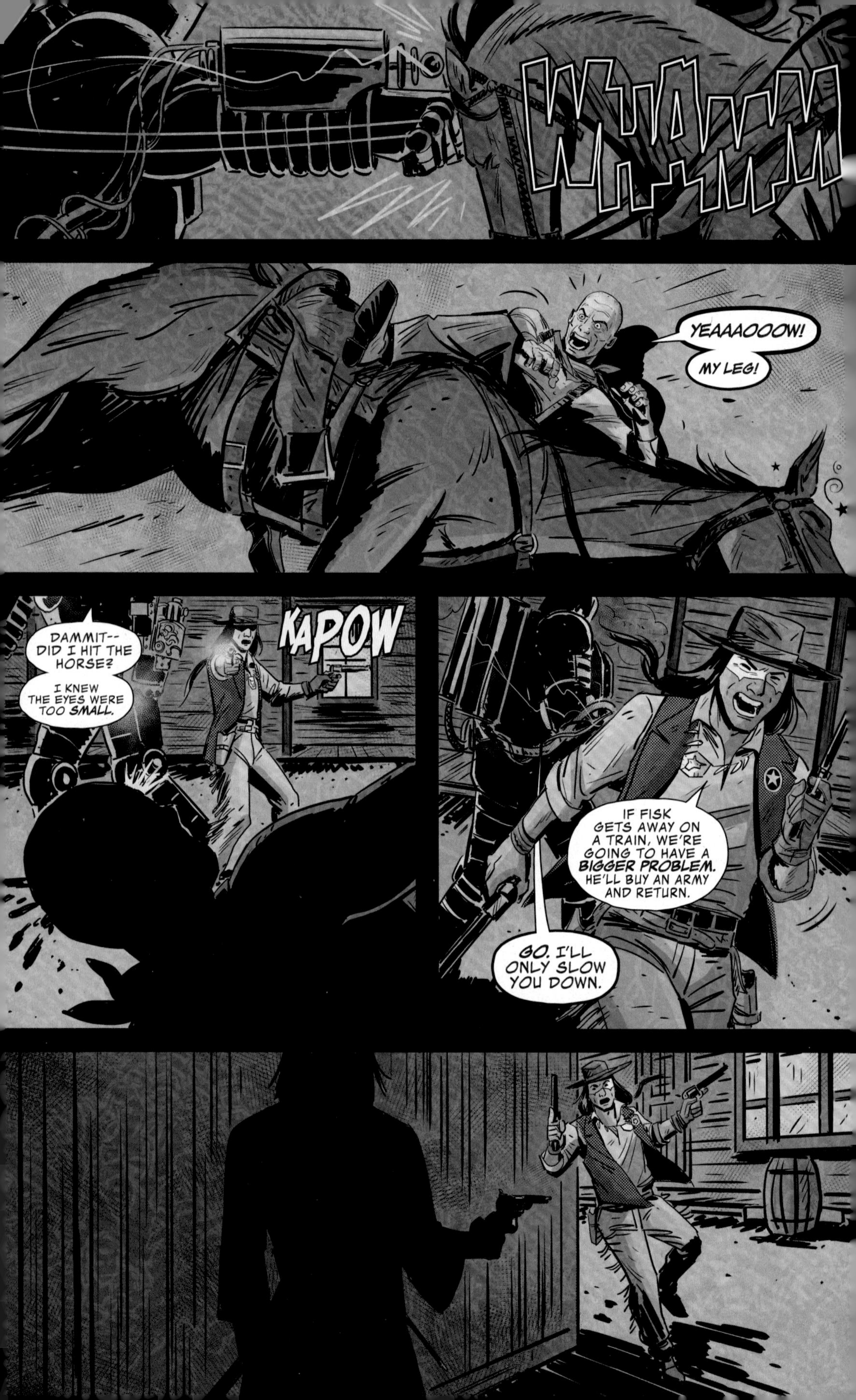
WHAMM
YEAAAOOOW!
MY LEG!
DAMMIT--
DID I HIT THE HORSE?
I KNEW THE EYES WERE TOO SMALL.
KAPOW
IF FISK GETS AWAY ON A TRAIN, WE'RE GOING TO HAVE A BIGGER PROBLEM. HE'LL BUY AN ARMY AND RETURN.
GO. I'LL ONLY SLOW YOU DOWN.

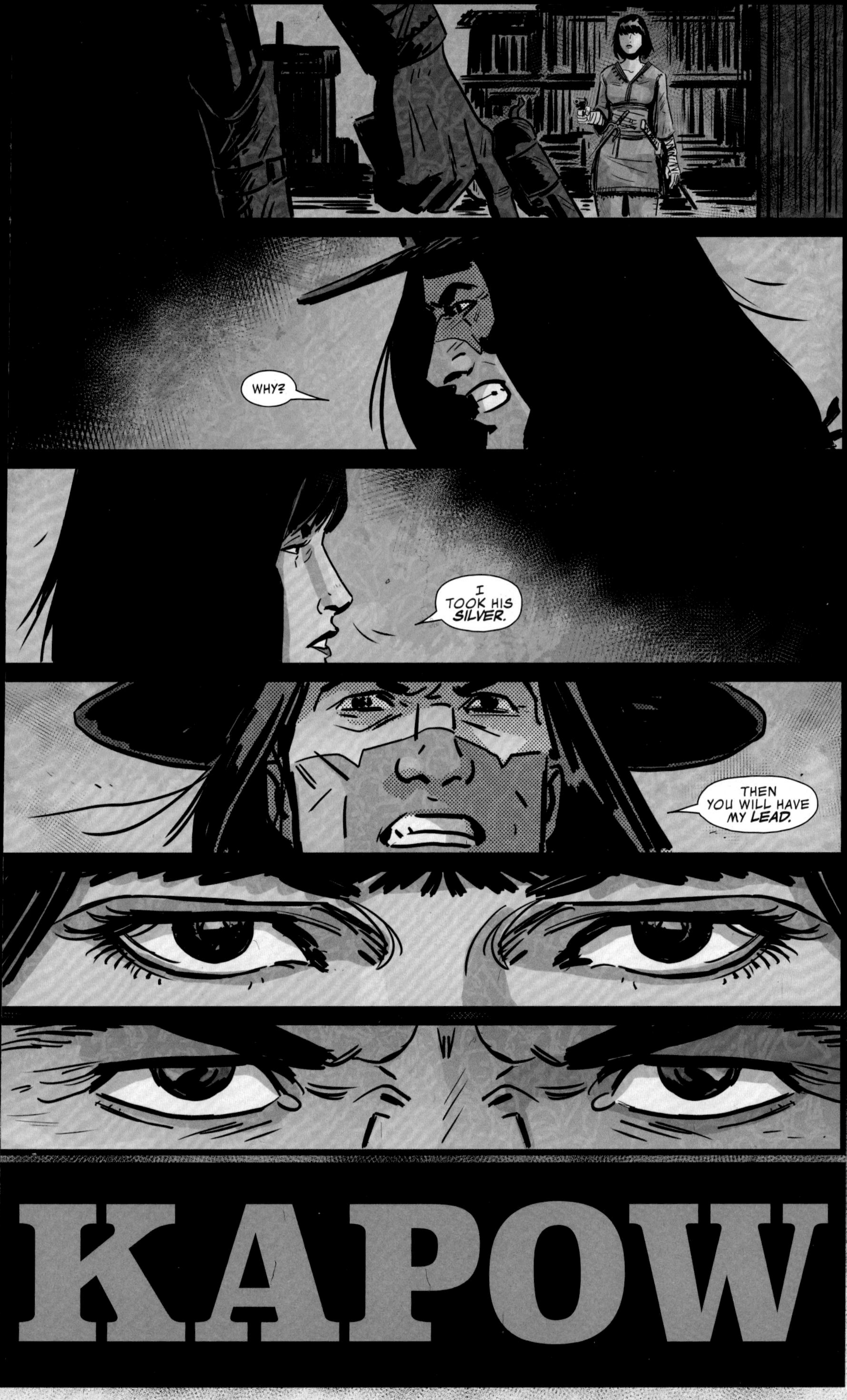
WHY?
I TOOK HIS SILVER.
THEN YOU WILL HAVE MY LEAD.
KAPOW

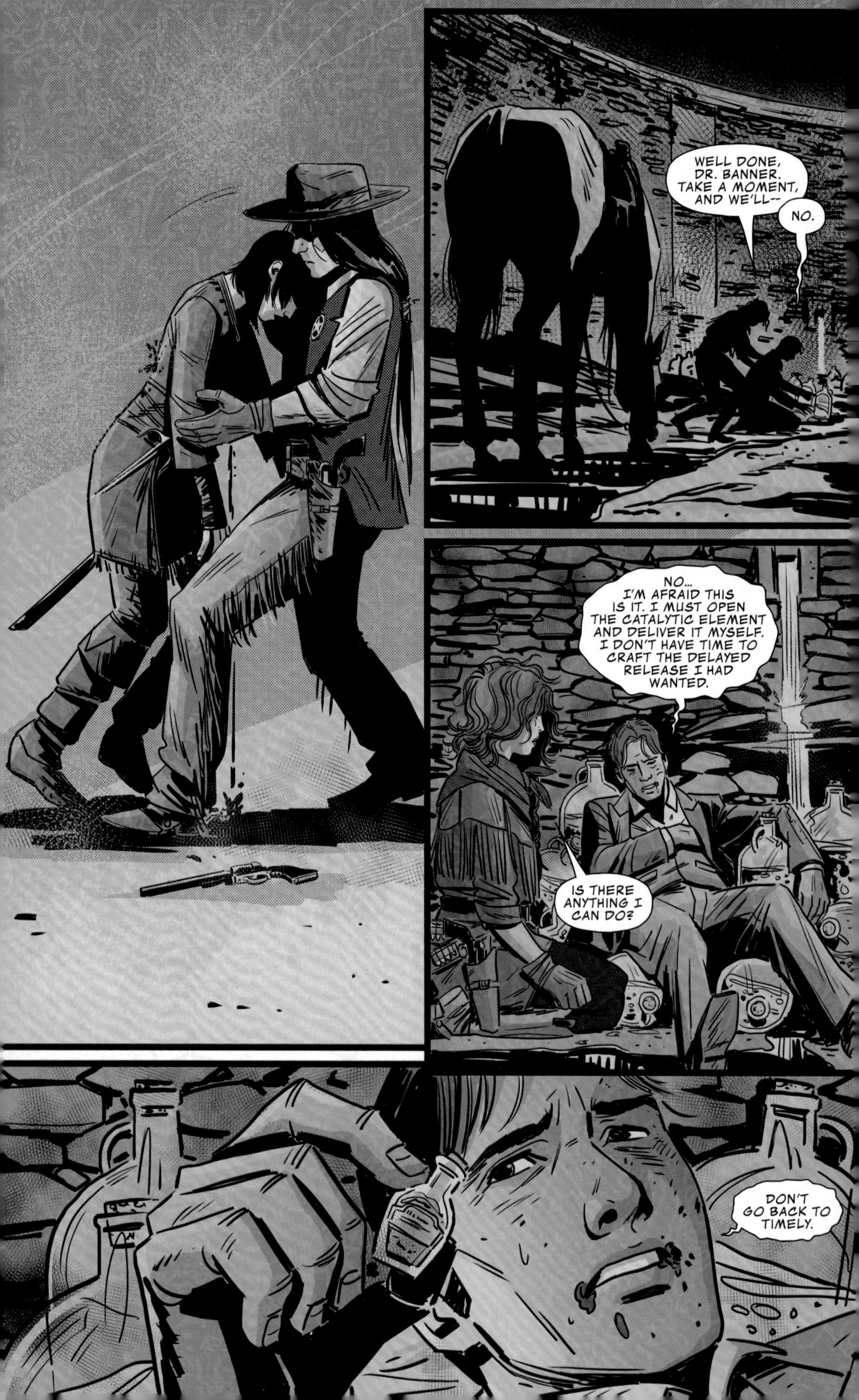
WELL DONE, DR. BANNER. TAKE A MOMENT, AND WE'LL--
NO.
NO... I'M AFRAID THIS IS IT. I MUST OPEN THE CATALYTIC ELEMENT AND DELIVER IT MYSELF. I DON'T HAVE TIME TO CRAFT THE DELAYED RELEASE I HAD WANTED.
IS THERE ANYTHING I CAN DO?
DON'T GO BACK TO TIMELY.

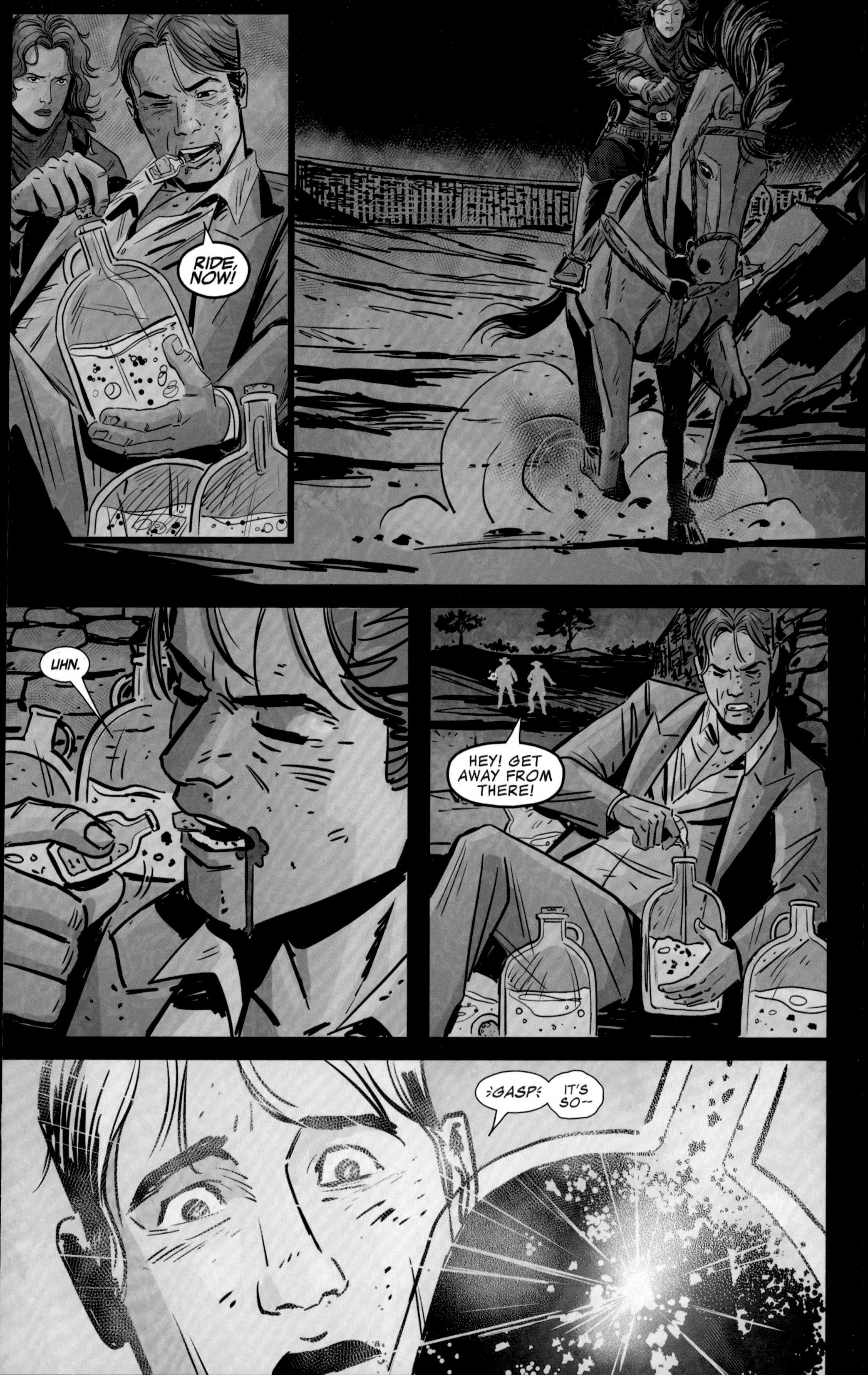
RIDE, NOW!
UHN.
HEY! GET AWAY FROM THERE!
:GASP: IT'S SO--

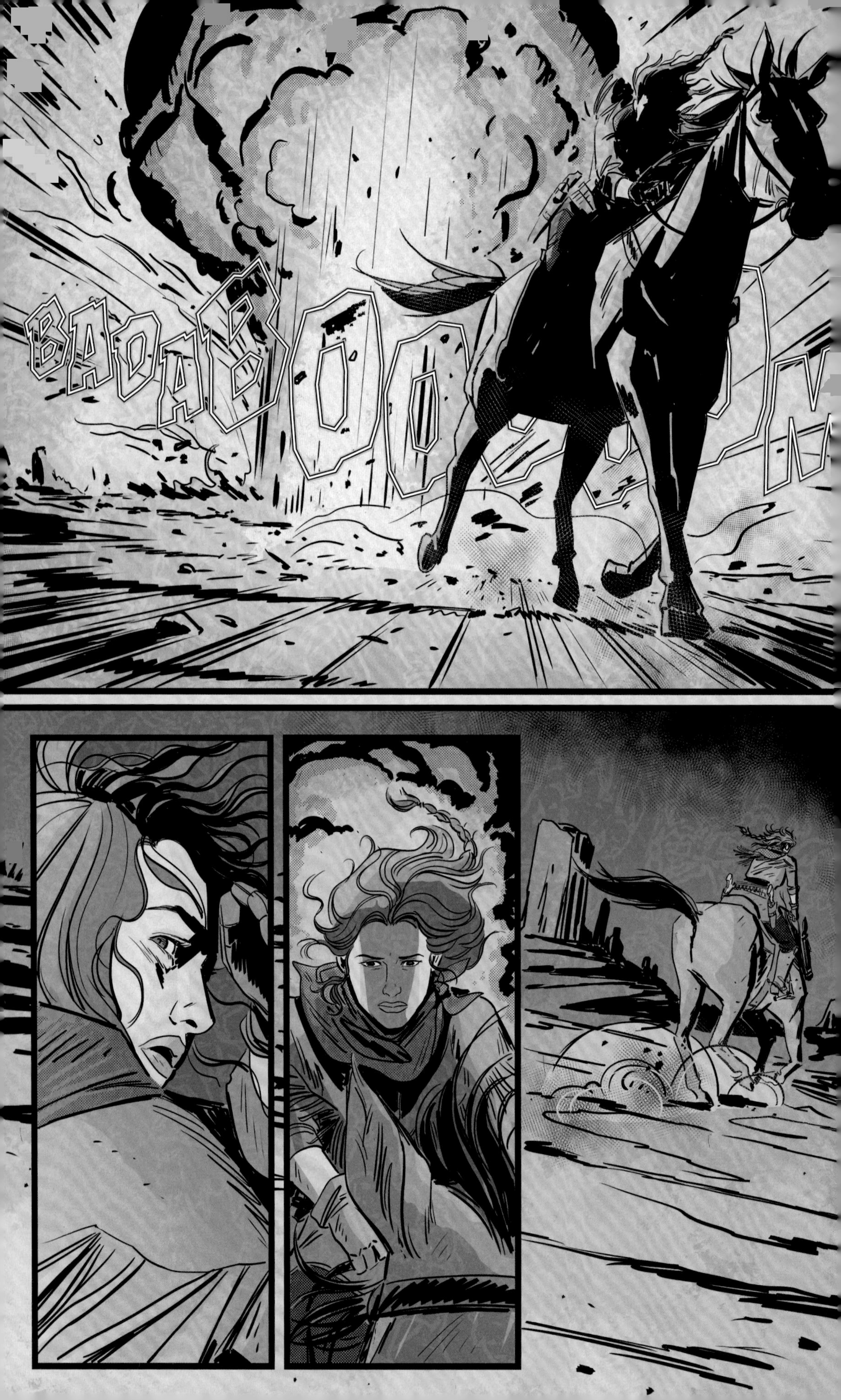
BADABOOOOOM

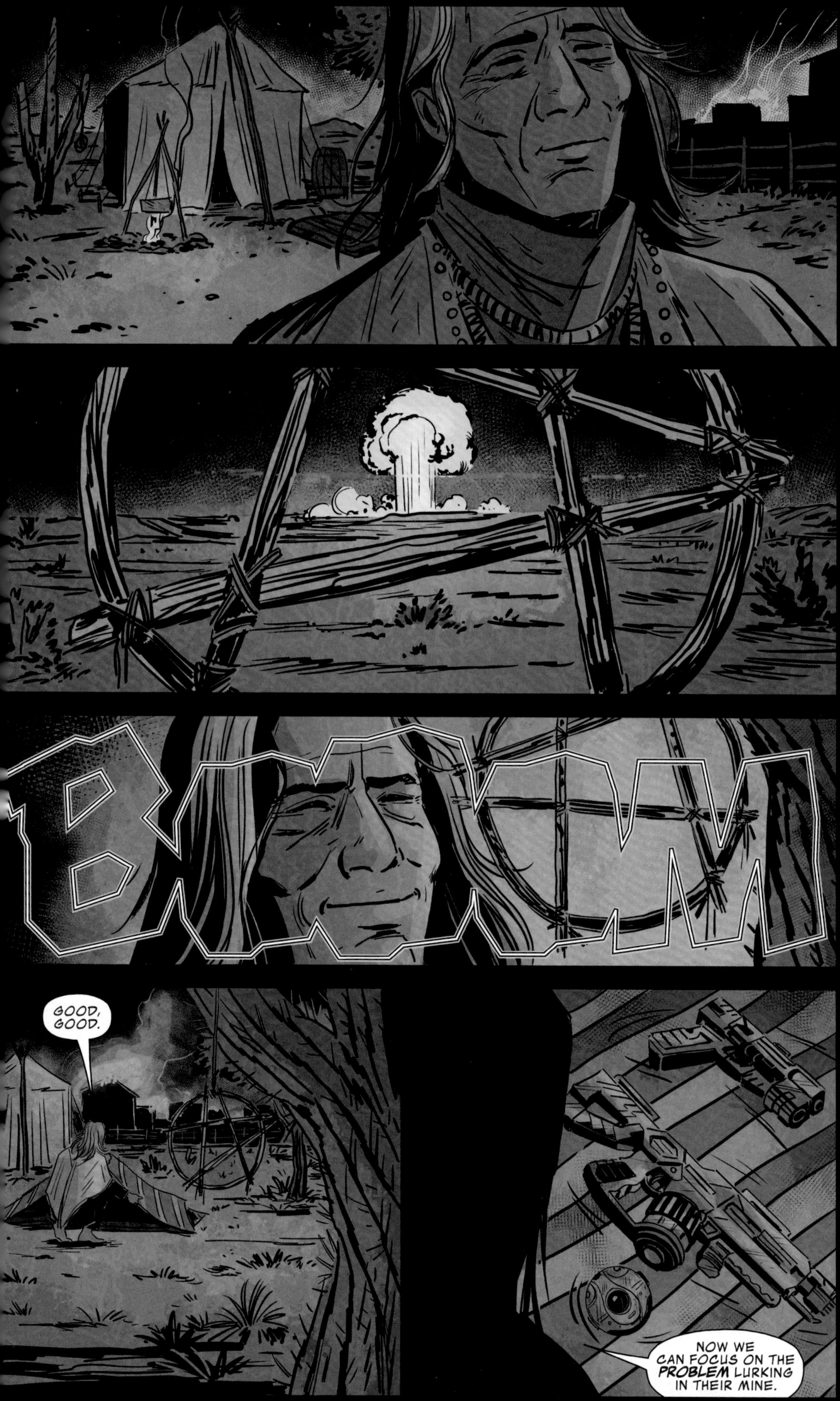
BOOM
GOOD, GOOD.
NOW WE CAN FOCUS ON THE PROBLEM LURKING IN THEIR MINE.

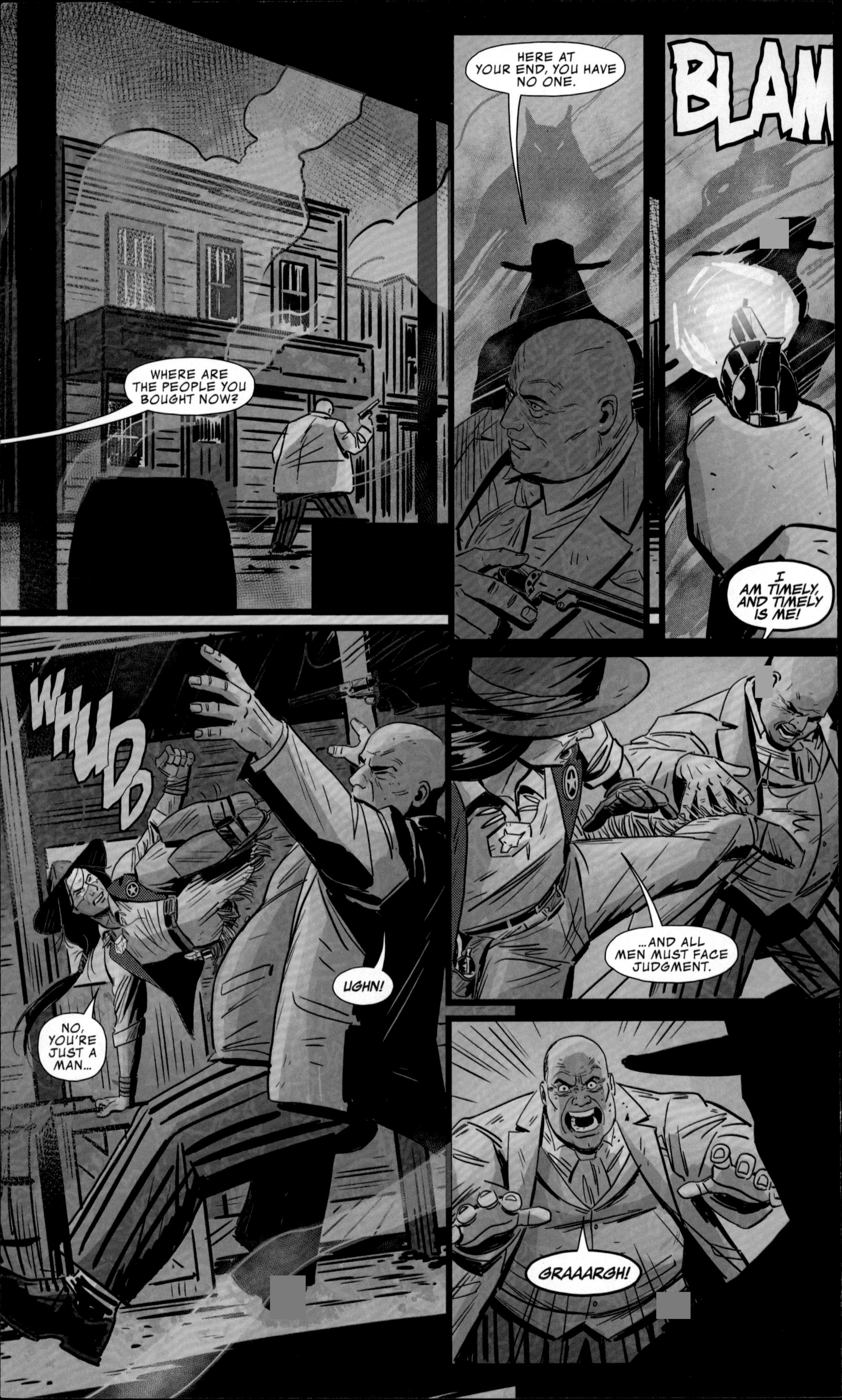
WHERE ARE THE PEOPLE YOU BOUGHT NOW?
HERE AT YOUR END, YOU HAVE NO ONE.
BLAM
I AM TIMELY, AND TIMELY IS ME!
WHUDD
UGHN!
NO, YOU'RE JUST A MAN...
...AND ALL MEN MUST FACE JUDGMENT.
GRAAARGH!

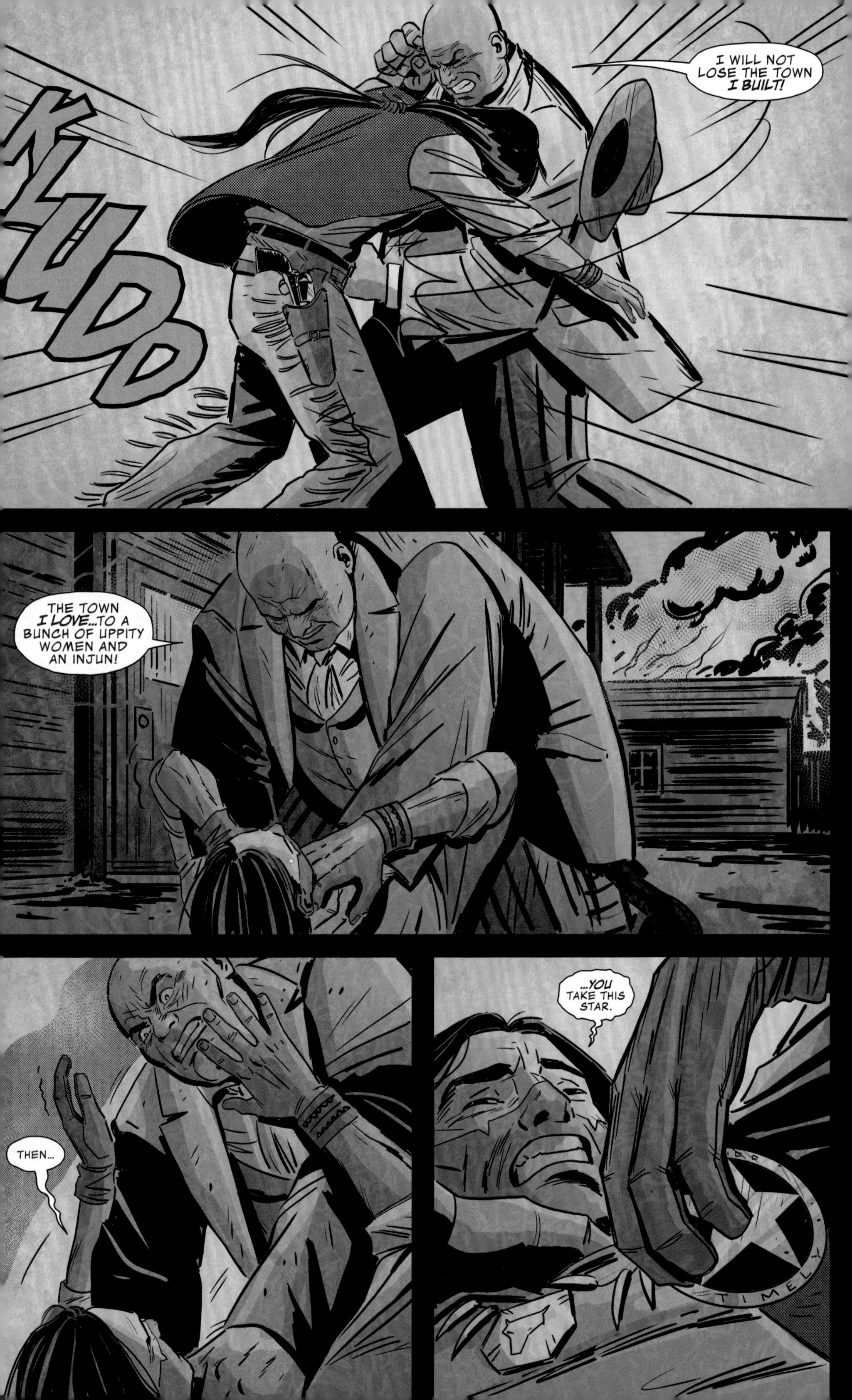
KLUDD
I WILL NOT LOSE THE TOWN I BUILT!
THE TOWN I LOVE...TO A BUNCH OF UPPITY WOMEN AND AN INJUN!
THEN...
...YOU TAKE THIS STAR.
TIMELY

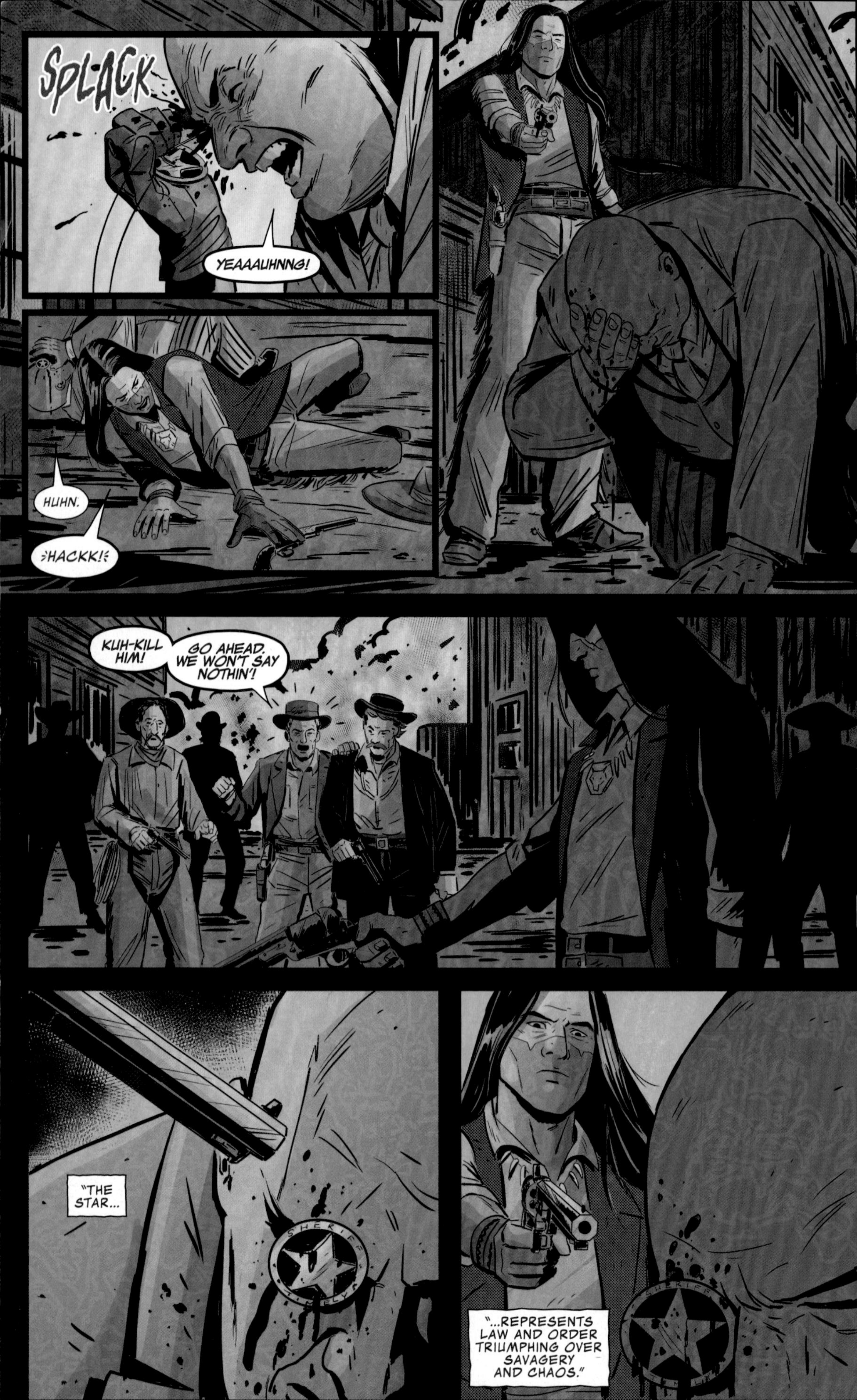
SPLACK
YEAAAUHNNG!
HUHN.
HACKK!
KUH-KILL HIM!
GO AHEAD. WE WON'T SAY NOTHIN'!
"THE STAR...
"...REPRESENTS LAW AND ORDER TRIUMPHING OVER SAVAGERY AND CHAOS."

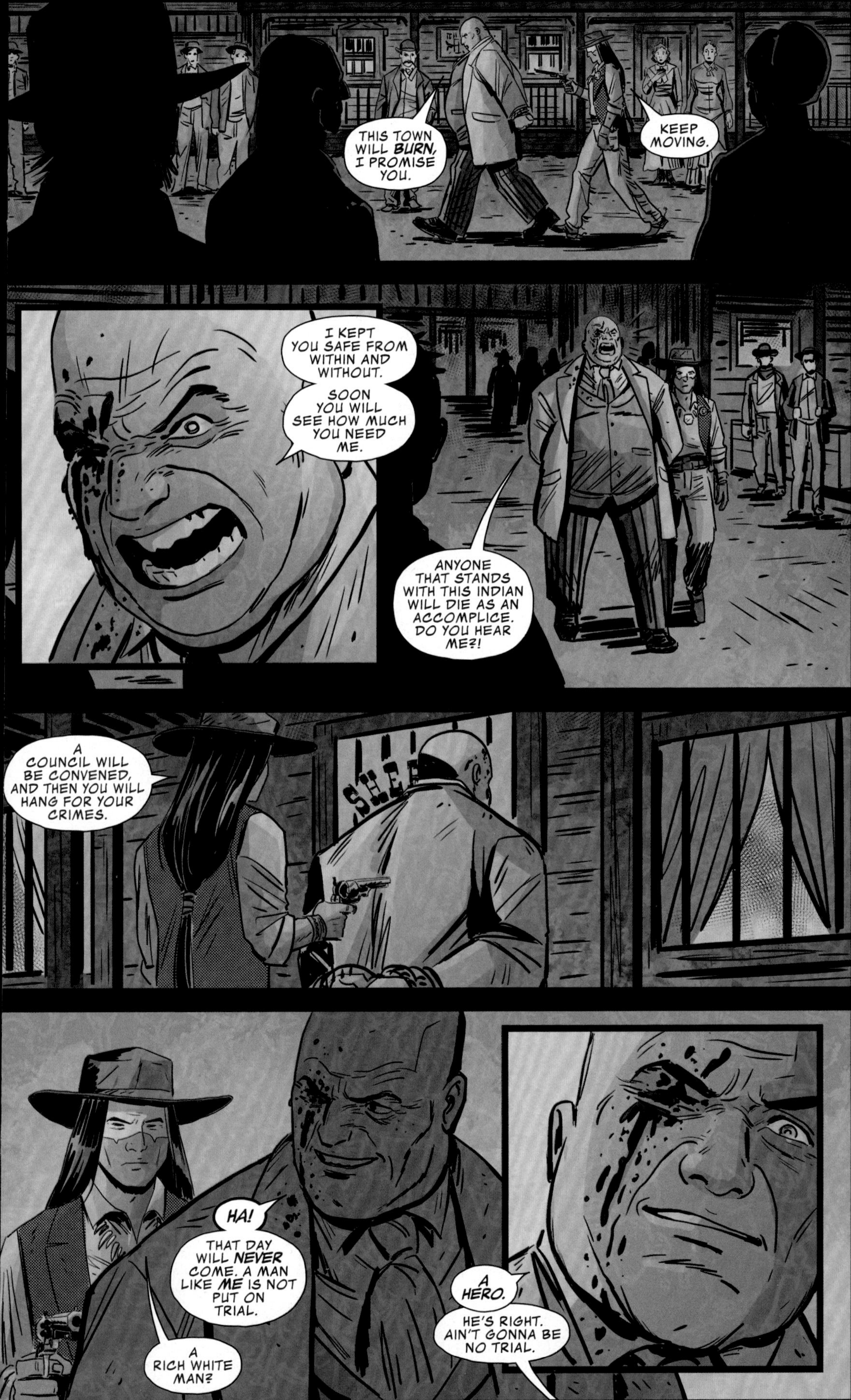
THIS TOWN WILL BURN, I PROMISE YOU.
KEEP MOVING.
I KEPT YOU SAFE FROM WITHIN AND WITHOUT.
SOON YOU WILL SEE HOW MUCH YOU NEED ME.
ANYONE THAT STANDS WITH THIS INDIAN WILL DIE AS AN ACCOMPLICE. DO YOU HEAR ME?!
A COUNCIL WILL BE CONVENED, AND THEN YOU WILL HANG FOR YOUR CRIMES.
HA!
THAT DAY WILL NEVER COME. A MAN LIKE ME IS NOT PUT ON TRIAL.
A RICH WHITE MAN?
A HERO.
HE'S RIGHT. AIN'T GONNA BE NO TRIAL.

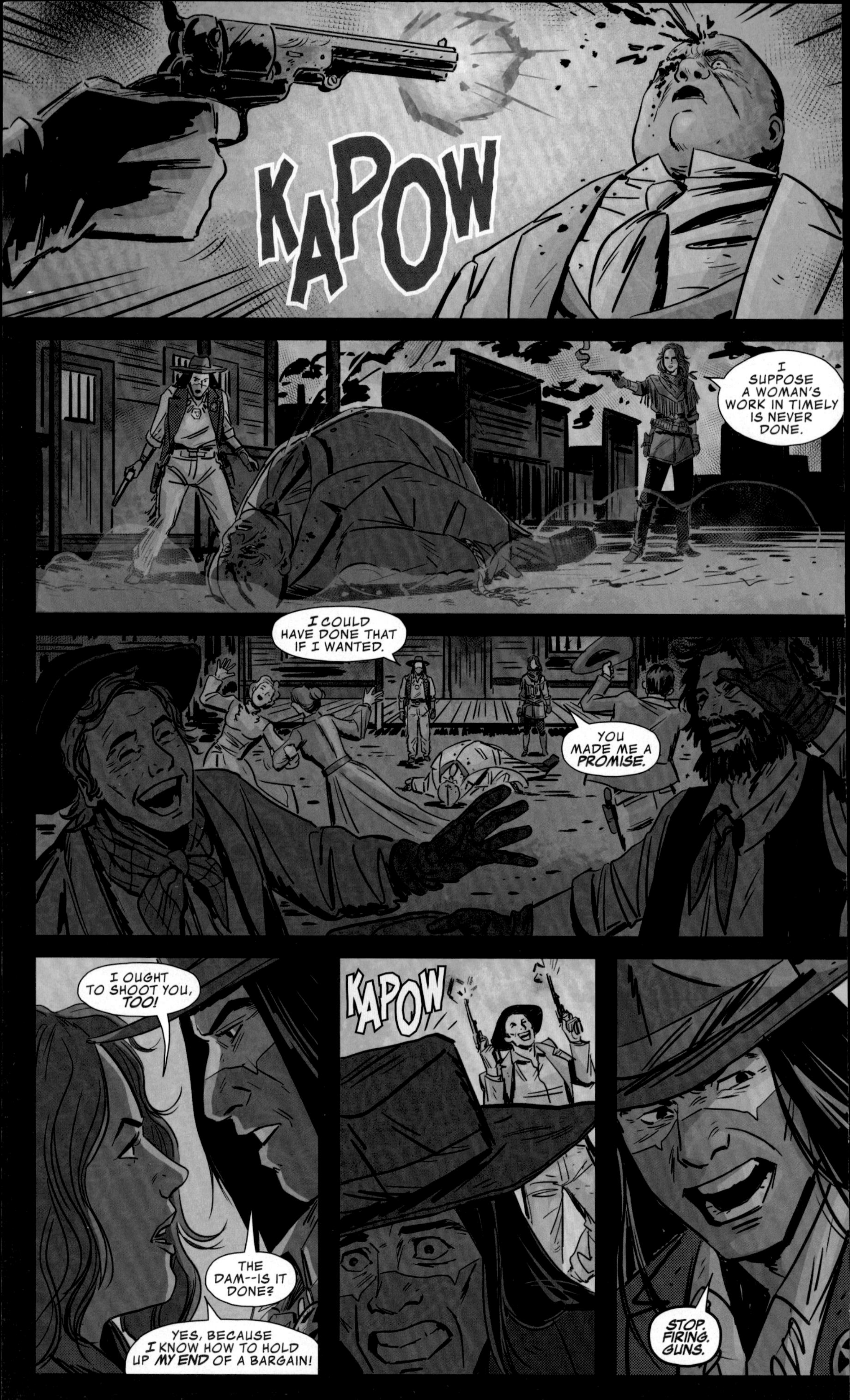
KAPOW
I SUPPOSE A WOMAN'S WORK IN TIMELY IS NEVER DONE.
I COULD HAVE DONE THAT IF I WANTED.
YOU MADE ME A PROMISE.
I OUGHT TO SHOOT YOU, TOO!
THE DAM--IS IT DONE?
YES, BECAUSE I KNOW HOW TO HOLD UP MY END OF A BARGAIN!
KAPOW
STOP. FIRING. GUNS.

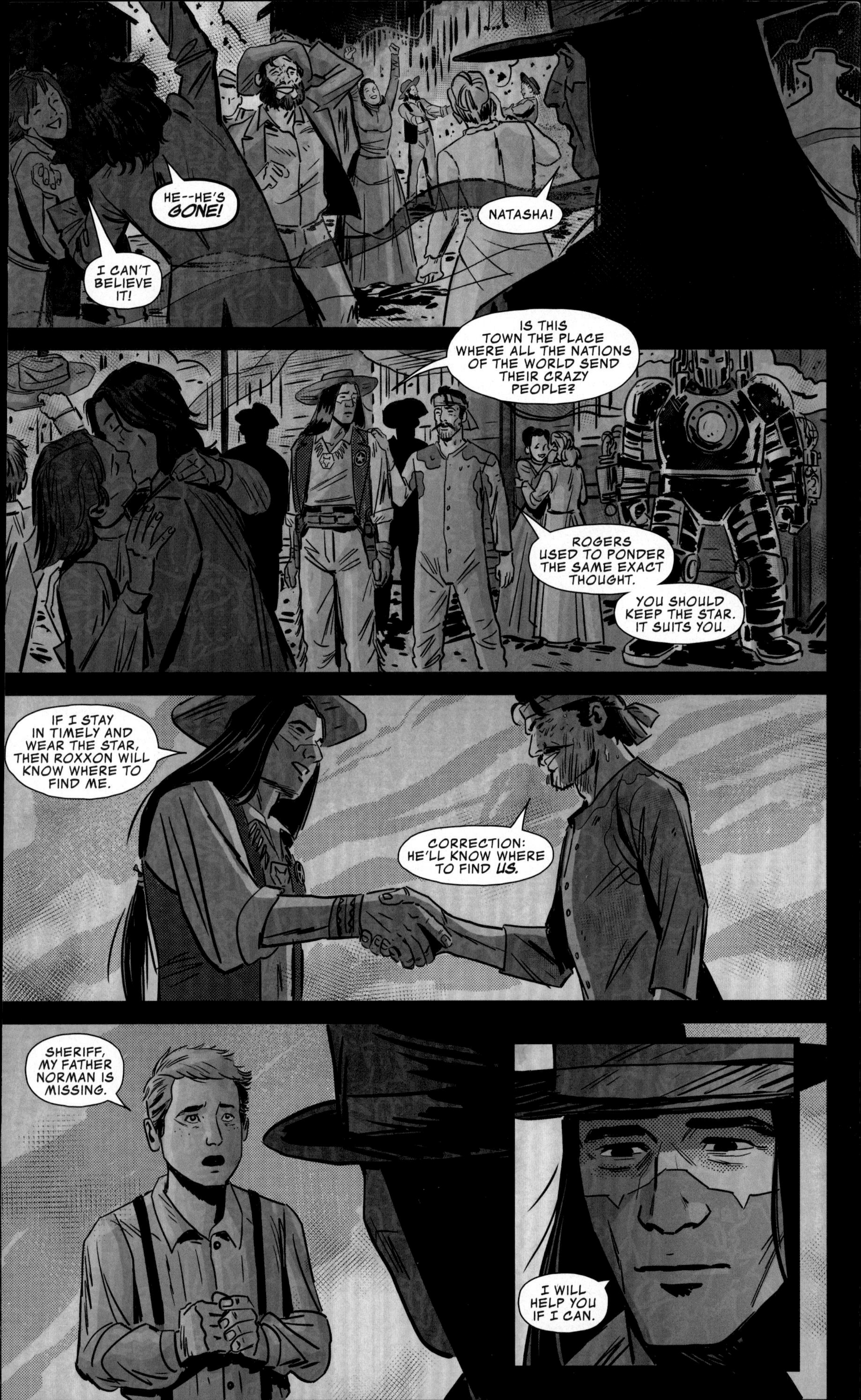
HE--HE'S GONE!
I CAN'T BELIEVE IT!
NATASHA!
IS THIS TOWN THE PLACE WHERE ALL THE NATIONS OF THE WORLD SEND THEIR CRAZY PEOPLE?
ROGERS USED TO PONDER THE SAME EXACT THOUGHT.
YOU SHOULD KEEP THE STAR. IT SUITS YOU.
IF I STAY IN TIMELY AND WEAR THE STAR, THEN ROXXON WILL KNOW WHERE TO FIND ME.
CORRECTION: HE'LL KNOW WHERE TO FIND US.
SHERIFF, MY FATHER NORMAN IS MISSING.
I WILL HELP YOU IF I CAN.

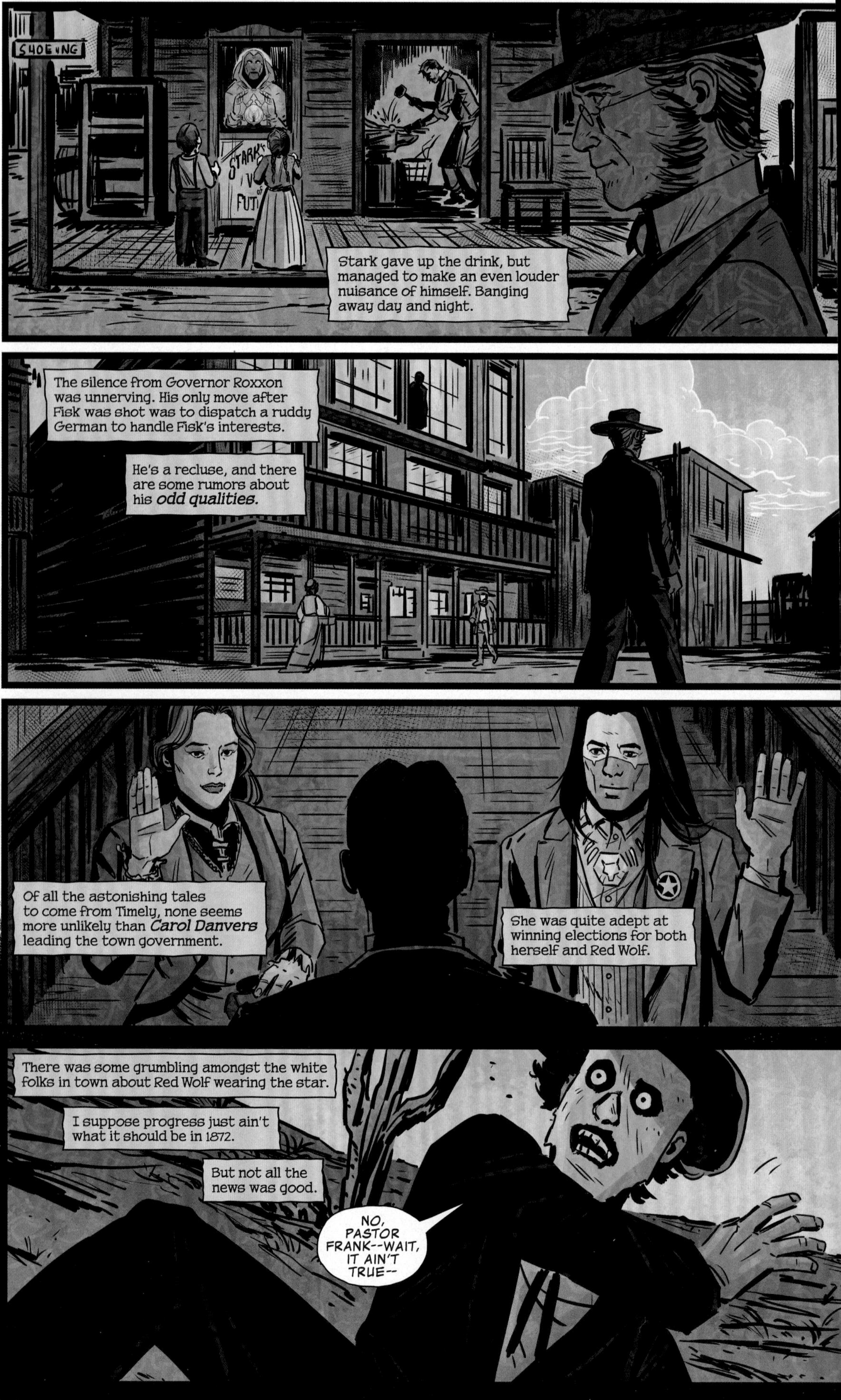
SHOEING
STARK'S
Stark gave up the drink, but managed to make an even louder nuisance of himself. Banging away day and night.
The silence from Governor Roxxon was unnerving. His only move after Fisk was shot was to dispatch a ruddy German to handle Fisk's interests.
He's a recluse, and there are some rumors about his *odd qualities.*
Of all the astonishing tales to come from Timely, none seems more unlikely than *Carol Danvers* leading the town government.
She was quite adept at winning elections for both herself and Red Wolf.
There was some grumbling amongst the white folks in town about Red Wolf wearing the star.
I suppose progress just ain't what it should be in 1872.
But not all the news was good.
NO, PASTOR FRANK--WAIT, IT AIN'T TRUE--

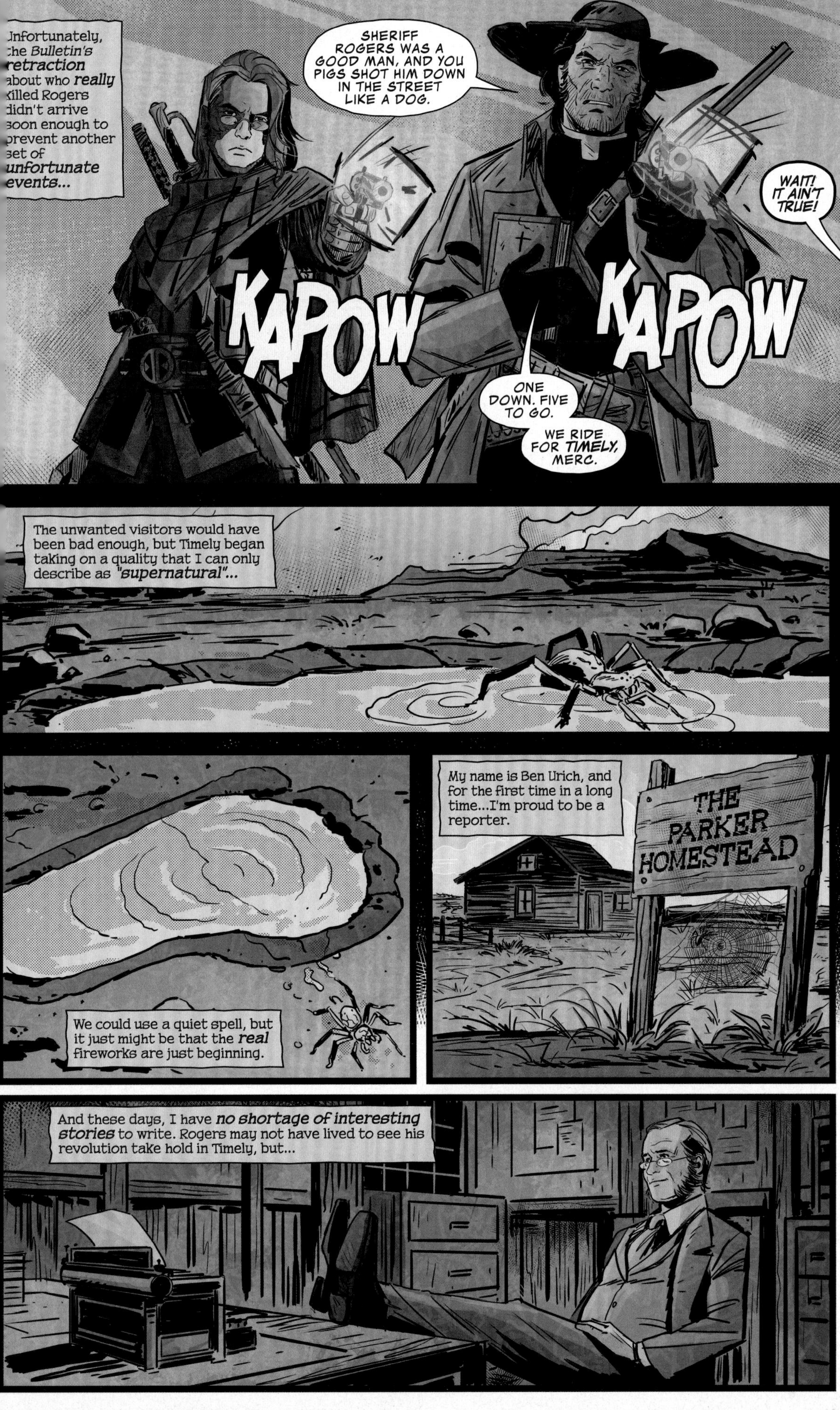

Unfortunately, the Bulletin's retraction about who really killed Rogers didn't arrive soon enough to prevent another set of unfortunate events...
SHERIFF ROGERS WAS A GOOD MAN, AND YOU PIGS SHOT HIM DOWN IN THE STREET LIKE A DOG.
WAIT! IT AIN'T TRUE!
KAPOW
KAPOW
ONE DOWN. FIVE TO GO.
WE RIDE FOR TIMELY, MERC.
The unwanted visitors would have been bad enough, but Timely began taking on a quality that I can only describe as "supernatural"...
We could use a quiet spell, but it just might be that the real fireworks are just beginning.
My name is Ben Urich, and for the first time in a long time...I'm proud to be a reporter.
THE PARKER HOMESTEAD
And these days, I have no shortage of interesting stories to write. Rogers may not have lived to see his revolution take hold in Timely, but...

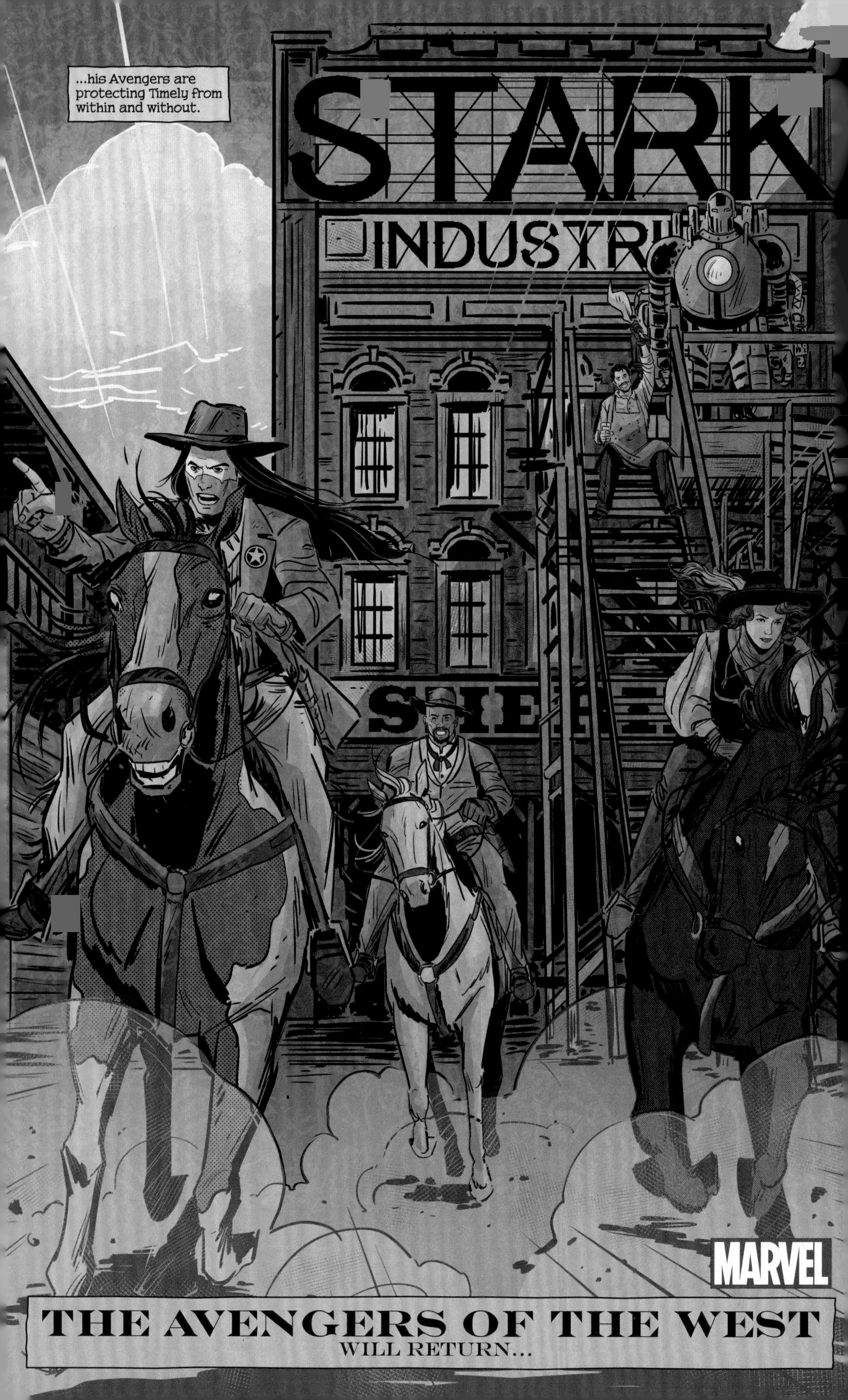
...his Avengers are protecting Timely from within and without.
STARK
INDUSTRI
THE AVENGERS OF THE WEST
WILL RETURN...

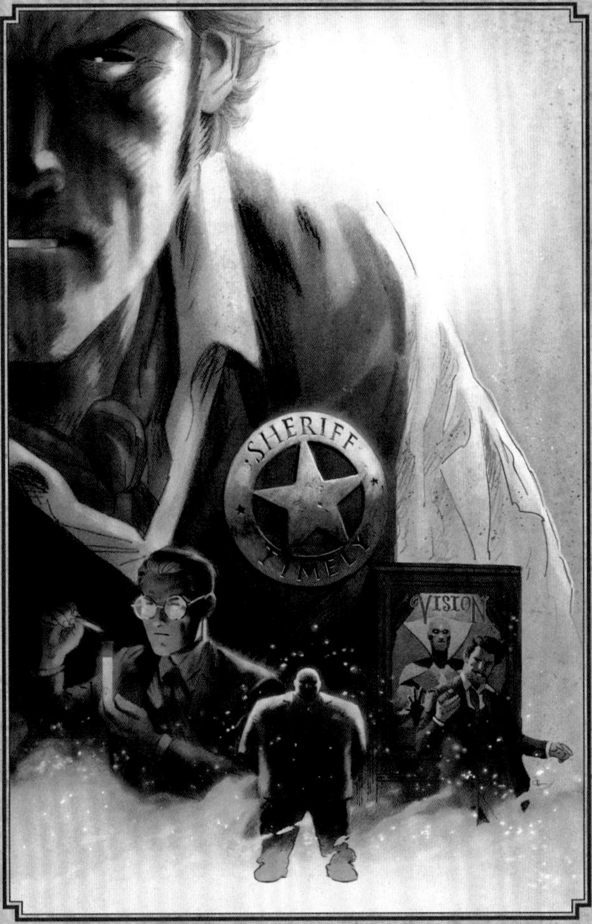
SHERIFF
VISION

1872 #1 VARIANT COVER
BY EVAN "DOC" SHANER

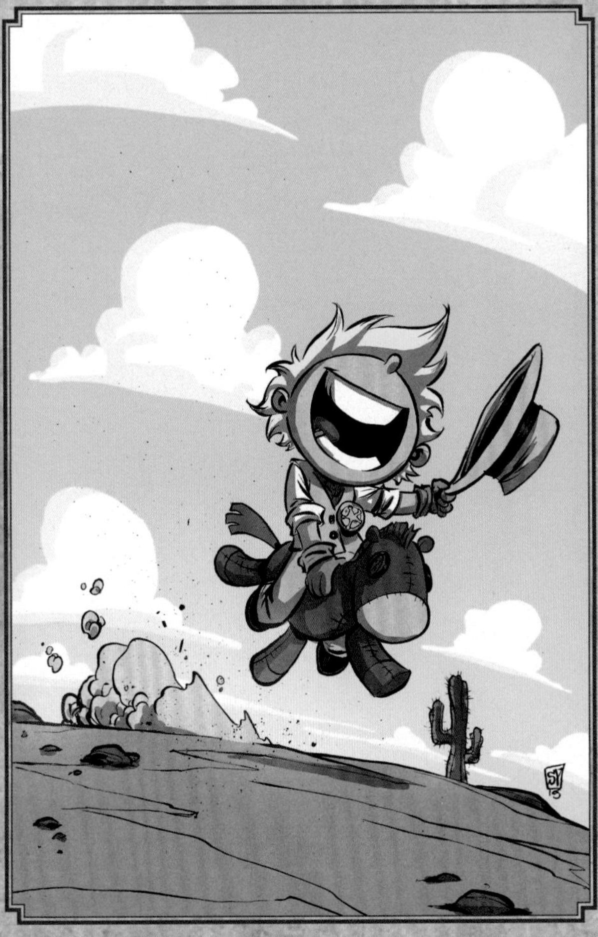

1872 #1 VARIANT COVER
BY SKOTTIE YOUNG

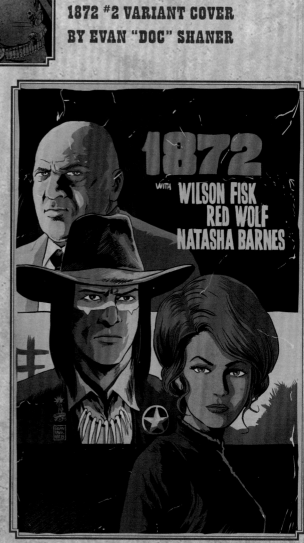

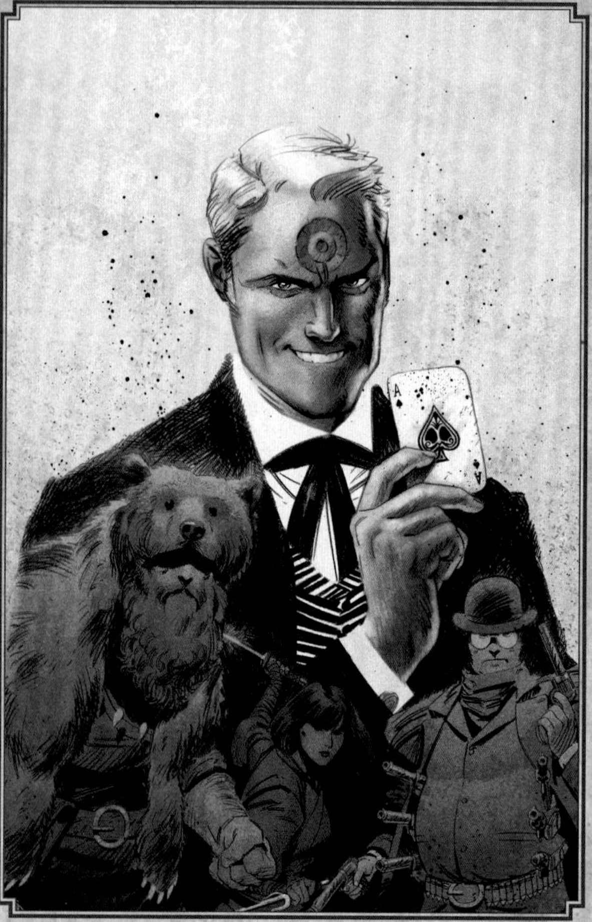

1872 #2 VARIANT COVER
BY EVAN "DOC" SHANER

1872
WITH
WILSON FISK
RED WOLF
NATASHA BARNES

1872 #3 VARIANT COVER
BY FRANCESCO FRANCAVILLA

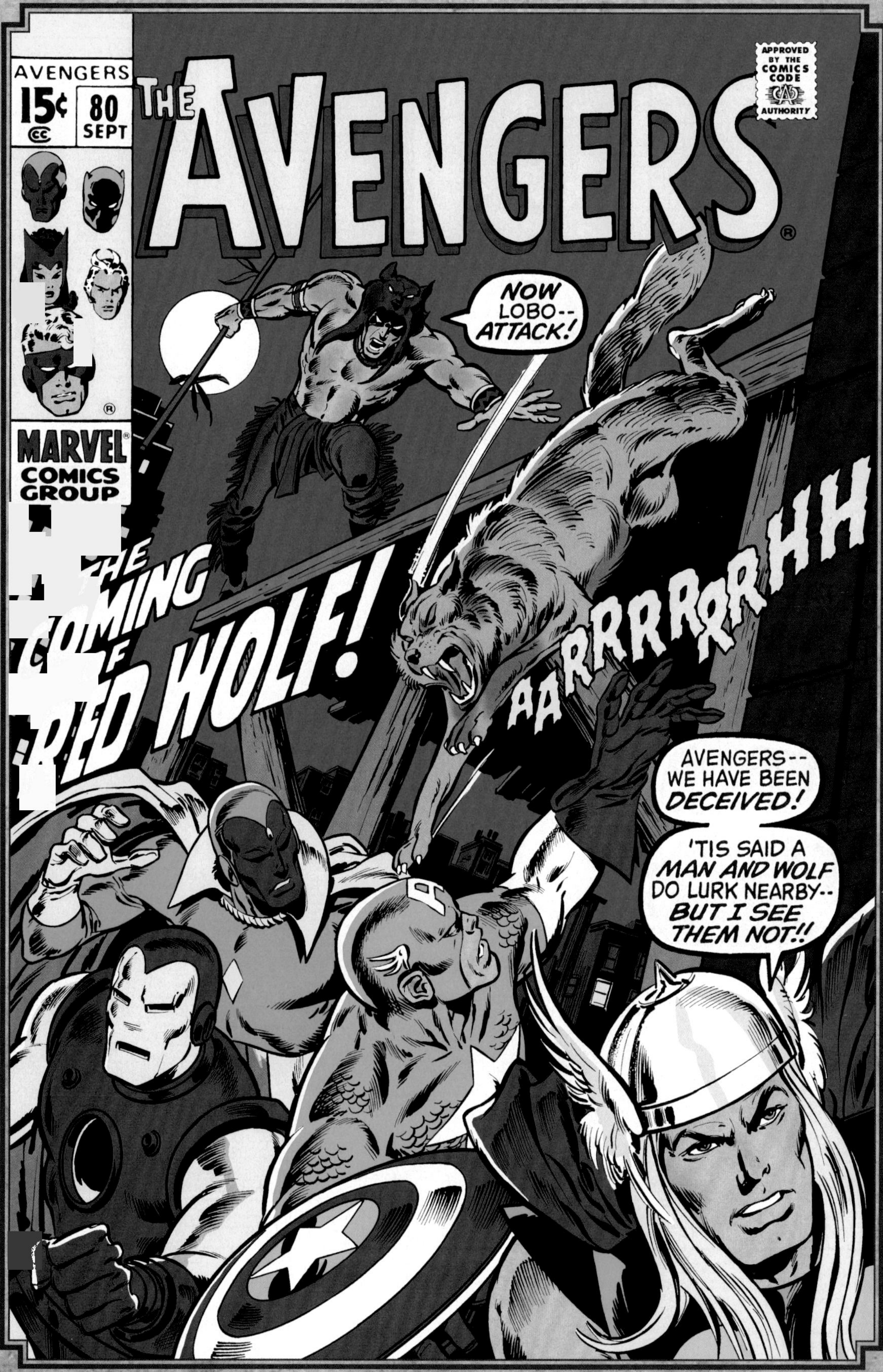

AVENGERS
15¢
80
SEPT
THE AVENGERS
MARVEL COMICS GROUP
APPROVED BY THE COMICS CODE AUTHORITY
NOW LOBO-- ATTACK!
HE
COMING
F
ED WOLF!
AARRRRRRHH
AVENGERS-- WE HAVE BEEN DECEIVED!
'TIS SAID A MAN AND WOLF DO LURK NEARBY-- BUT I SEE THEM NOT!!

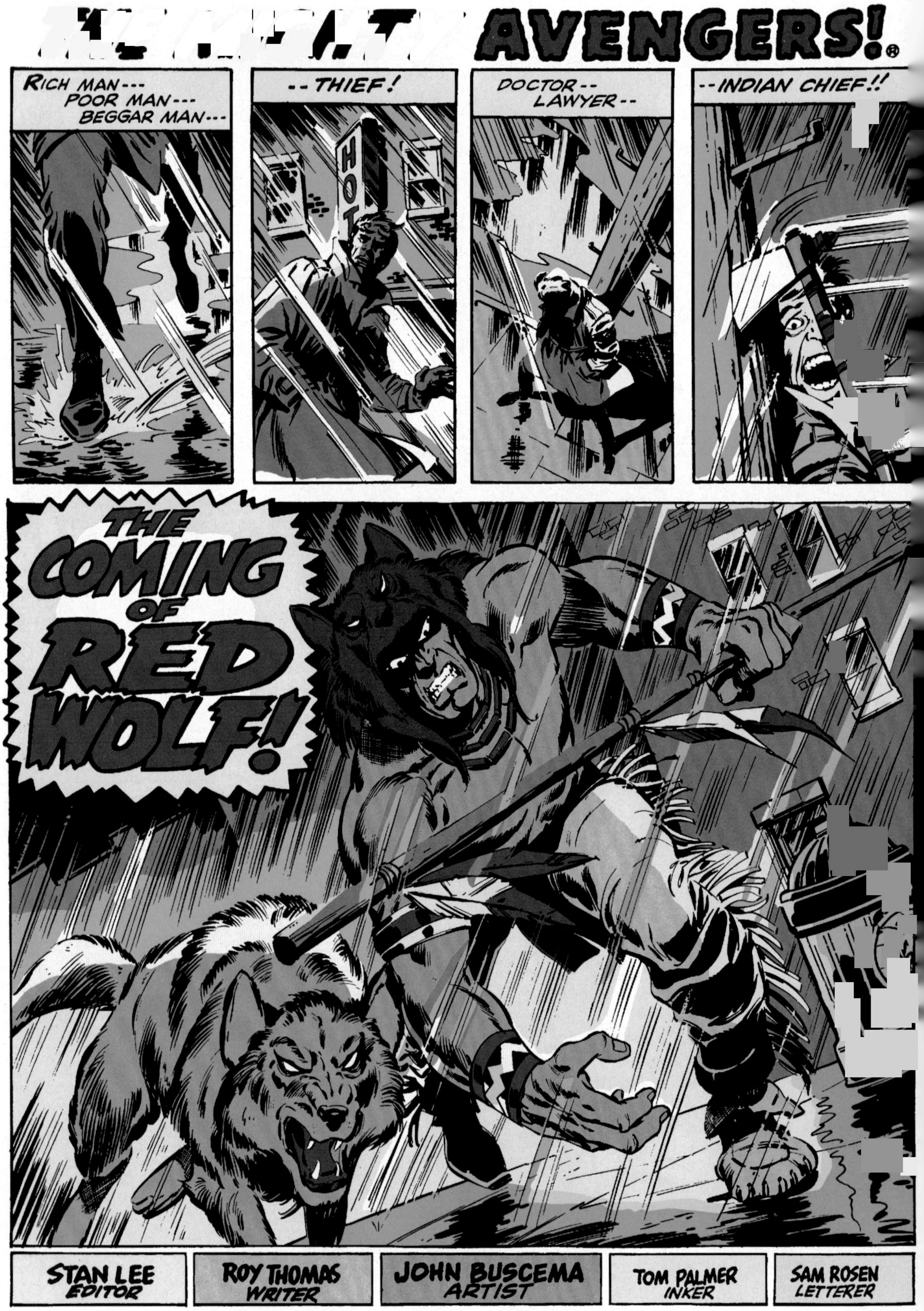
AVENGERS!
RICH MAN--- POOR MAN--- BEGGAR MAN---
--THIEF!
DOCTOR-- LAWYER--
--INDIAN CHIEF!!
HOT
THE COMING OF RED WOLF!
STAN LEE EDITOR
ROY THOMAS WRITER
JOHN BUSCEMA ARTIST
TOM PALMER INKER
SAM ROSEN LETTERER

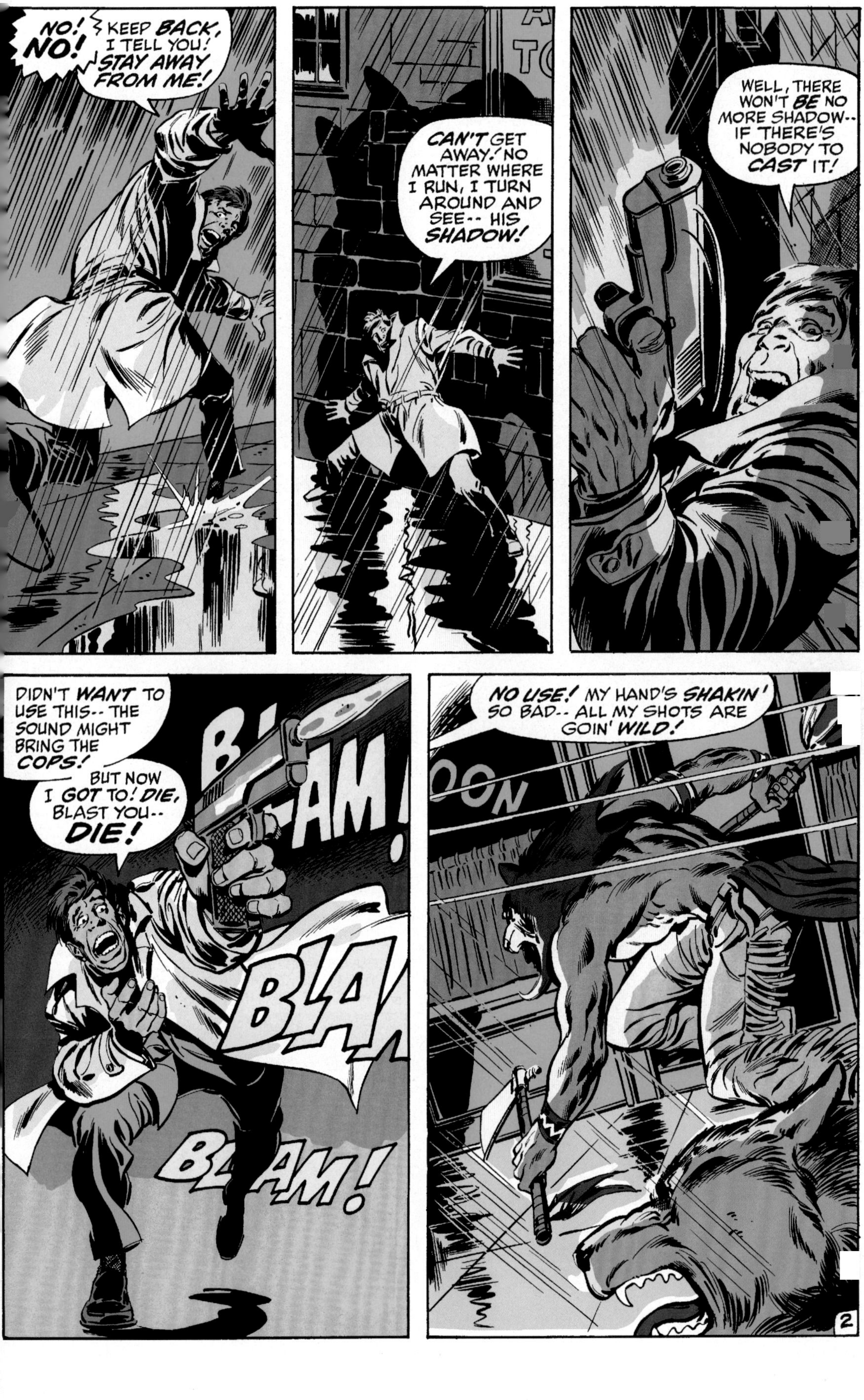
NO! NO!
KEEP BACK, I TELL YOU! STAY AWAY FROM ME!
CAN'T GET AWAY! NO MATTER WHERE I RUN, I TURN AROUND AND SEE-- HIS SHADOW!
WELL, THERE WON'T BE NO MORE SHADOW-- IF THERE'S NOBODY TO CAST IT!
DIDN'T WANT TO USE THIS-- THE SOUND MIGHT BRING THE COPS!
BUT NOW I GOT TO! DIE, BLAST YOU-- DIE!
BLAM!
BLA
BLAM!
NO USE! MY HAND'S SHAKIN' SO BAD-- ALL MY SHOTS ARE GOIN' WILD!
2

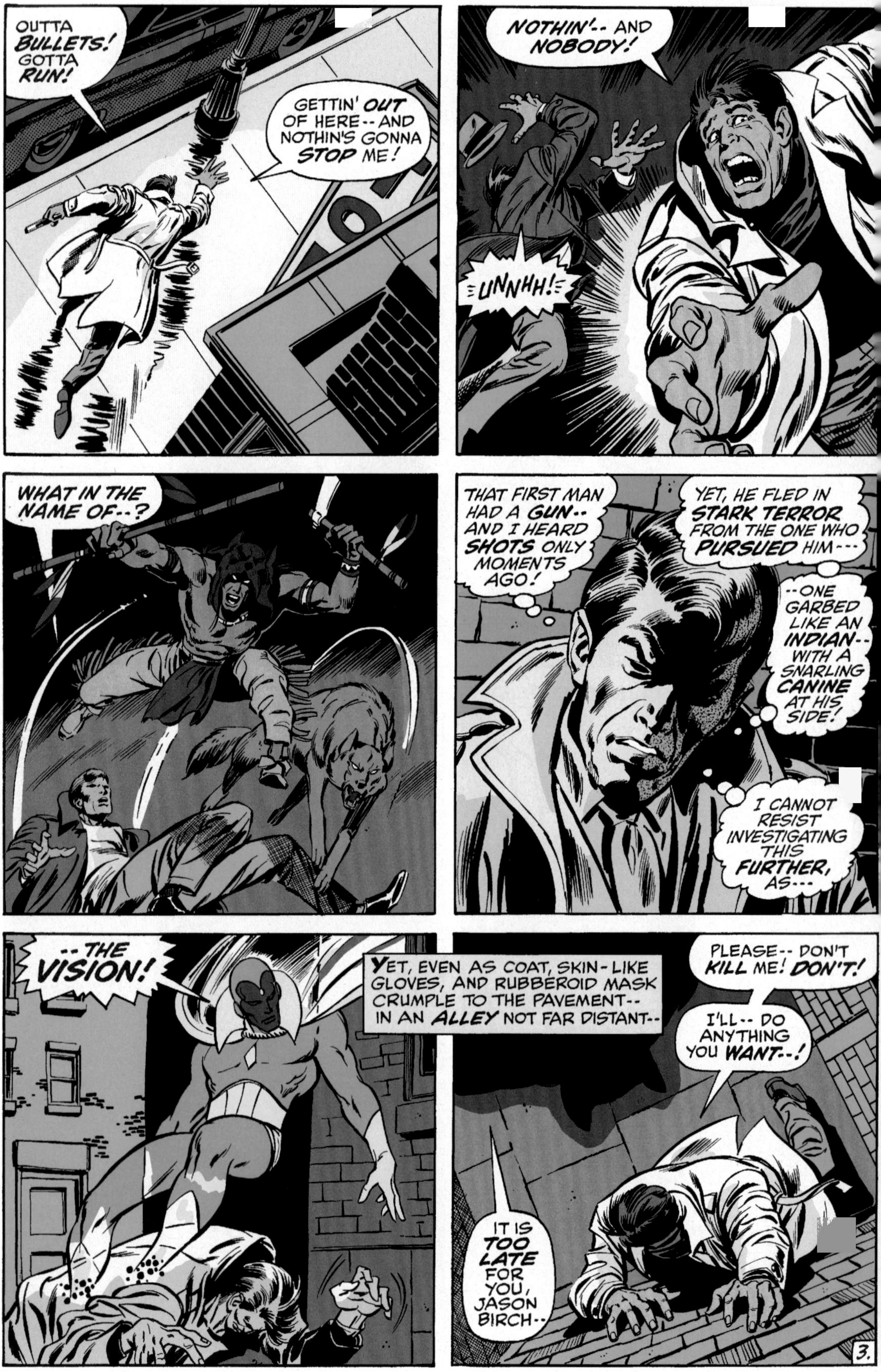

OUTTA BULLETS! GOTTA RUN!
GETTIN' OUT OF HERE-- AND NOTHIN'S GONNA STOP ME!
NOTHIN'-- AND NOBODY!
UNNHH!
WHAT IN THE NAME OF--?
THAT FIRST MAN HAD A GUN-- AND I HEARD SHOTS ONLY MOMENTS AGO!
YET, HE FLED IN STARK TERROR FROM THE ONE WHO PURSUED HIM---
--ONE GARBED LIKE AN INDIAN-- WITH A SNARLING CANINE AT HIS SIDE!
I CANNOT RESIST INVESTIGATING THIS FURTHER, AS---
--THE VISION!
YET, EVEN AS COAT, SKIN-LIKE GLOVES, AND RUBBEROID MASK CRUMPLE TO THE PAVEMENT-- IN AN ALLEY NOT FAR DISTANT--
PLEASE-- DON'T KILL ME! DON'T!
I'LL-- DO ANYTHING YOU WANT--!
IT IS TOO LATE FOR YOU, JASON BIRCH--
3.

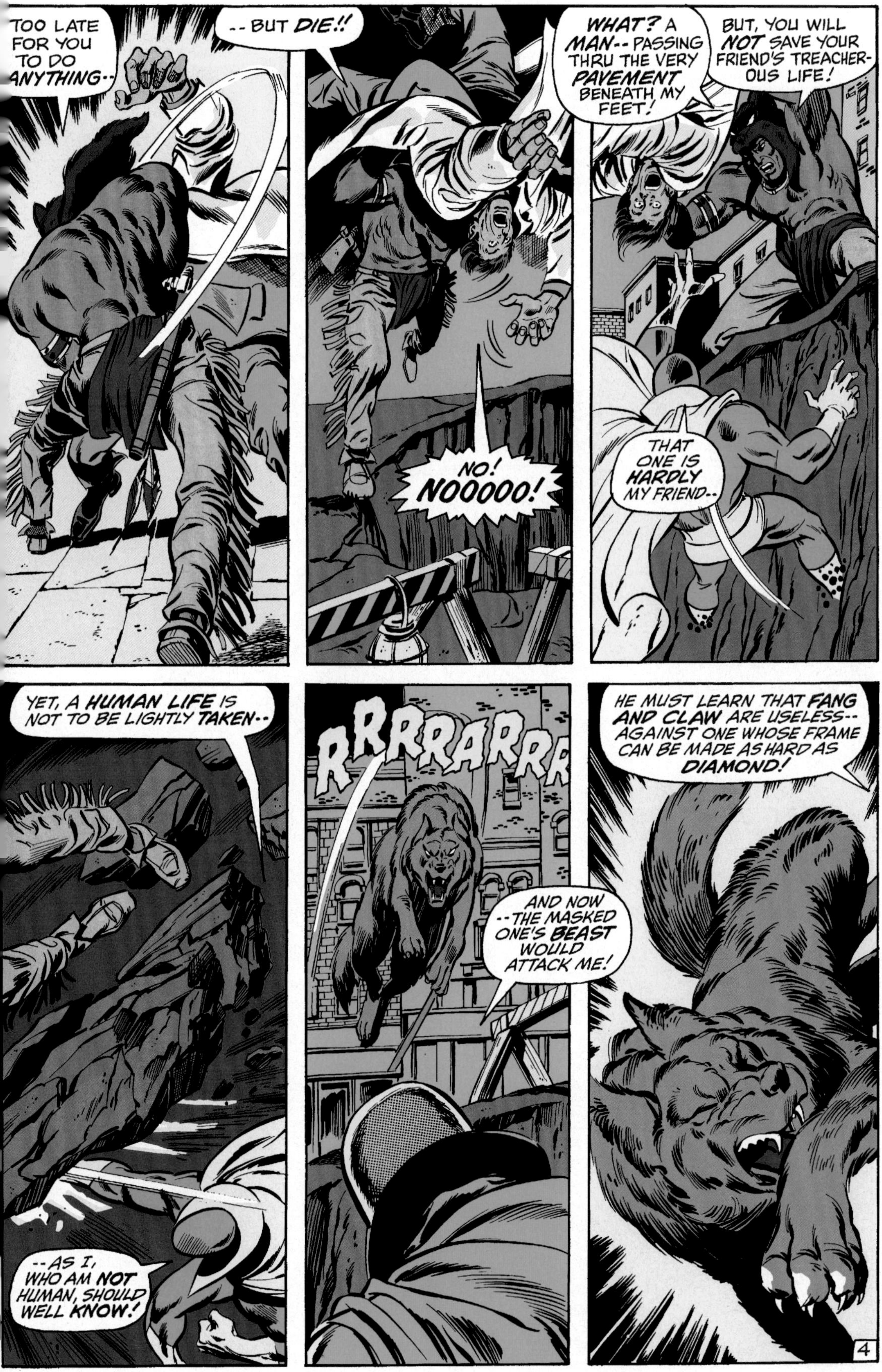

TOO LATE FOR YOU TO DO ANYTHING--
--BUT DIE!!
NO! NOOOOO!
WHAT? A MAN--PASSING THRU THE VERY PAVEMENT BENEATH MY FEET!
BUT, YOU WILL NOT SAVE YOUR FRIEND'S TREACHEROUS LIFE!
THAT ONE IS HARDLY MY FRIEND--
YET, A HUMAN LIFE IS NOT TO BE LIGHTLY TAKEN--
--AS I, WHO AM NOT HUMAN, SHOULD WELL KNOW!
RRRRARRR
AND NOW--THE MASKED ONE'S BEAST WOULD ATTACK ME!
HE MUST LEARN THAT FANG AND CLAW ARE USELESS--AGAINST ONE WHOSE FRAME CAN BE MADE AS HARD AS DIAMOND!
4

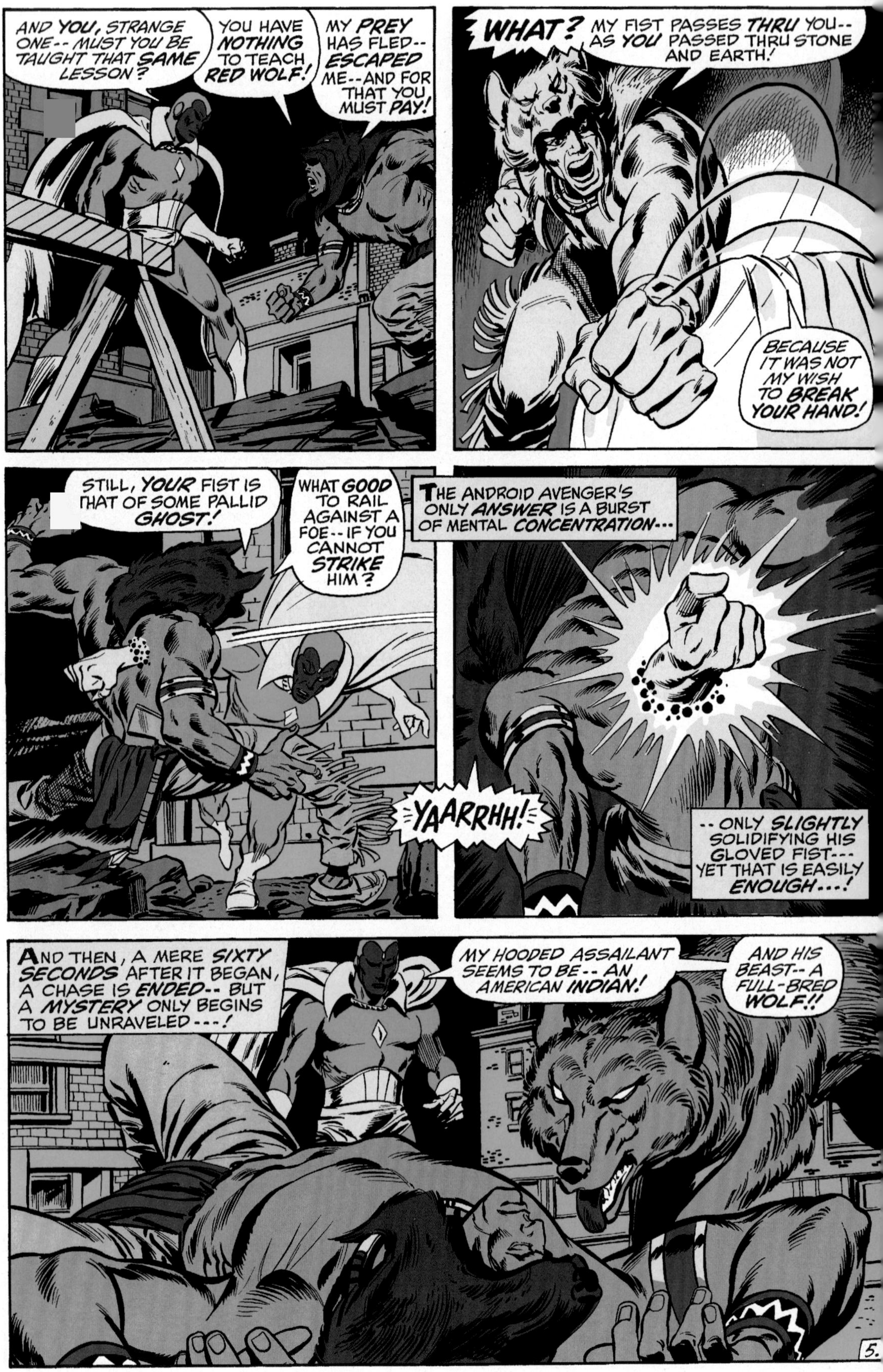

AND YOU, STRANGE ONE-- MUST YOU BE TAUGHT THAT SAME LESSON?
YOU HAVE NOTHING TO TEACH RED WOLF!
MY PREY HAS FLED-- ESCAPED ME--AND FOR THAT YOU MUST PAY!
WHAT? MY FIST PASSES THRU YOU-- AS YOU PASSED THRU STONE AND EARTH!
BECAUSE IT WAS NOT MY WISH TO BREAK YOUR HAND!
STILL, YOUR FIST IS THAT OF SOME PALLID GHOST!
WHAT GOOD TO RAIL AGAINST A FOE-- IF YOU CANNOT STRIKE HIM?
THE ANDROID AVENGER'S ONLY ANSWER IS A BURST OF MENTAL CONCENTRATION...
YAARRHH!
-- ONLY SLIGHTLY SOLIDIFYING HIS GLOVED FIST--- YET THAT IS EASILY ENOUGH...!
AND THEN, A MERE SIXTY SECONDS AFTER IT BEGAN, A CHASE IS ENDED-- BUT A MYSTERY ONLY BEGINS TO BE UNRAVELED---!
MY HOODED ASSAILANT SEEMS TO BE-- AN AMERICAN INDIAN!
AND HIS BEAST-- A FULL-BRED WOLF!!
5.

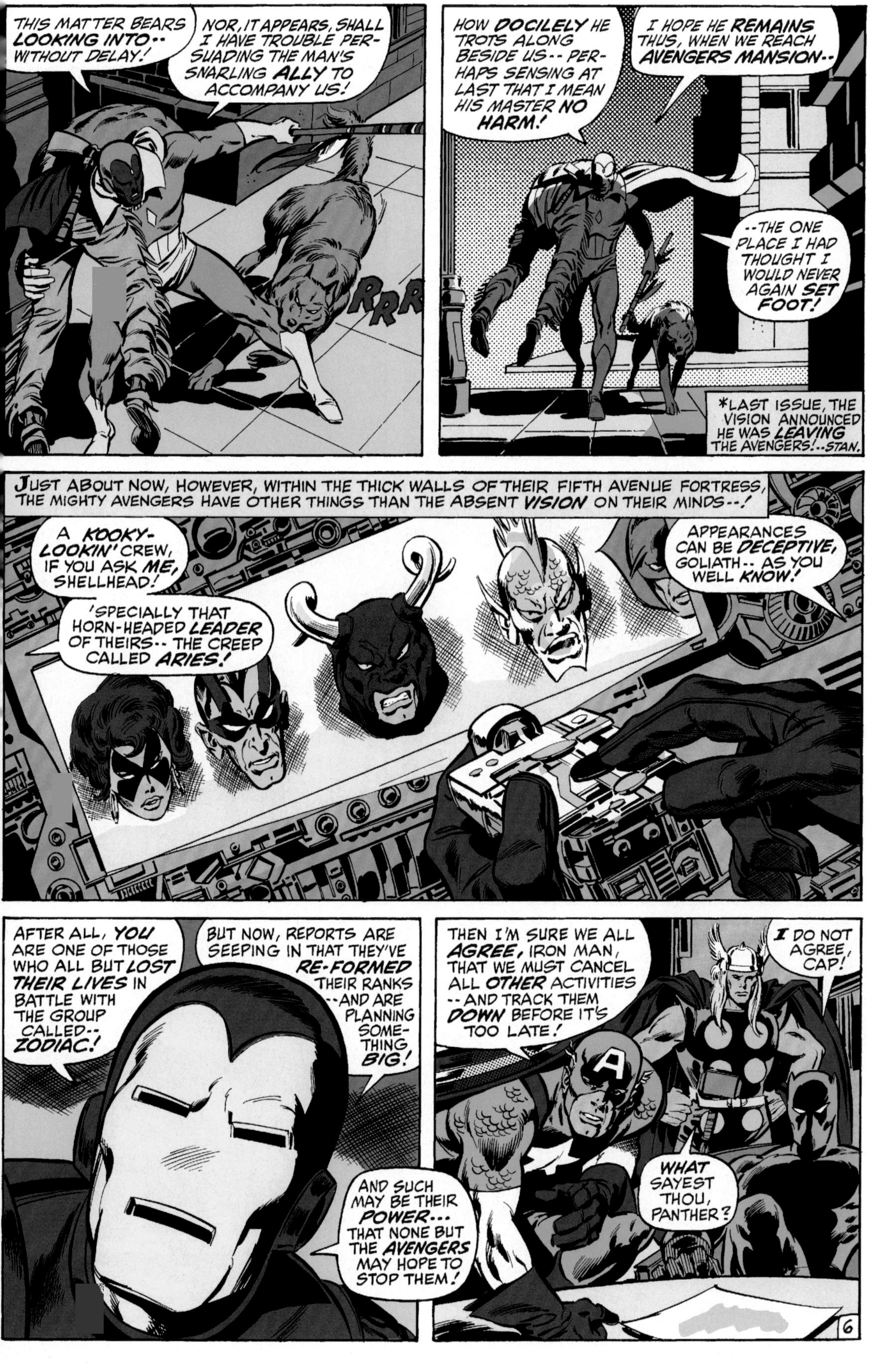

THIS MATTER BEARS LOOKING INTO-- WITHOUT DELAY!
NOR, IT APPEARS, SHALL I HAVE TROUBLE PERSUADING THE MAN'S SNARLING ALLY TO ACCOMPANY US!
RRR
HOW DOCILELY HE TROTS ALONG BESIDE US-- PERHAPS SENSING AT LAST THAT I MEAN HIS MASTER NO HARM!
I HOPE HE REMAINS THUS, WHEN WE REACH AVENGERS MANSION--
--THE ONE PLACE I HAD THOUGHT I WOULD NEVER AGAIN SET FOOT!
*LAST ISSUE, THE VISION ANNOUNCED HE WAS LEAVING THE AVENGERS!--STAN.
JUST ABOUT NOW, HOWEVER, WITHIN THE THICK WALLS OF THEIR FIFTH AVENUE FORTRESS, THE MIGHTY AVENGERS HAVE OTHER THINGS THAN THE ABSENT VISION ON THEIR MINDS--!
A KOOKY-LOOKIN' CREW, IF YOU ASK ME, SHELLHEAD!
'SPECIALLY THAT HORN-HEADED LEADER OF THEIRS-- THE CREEP CALLED ARIES!
APPEARANCES CAN BE DECEPTIVE, GOLIATH-- AS YOU WELL KNOW!
AFTER ALL, YOU ARE ONE OF THOSE WHO ALL BUT LOST THEIR LIVES IN BATTLE WITH THE GROUP CALLED-- ZODIAC!
BUT NOW, REPORTS ARE SEEPING IN THAT THEY'VE RE-FORMED THEIR RANKS --AND ARE PLANNING SOMETHING BIG!
AND SUCH MAY BE THEIR POWER... THAT NONE BUT THE AVENGERS MAY HOPE TO STOP THEM!
THEN I'M SURE WE ALL AGREE, IRON MAN, THAT WE MUST CANCEL ALL OTHER ACTIVITIES -- AND TRACK THEM DOWN BEFORE IT'S TOO LATE!
I DO NOT AGREE, CAP!
WHAT SAYEST THOU, PANTHER?
6

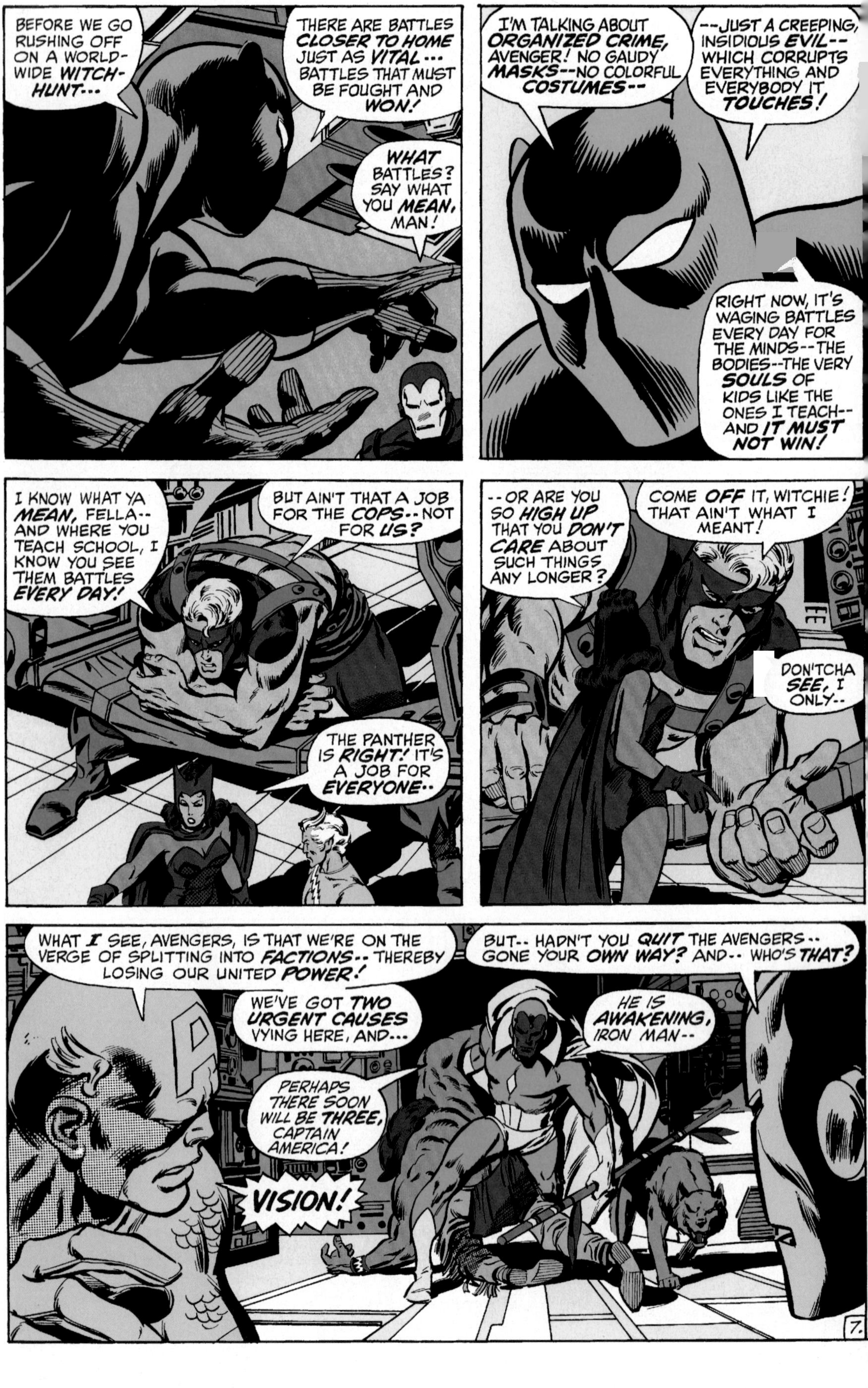
BEFORE WE GO RUSHING OFF ON A WORLD-WIDE WITCH-HUNT...
THERE ARE BATTLES CLOSER TO HOME JUST AS VITAL... BATTLES THAT MUST BE FOUGHT AND WON!
WHAT BATTLES? SAY WHAT YOU MEAN, MAN!
I'M TALKING ABOUT ORGANIZED CRIME, AVENGER! NO GAUDY MASKS--NO COLORFUL COSTUMES--
--JUST A CREEPING, INSIDIOUS EVIL--WHICH CORRUPTS EVERYTHING AND EVERYBODY IT TOUCHES!
RIGHT NOW, IT'S WAGING BATTLES EVERY DAY FOR THE MINDS--THE BODIES--THE VERY SOULS OF KIDS LIKE THE ONES I TEACH--AND IT MUST NOT WIN!
I KNOW WHAT YA MEAN, FELLA--AND WHERE YOU TEACH SCHOOL, I KNOW YOU SEE THEM BATTLES EVERY DAY!
BUT AIN'T THAT A JOB FOR THE COPS--NOT FOR US?
THE PANTHER IS RIGHT! IT'S A JOB FOR EVERYONE--
--OR ARE YOU SO HIGH UP THAT YOU DON'T CARE ABOUT SUCH THINGS ANY LONGER?
COME OFF IT, WITCHIE! THAT AIN'T WHAT I MEANT!
DON'TCHA SEE, I ONLY--
WHAT I SEE, AVENGERS, IS THAT WE'RE ON THE VERGE OF SPLITTING INTO FACTIONS-- THEREBY LOSING OUR UNITED POWER!
WE'VE GOT TWO URGENT CAUSES VYING HERE, AND...
PERHAPS THERE SOON WILL BE THREE, CAPTAIN AMERICA!
VISION!
BUT-- HADN'T YOU QUIT THE AVENGERS-- GONE YOUR OWN WAY? AND-- WHO'S THAT?
HE IS AWAKENING, IRON MAN--
7.

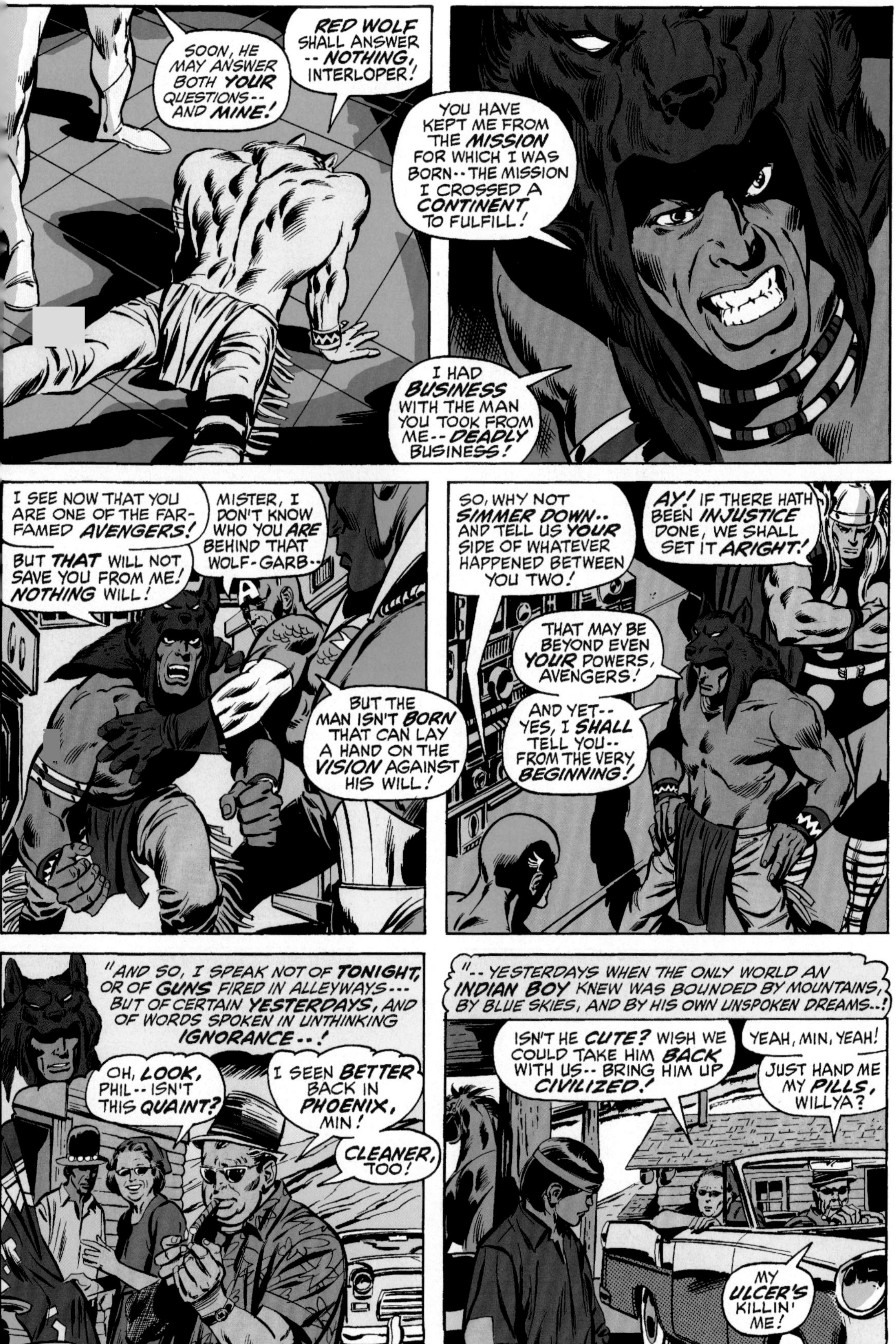
SOON, HE MAY ANSWER BOTH YOUR QUESTIONS -- AND MINE!
RED WOLF SHALL ANSWER -- NOTHING, INTERLOPER!
YOU HAVE KEPT ME FROM THE MISSION FOR WHICH I WAS BORN -- THE MISSION I CROSSED A CONTINENT TO FULFILL!
I HAD BUSINESS WITH THE MAN YOU TOOK FROM ME -- DEADLY BUSINESS!
I SEE NOW THAT YOU ARE ONE OF THE FAR-FAMED AVENGERS!
BUT THAT WILL NOT SAVE YOU FROM ME! NOTHING WILL!
MISTER, I DON'T KNOW WHO YOU ARE BEHIND THAT WOLF-GARB--
BUT THE MAN ISN'T BORN THAT CAN LAY A HAND ON THE VISION AGAINST HIS WILL!
SO, WHY NOT SIMMER DOWN.. AND TELL US YOUR SIDE OF WHATEVER HAPPENED BETWEEN YOU TWO!
AY! IF THERE HATH BEEN INJUSTICE DONE, WE SHALL SET IT ARIGHT!
THAT MAY BE BEYOND EVEN YOUR POWERS, AVENGERS!
AND YET-- YES, I SHALL TELL YOU-- FROM THE VERY BEGINNING!
"AND SO, I SPEAK NOT OF TONIGHT, OR OF GUNS FIRED IN ALLEYWAYS--- BUT OF CERTAIN YESTERDAYS, AND OF WORDS SPOKEN IN UNTHINKING IGNORANCE..!
OH, LOOK, PHIL -- ISN'T THIS QUAINT?
I SEEN BETTER BACK IN PHOENIX, MIN!
CLEANER, TOO!
"-- YESTERDAYS WHEN THE ONLY WORLD AN INDIAN BOY KNEW WAS BOUNDED BY MOUNTAINS, BY BLUE SKIES, AND BY HIS OWN UNSPOKEN DREAMS..!
ISN'T HE CUTE? WISH WE COULD TAKE HIM BACK WITH US -- BRING HIM UP CIVILIZED!
YEAH, MIN, YEAH!
JUST HAND ME MY PILLS, WILLYA?
MY ULCER'S KILLIN' ME!
8

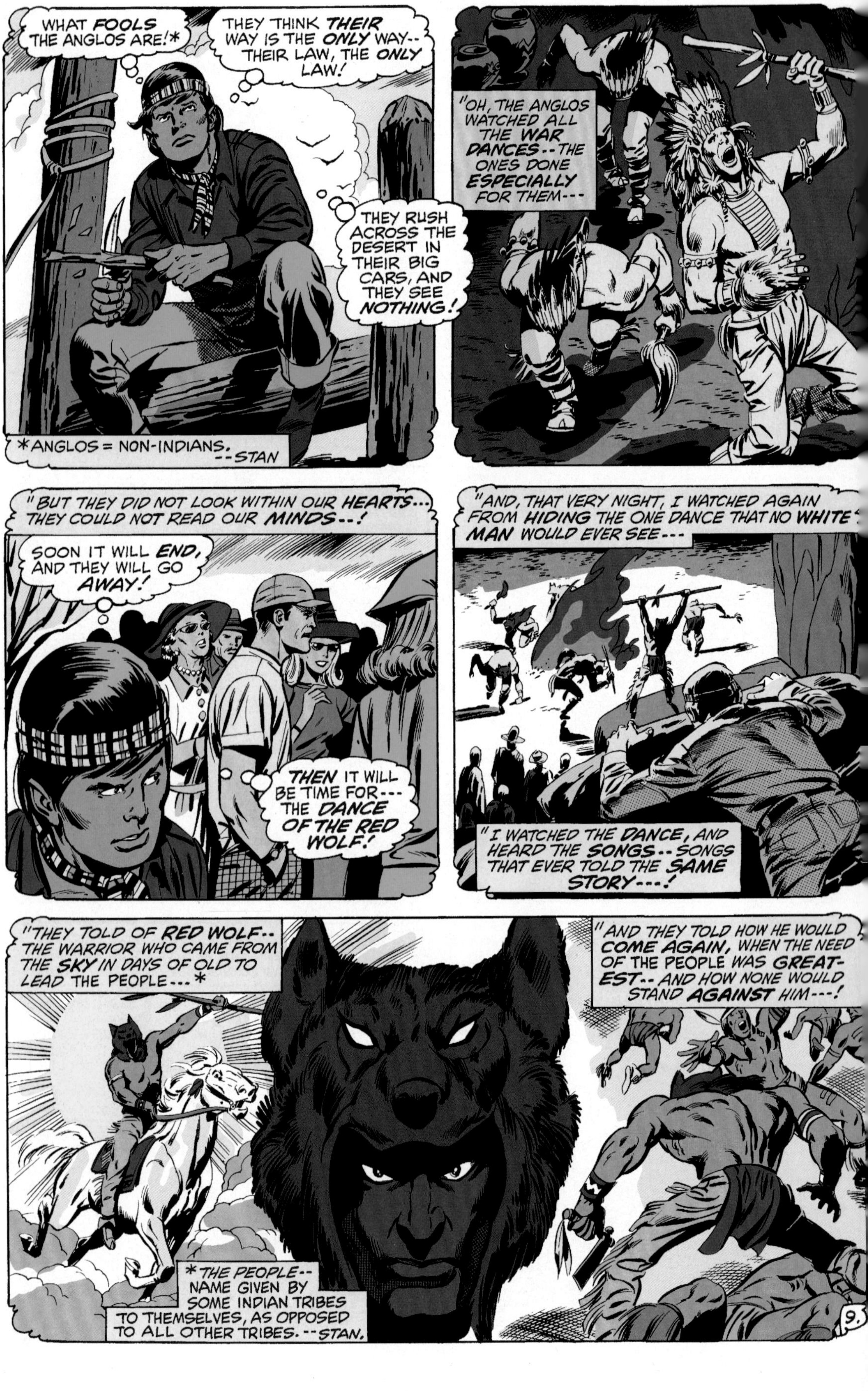
WHAT FOOLS THE ANGLOS ARE!*
THEY THINK THEIR WAY IS THE ONLY WAY-- THEIR LAW, THE ONLY LAW!
THEY RUSH ACROSS THE DESERT IN THEIR BIG CARS, AND THEY SEE NOTHING!
*ANGLOS = NON-INDIANS. --STAN
"OH, THE ANGLOS WATCHED ALL THE WAR DANCES--THE ONES DONE ESPECIALLY FOR THEM---
"BUT THEY DID NOT LOOK WITHIN OUR HEARTS... THEY COULD NOT READ OUR MINDS--!
SOON IT WILL END, AND THEY WILL GO AWAY!
THEN IT WILL BE TIME FOR--- THE DANCE OF THE RED WOLF!
"AND, THAT VERY NIGHT, I WATCHED AGAIN FROM HIDING THE ONE DANCE THAT NO WHITE MAN WOULD EVER SEE---
"I WATCHED THE DANCE, AND HEARD THE SONGS--SONGS THAT EVER TOLD THE SAME STORY---!
"THEY TOLD OF RED WOLF-- THE WARRIOR WHO CAME FROM THE SKY IN DAYS OF OLD TO LEAD THE PEOPLE---*
"AND THEY TOLD HOW HE WOULD COME AGAIN, WHEN THE NEED OF THE PEOPLE WAS GREAT-EST-- AND HOW NONE WOULD STAND AGAINST HIM---!
*THE PEOPLE-- NAME GIVEN BY SOME INDIAN TRIBES TO THEMSELVES, AS OPPOSED TO ALL OTHER TRIBES. --STAN.
9.

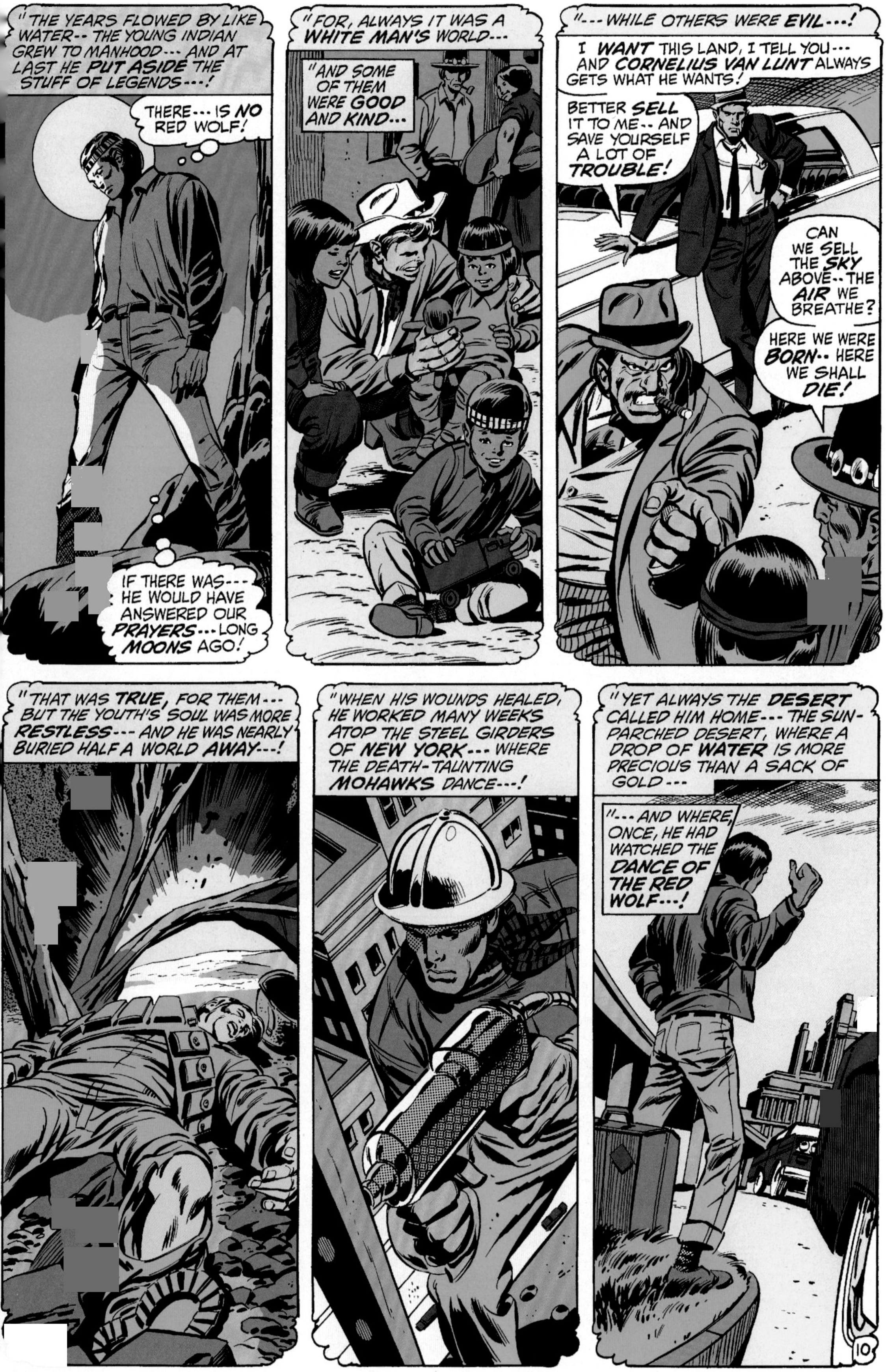
"THE YEARS FLOWED BY LIKE WATER-- THE YOUNG INDIAN GREW TO MANHOOD--- AND AT LAST HE PUT ASIDE THE STUFF OF LEGENDS---!
THERE--- IS NO RED WOLF!
IF THERE WAS--- HE WOULD HAVE ANSWERED OUR PRAYERS--- LONG MOONS AGO!
"FOR, ALWAYS IT WAS A WHITE MAN'S WORLD---
"AND SOME OF THEM WERE GOOD AND KIND---
"--- WHILE OTHERS WERE EVIL---!
I WANT THIS LAND, I TELL YOU--- AND CORNELIUS VAN LUNT ALWAYS GETS WHAT HE WANTS!
BETTER SELL IT TO ME-- AND SAVE YOURSELF A LOT OF TROUBLE!
CAN WE SELL THE SKY ABOVE-- THE AIR WE BREATHE?
HERE WE WERE BORN-- HERE WE SHALL DIE!
"THAT WAS TRUE, FOR THEM--- BUT THE YOUTH'S SOUL WAS MORE RESTLESS--- AND HE WAS NEARLY BURIED HALF A WORLD AWAY---!
"WHEN HIS WOUNDS HEALED, HE WORKED MANY WEEKS ATOP THE STEEL GIRDERS OF NEW YORK--- WHERE THE DEATH-TAUNTING MOHAWKS DANCE---!
"YET ALWAYS THE DESERT CALLED HIM HOME--- THE SUN-PARCHED DESERT, WHERE A DROP OF WATER IS MORE PRECIOUS THAN A SACK OF GOLD---
"--- AND WHERE, ONCE, HE HAD WATCHED THE DANCE OF THE RED WOLF---!
10

"BUT, HIS HOMECOMING WAS DESTINED BY THE GODS TO BE A *GRIM* ONE---

WHY DOES THE CAR OF THE MAN *VAN LUNT* STAND BEFORE MY FATHER'S HOUSE?

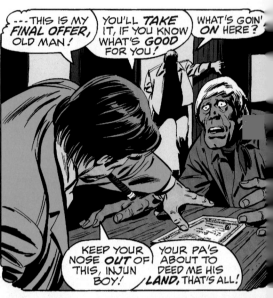

---THIS IS MY *FINAL* OFFER, OLD MAN!

YOU'LL *TAKE* IT, IF YOU KNOW WHAT'S *GOOD* FOR YOU!

WHAT'S GOIN' *ON* HERE?

KEEP YOUR NOSE *OUT* OF THIS, INJUN BOY!

YOUR PA'S ABOUT TO DEED ME HIS *LAND,* THAT'S ALL!

YOU ROTTEN *LIAR!*

LET *ME* TAKE CARE'A THIS CREEP, BOSS!

NO, JASON-- NOT *HERE--* NOT *NOW!*

GET *OUT* OF HERE-- BEFORE I *KILL* YOU!

WE'RE *LEAVING,* BOY-- BUT *HEAR* ME OUT!

YOU MADE MY MAN *JASON BIRCH* HERE AWFULLY *MAD--*

AND I CAN'T BE HELD *RESPONSIBLE* FOR ANYTHING HE MIGHT *DO--* SOMETIME WHEN I'M NOT AROUND TO *PROTECT* YOU!

"IT DID NOT TAKE MORE THAN *ONE NIGHT* FOR THE YOUTH TO LEARN THE FULL *MEANING* OF VAN LUNT'S THREAT---!

HAW! JUST LIKE SHOOTIN' FISH IN A *BARREL,* JASE!

SHUT UP, AN' *KEEP SHOOTIN'!*

NOBODY CAN *PIN* NOTHIN' ON US-- IF THERE'S NOBODY ALIVE TO DO ANY *TALKIN'!*

KA-BRAK

BRAKK

11.

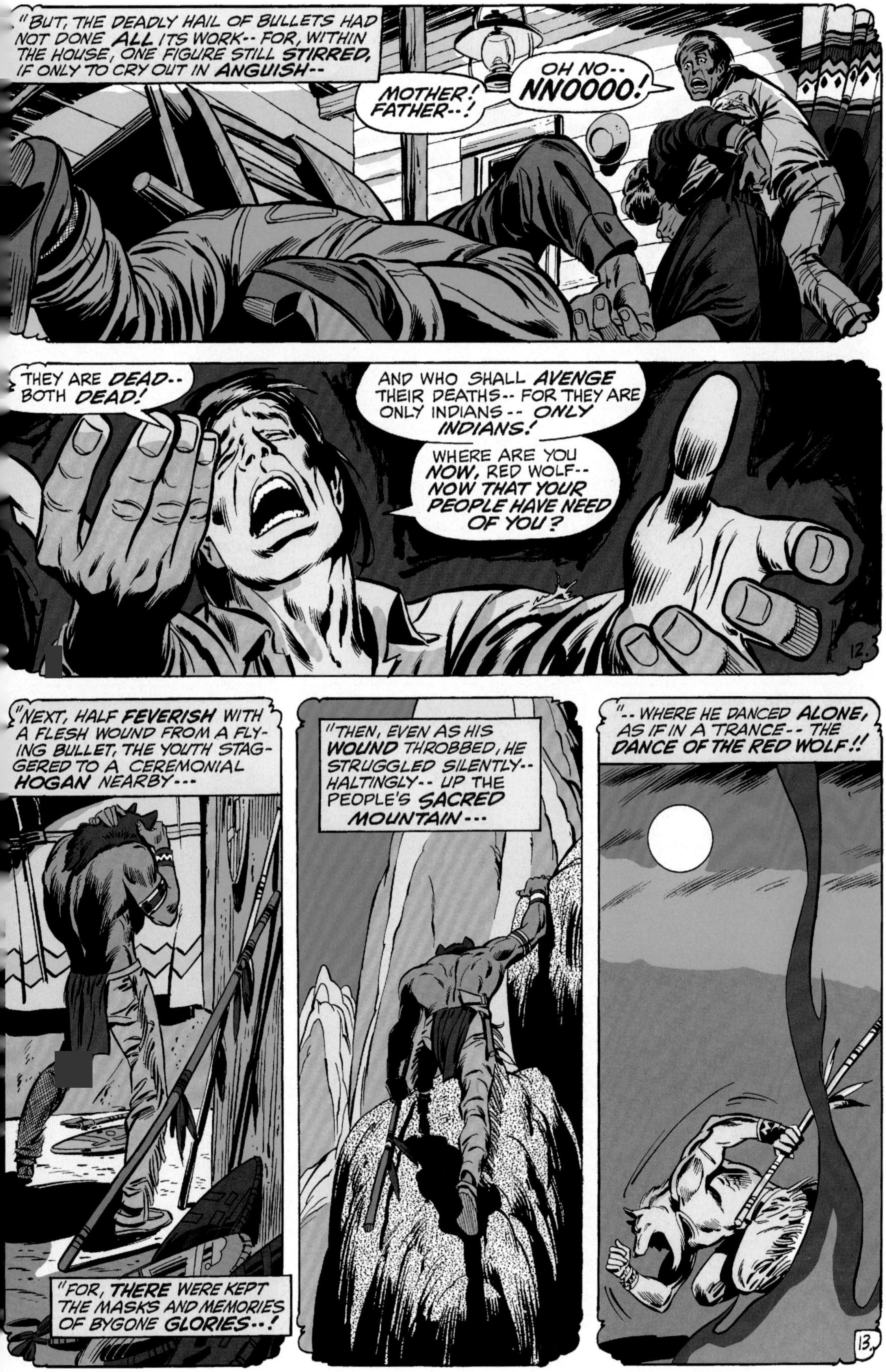
"BUT, THE DEADLY HAIL OF BULLETS HAD NOT DONE ALL ITS WORK-- FOR, WITHIN THE HOUSE, ONE FIGURE STILL STIRRED, IF ONLY TO CRY OUT IN ANGUISH--
MOTHER! FATHER--!
OH NO-- NNOOOO!
THEY ARE DEAD-- BOTH DEAD!
AND WHO SHALL AVENGE THEIR DEATHS-- FOR THEY ARE ONLY INDIANS-- ONLY INDIANS!
WHERE ARE YOU NOW, RED WOLF-- NOW THAT YOUR PEOPLE HAVE NEED OF YOU?
12.
"NEXT, HALF FEVERISH WITH A FLESH WOUND FROM A FLYING BULLET, THE YOUTH STAGGERED TO A CEREMONIAL HOGAN NEARBY---
"FOR, THERE WERE KEPT THE MASKS AND MEMORIES OF BYGONE GLORIES--!
"THEN, EVEN AS HIS WOUND THROBBED, HE STRUGGLED SILENTLY-- HALTINGLY-- UP THE PEOPLE'S SACRED MOUNTAIN---
"-- WHERE HE DANCED ALONE, AS IF IN A TRANCE-- THE DANCE OF THE RED WOLF!!
13.

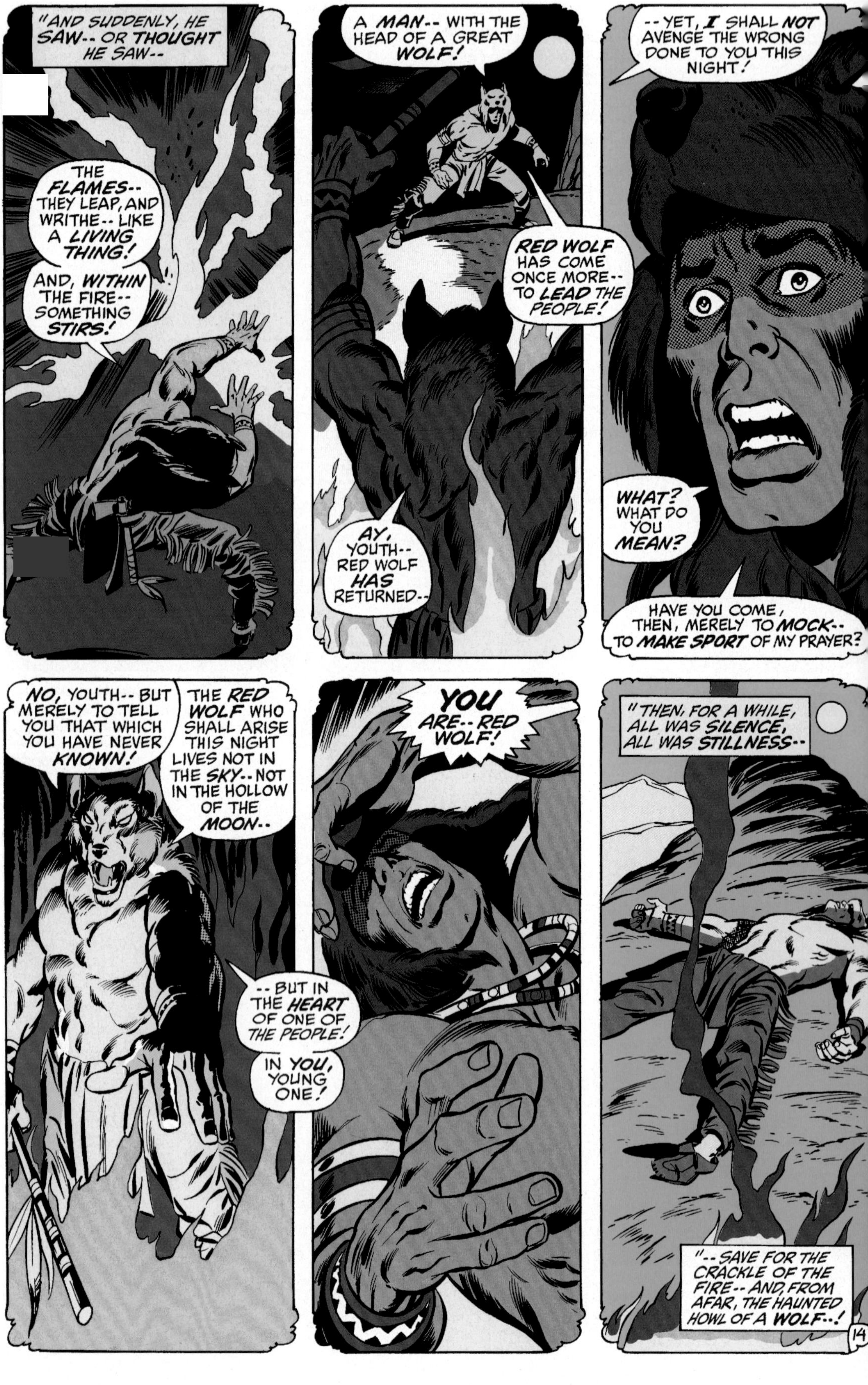
"AND SUDDENLY, HE SAW-- OR THOUGHT HE SAW--
THE FLAMES-- THEY LEAP, AND WRITHE-- LIKE A LIVING THING!
AND, WITHIN THE FIRE-- SOMETHING STIRS!
A MAN-- WITH THE HEAD OF A GREAT WOLF!
RED WOLF HAS COME ONCE MORE-- TO LEAD THE PEOPLE!
AY, YOUTH-- RED WOLF HAS RETURNED--
--YET, I SHALL NOT AVENGE THE WRONG DONE TO YOU THIS NIGHT!
WHAT? WHAT DO YOU MEAN?
HAVE YOU COME, THEN, MERELY TO MOCK-- TO MAKE SPORT OF MY PRAYER?
NO, YOUTH-- BUT MERELY TO TELL YOU THAT WHICH YOU HAVE NEVER KNOWN!
THE RED WOLF WHO SHALL ARISE THIS NIGHT LIVES NOT IN THE SKY-- NOT IN THE HOLLOW OF THE MOON--
-- BUT IN THE HEART OF ONE OF THE PEOPLE!
IN YOU, YOUNG ONE!
YOU ARE-- RED WOLF!
"THEN, FOR A WHILE, ALL WAS SILENCE, ALL WAS STILLNESS--
"-- SAVE FOR THE CRACKLE OF THE FIRE-- AND, FROM AFAR, THE HAUNTED HOWL OF A WOLF--!
14

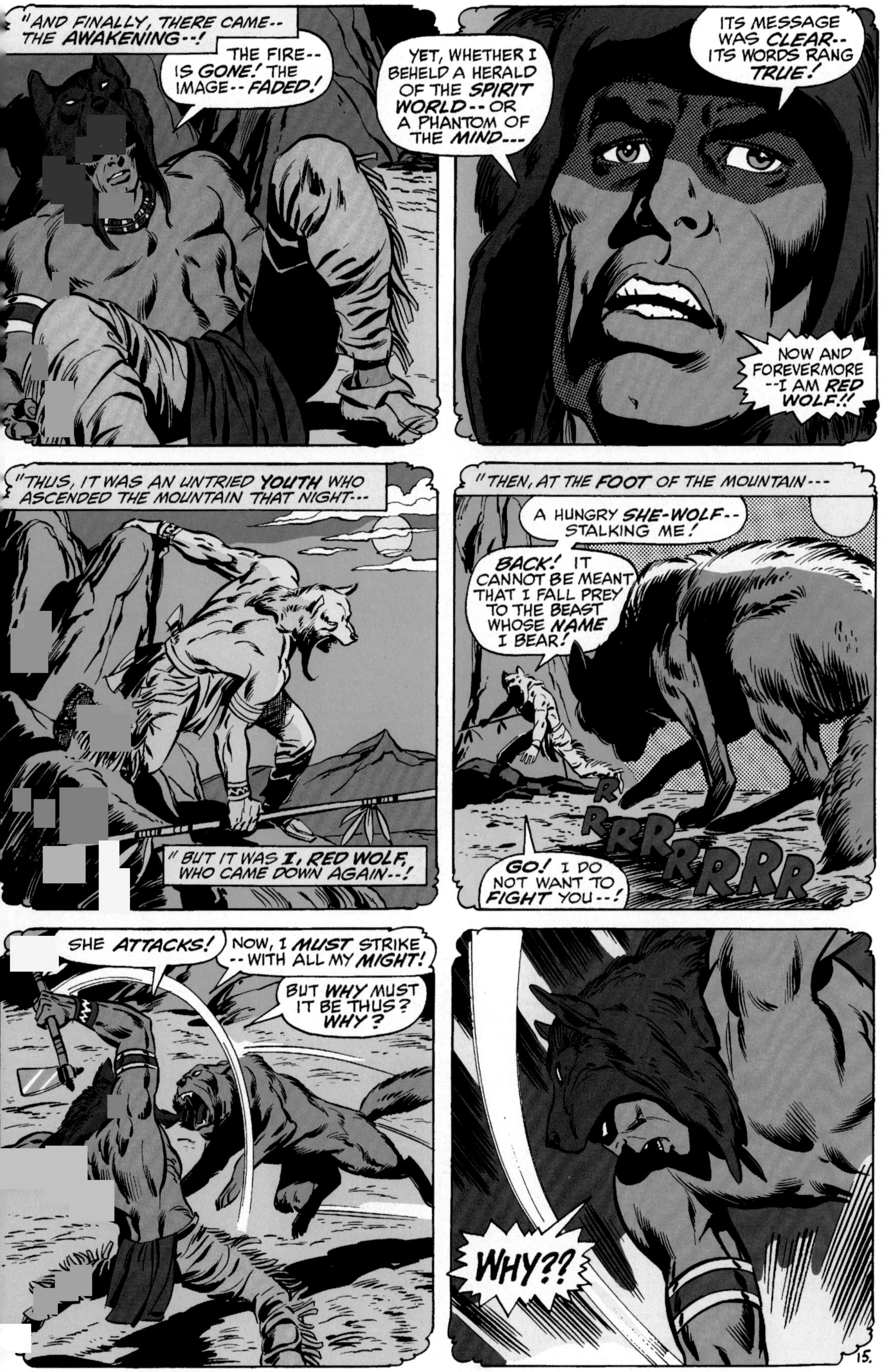
"AND FINALLY, THERE CAME-- THE AWAKENING--!
THE FIRE-- IS GONE! THE IMAGE-- FADED!
YET, WHETHER I BEHELD A HERALD OF THE SPIRIT WORLD-- OR A PHANTOM OF THE MIND---
ITS MESSAGE WAS CLEAR-- ITS WORDS RANG TRUE!
NOW AND FOREVERMORE --I AM RED WOLF!!
"THUS, IT WAS AN UNTRIED YOUTH WHO ASCENDED THE MOUNTAIN THAT NIGHT--
"BUT IT WAS I, RED WOLF, WHO CAME DOWN AGAIN--!
"THEN, AT THE FOOT OF THE MOUNTAIN---
A HUNGRY SHE-WOLF-- STALKING ME!
BACK! IT CANNOT BE MEANT THAT I FALL PREY TO THE BEAST WHOSE NAME I BEAR!
RRRRRRRRR
GO! I DO NOT WANT TO FIGHT YOU--!
SHE ATTACKS!
NOW, I MUST STRIKE --WITH ALL MY MIGHT!
BUT WHY MUST IT BE THUS? WHY?
WHY??

SHE IS *DEAD!* WEAK FROM HUNGER, SHE WAS *NO MATCH* FOR MY TOMAHAWK!

SURELY, THE *SPIRIT-WOLF* SENT HER AGAINST ME FOR A *REASON!* YET *WHAT--?*

WAIT! THAT *CRY* FROM WITHIN THE CAVE!

THERE IS THE *REASON--!*

SHE FOUGHT TO PROTECT-- HER *CUB!*

HE IS A *SIGN--* A LIVING OMEN OF THE *MISSION* I MUST FULFILL!

AND HE SHALL BE CALLED--- *LOBO!*

"*LONG MONTHS* I SPENT, IN *SECLUSION,* ON THE SUN-SCORCHED *DESERT,* PREPARING FOR WHAT WAS TO COME--!"

"*THEN,* AT *LAST,* I CAME AGAIN TO THIS *CITY--!*"

ROOM FOR RENT

"*ONCE MORE,* I LABORED AMONG MAN-MADE *PEAKS--*"

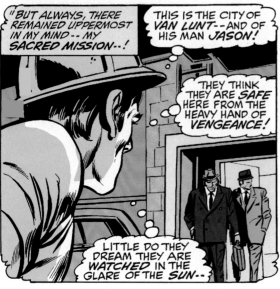

"*BUT ALWAYS,* THERE REMAINED UPPERMOST IN MY MIND -- MY *SACRED MISSION--!*"

THIS IS THE CITY OF VAN LUNT-- AND OF HIS MAN *JASON!*

THEY THINK THEY ARE *SAFE* HERE FROM THE HEAVY HAND OF *VENGEANCE!*

LITTLE DO THEY DREAM THEY ARE *WATCHED* IN THE GLARE OF THE *SUN--*

-- AND IN THE GLOW OF THE *MOON!*

16

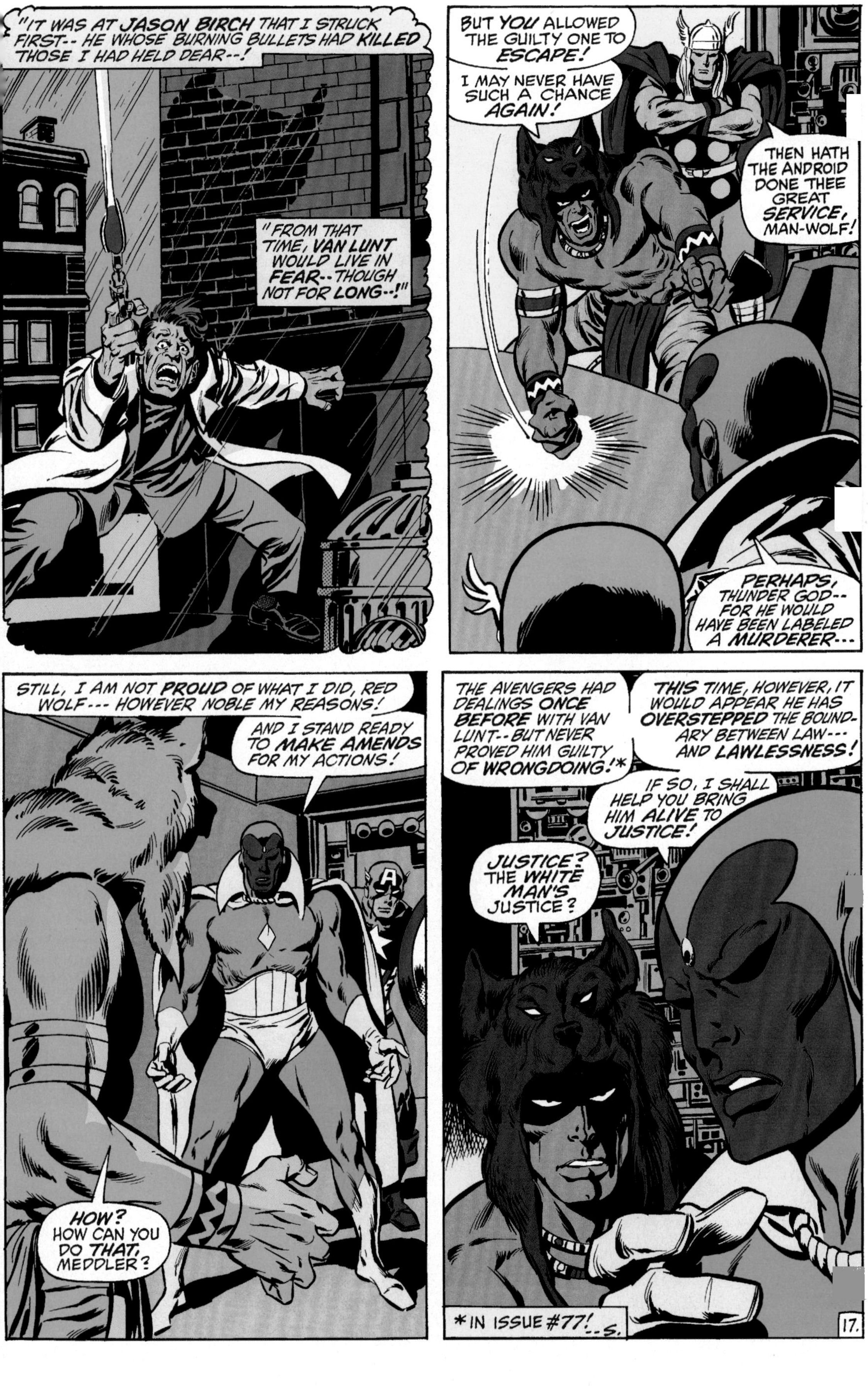
"IT WAS AT JASON BIRCH THAT I STRUCK FIRST-- HE WHOSE BURNING BULLETS HAD KILLED THOSE I HAD HELD DEAR--!
"FROM THAT TIME, VAN LUNT WOULD LIVE IN FEAR--THOUGH NOT FOR LONG--!"
BUT YOU ALLOWED THE GUILTY ONE TO ESCAPE!
I MAY NEVER HAVE SUCH A CHANCE AGAIN!
THEN HATH THE ANDROID DONE THEE GREAT SERVICE, MAN-WOLF!
PERHAPS, THUNDER GOD-- FOR HE WOULD HAVE BEEN LABELED A MURDERER--
STILL, I AM NOT PROUD OF WHAT I DID, RED WOLF--- HOWEVER NOBLE MY REASONS!
AND I STAND READY TO MAKE AMENDS FOR MY ACTIONS!
HOW? HOW CAN YOU DO THAT, MEDDLER?
THE AVENGERS HAD DEALINGS ONCE BEFORE WITH VAN LUNT--BUT NEVER PROVED HIM GUILTY OF WRONGDOING!*
THIS TIME, HOWEVER, IT WOULD APPEAR HE HAS OVERSTEPPED THE BOUNDARY BETWEEN LAW--- AND LAWLESSNESS!
IF SO, I SHALL HELP YOU BRING HIM ALIVE TO JUSTICE!
JUSTICE? THE WHITE MAN'S JUSTICE?
*IN ISSUE #77! --S.

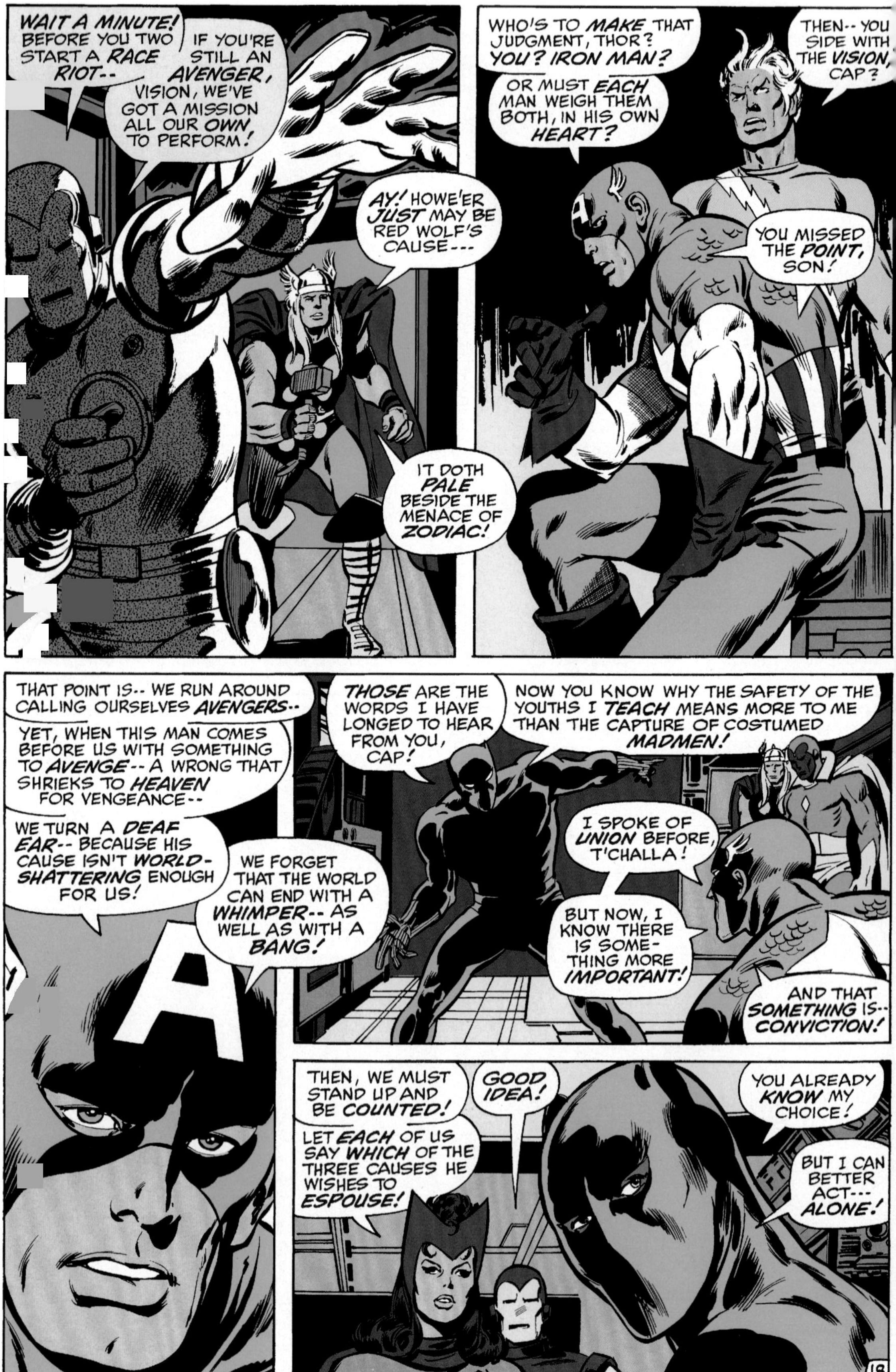

WAIT A MINUTE! BEFORE YOU TWO START A RACE RIOT--
IF YOU'RE STILL AN AVENGER, VISION, WE'VE GOT A MISSION ALL OUR OWN, TO PERFORM!
AY! HOWE'ER JUST MAY BE RED WOLF'S CAUSE---
IT DOTH PALE BESIDE THE MENACE OF ZODIAC!
WHO'S TO MAKE THAT JUDGMENT, THOR? YOU? IRON MAN?
OR MUST EACH MAN WEIGH THEM BOTH, IN HIS OWN HEART?
THEN-- YOU SIDE WITH THE VISION, CAP?
YOU MISSED THE POINT, SON!
THAT POINT IS-- WE RUN AROUND CALLING OURSELVES AVENGERS--
YET, WHEN THIS MAN COMES BEFORE US WITH SOMETHING TO AVENGE-- A WRONG THAT SHRIEKS TO HEAVEN FOR VENGEANCE--
WE TURN A DEAF EAR-- BECAUSE HIS CAUSE ISN'T WORLD-SHATTERING ENOUGH FOR US!
WE FORGET THAT THE WORLD CAN END WITH A WHIMPER-- AS WELL AS WITH A BANG!
THOSE ARE THE WORDS I HAVE LONGED TO HEAR FROM YOU, CAP!
NOW YOU KNOW WHY THE SAFETY OF THE YOUTHS I TEACH MEANS MORE TO ME THAN THE CAPTURE OF COSTUMED MADMEN!
I SPOKE OF UNION BEFORE, T'CHALLA!
BUT NOW, I KNOW THERE IS SOME-THING MORE IMPORTANT!
AND THAT SOMETHING IS-- CONVICTION!
THEN, WE MUST STAND UP AND BE COUNTED!
LET EACH OF US SAY WHICH OF THE THREE CAUSES HE WISHES TO ESPOUSE!
GOOD IDEA!
YOU ALREADY KNOW MY CHOICE!
BUT I CAN BETTER ACT--- ALONE!

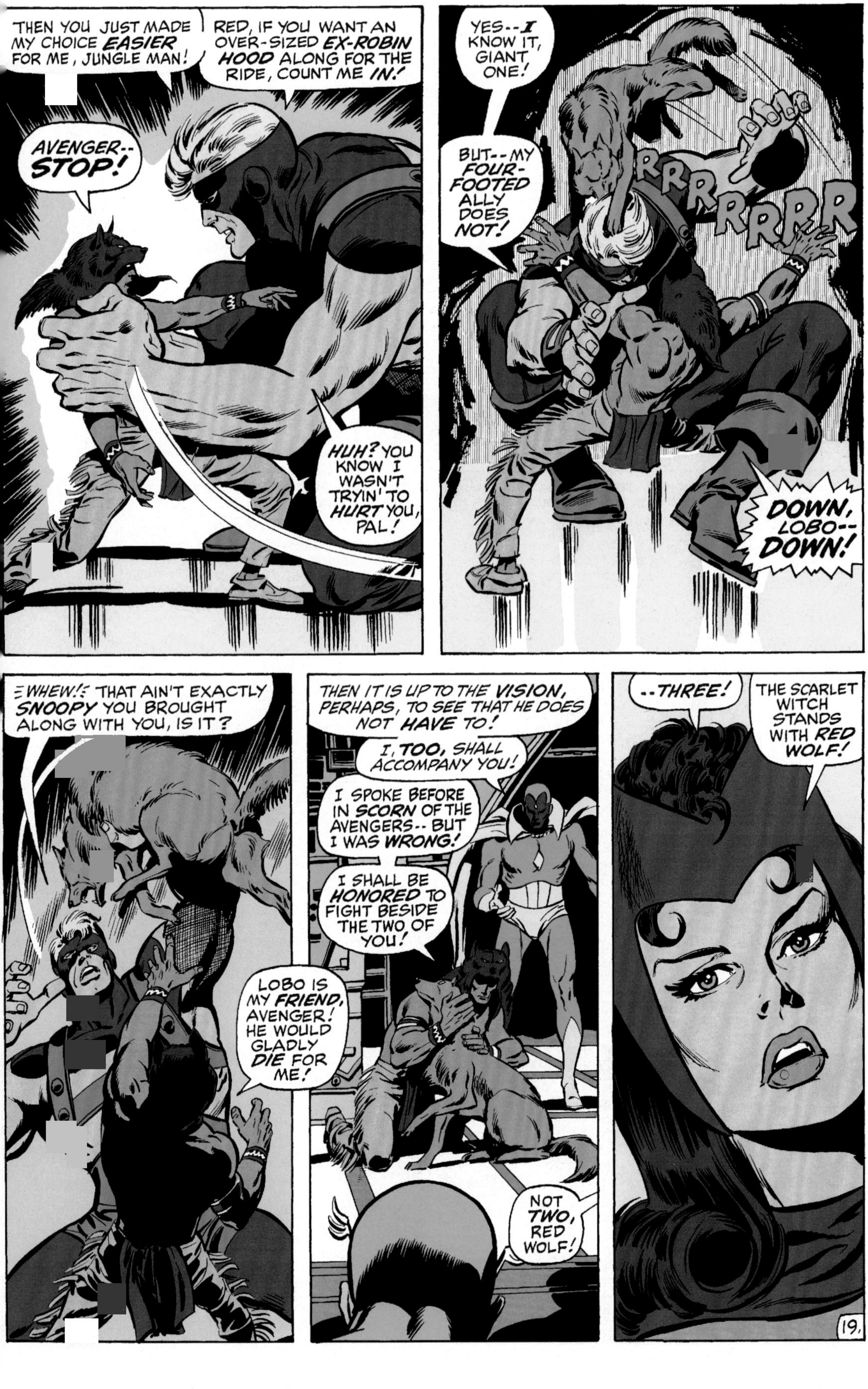
THEN YOU JUST MADE MY CHOICE EASIER FOR ME, JUNGLE MAN!
RED, IF YOU WANT AN OVER-SIZED EX-ROBIN HOOD ALONG FOR THE RIDE, COUNT ME IN!
AVENGER-- STOP!
HUH? YOU KNOW I WASN'T TRYIN' TO HURT YOU, PAL!
YES-- I KNOW IT, GIANT ONE!
BUT-- MY FOUR-FOOTED ALLY DOES NOT!
RRRRRRRRR
DOWN, LOBO-- DOWN!
WHEW! THAT AIN'T EXACTLY SNOOPY YOU BROUGHT ALONG WITH YOU, IS IT?
LOBO IS MY FRIEND, AVENGER! HE WOULD GLADLY DIE FOR ME!
THEN IT IS UP TO THE VISION, PERHAPS, TO SEE THAT HE DOES NOT HAVE TO!
I, TOO, SHALL ACCOMPANY YOU!
I SPOKE BEFORE IN SCORN OF THE AVENGERS-- BUT I WAS WRONG!
I SHALL BE HONORED TO FIGHT BESIDE THE TWO OF YOU!
NOT TWO, RED WOLF!
--THREE!
THE SCARLET WITCH STANDS WITH RED WOLF!

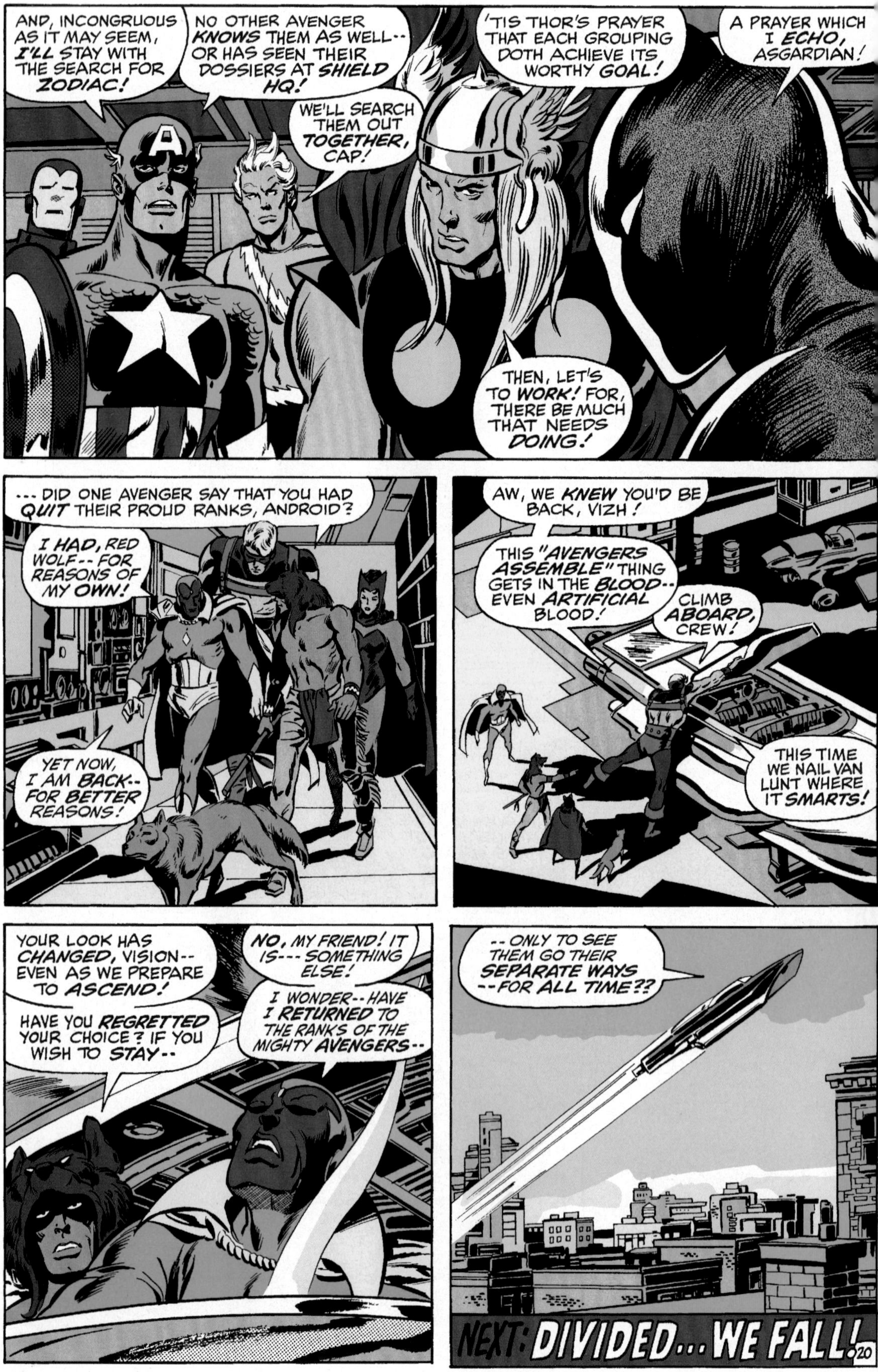
AND, INCONGRUOUS AS IT MAY SEEM, I'LL STAY WITH THE SEARCH FOR ZODIAC!
NO OTHER AVENGER KNOWS THEM AS WELL-- OR HAS SEEN THEIR DOSSIERS AT SHIELD HQ!
WE'LL SEARCH THEM OUT TOGETHER, CAP!
'TIS THOR'S PRAYER THAT EACH GROUPING DOTH ACHIEVE ITS WORTHY GOAL!
A PRAYER WHICH I ECHO, ASGARDIAN!
THEN, LET'S TO WORK! FOR, THERE BE MUCH THAT NEEDS DOING!
... DID ONE AVENGER SAY THAT YOU HAD QUIT THEIR PROUD RANKS, ANDROID?
I HAD, RED WOLF-- FOR REASONS OF MY OWN!
YET NOW, I AM BACK-- FOR BETTER REASONS!
AW, WE KNEW YOU'D BE BACK, VIZH!
THIS "AVENGERS ASSEMBLE" THING GETS IN THE BLOOD-- EVEN ARTIFICIAL BLOOD!
CLIMB ABOARD, CREW!
THIS TIME WE NAIL VAN LUNT WHERE IT SMARTS!
YOUR LOOK HAS CHANGED, VISION-- EVEN AS WE PREPARE TO ASCEND!
HAVE YOU REGRETTED YOUR CHOICE? IF YOU WISH TO STAY--
NO, MY FRIEND! IT IS--- SOMETHING ELSE!
I WONDER-- HAVE I RETURNED TO THE RANKS OF THE MIGHTY AVENGERS--
--ONLY TO SEE THEM GO THEIR SEPARATE WAYS --FOR ALL TIME??
NEXT: DIVIDED... WE FALL!
20

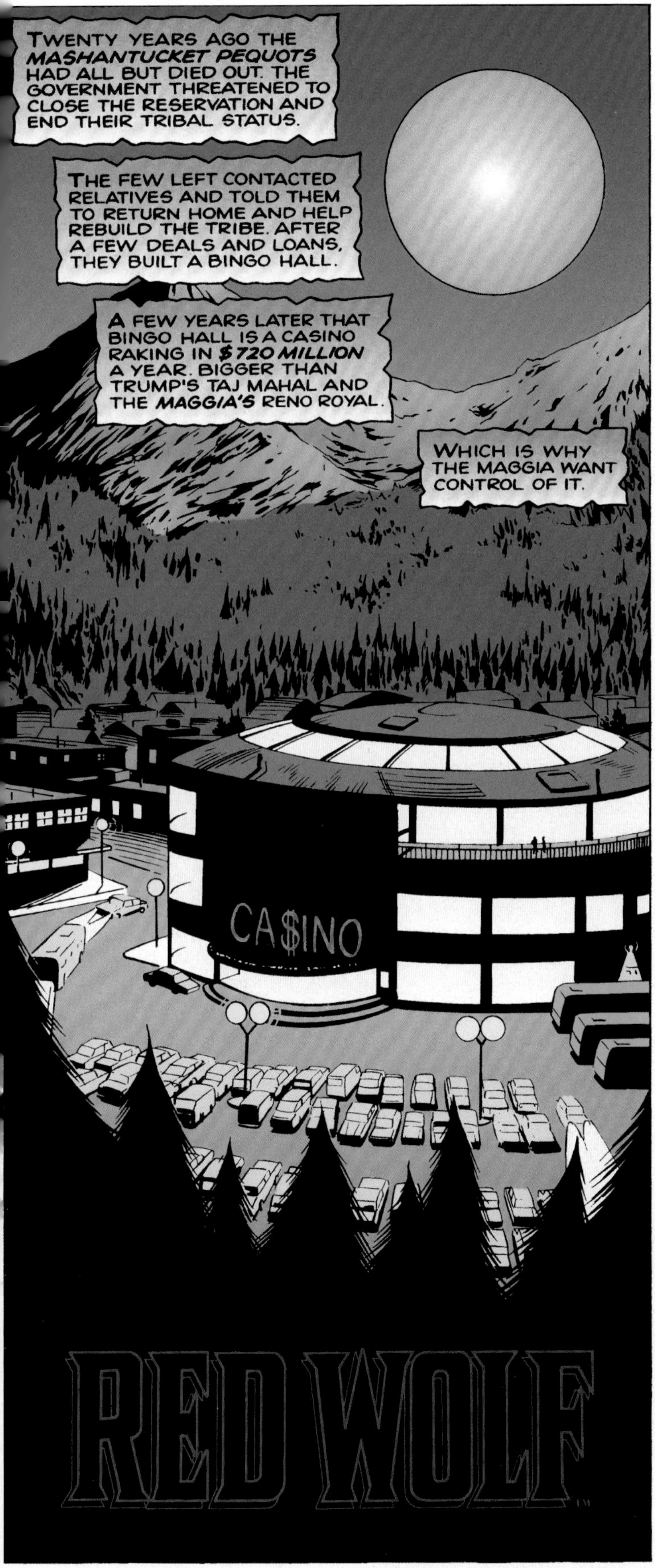
TWENTY YEARS AGO THE MASHANTUCKET PEQUOTS HAD ALL BUT DIED OUT. THE GOVERNMENT THREATENED TO CLOSE THE RESERVATION AND END THEIR TRIBAL STATUS.
THE FEW LEFT CONTACTED RELATIVES AND TOLD THEM TO RETURN HOME AND HELP REBUILD THE TRIBE. AFTER A FEW DEALS AND LOANS, THEY BUILT A BINGO HALL.
A FEW YEARS LATER THAT BINGO HALL IS A CASINO RAKING IN $720 MILLION A YEAR. BIGGER THAN TRUMP'S TAJ MAHAL AND THE MAGGIA'S RENO ROYAL.
WHICH IS WHY THE MAGGIA WANT CONTROL OF IT.
CA$INO
RED WOLF

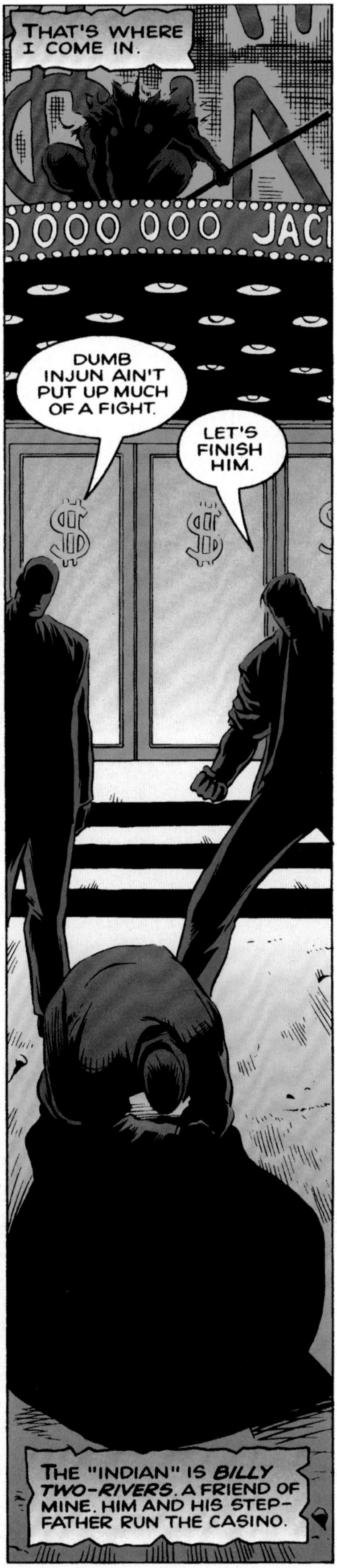
THAT'S WHERE I COME IN.
000 000 JAC
DUMB INJUN AIN'T PUT UP MUCH OF A FIGHT.
LET'S FINISH HIM.
THE "INDIAN" IS BILLY TWO-RIVERS. A FRIEND OF MINE. HIM AND HIS STEP-FATHER RUN THE CASINO.

Writer: Alan Cowsill • Pencils: Jimmy Chung • Inks: Martin Griffiths • Letters: Pat Prentice
Colors: Frank Lopez • Assistant Editor: Michael Kraiger • Editor: Richard Ashford

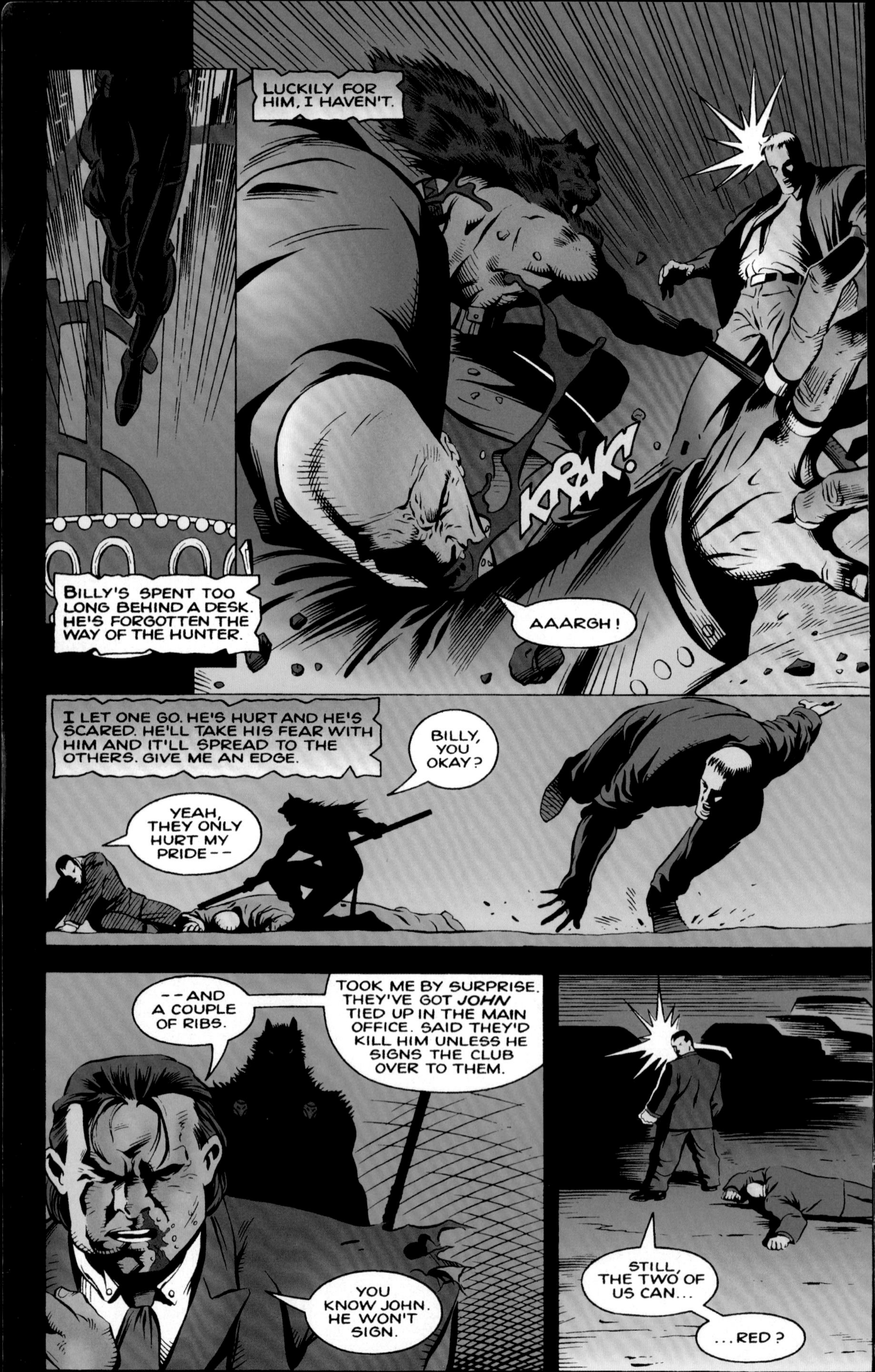
LUCKILY FOR HIM, I HAVEN'T.
BILLY'S SPENT TOO LONG BEHIND A DESK. HE'S FORGOTTEN THE WAY OF THE HUNTER.
KRAK!
AAARGH!
I LET ONE GO. HE'S HURT AND HE'S SCARED. HE'LL TAKE HIS FEAR WITH HIM AND IT'LL SPREAD TO THE OTHERS. GIVE ME AN EDGE.
BILLY, YOU OKAY?
YEAH, THEY ONLY HURT MY PRIDE--
--AND A COUPLE OF RIBS.
TOOK ME BY SURPRISE. THEY'VE GOT JOHN TIED UP IN THE MAIN OFFICE. SAID THEY'D KILL HIM UNLESS HE SIGNS THE CLUB OVER TO THEM.
YOU KNOW JOHN. HE WON'T SIGN.
STILL, THE TWO OF US CAN...
...RED?

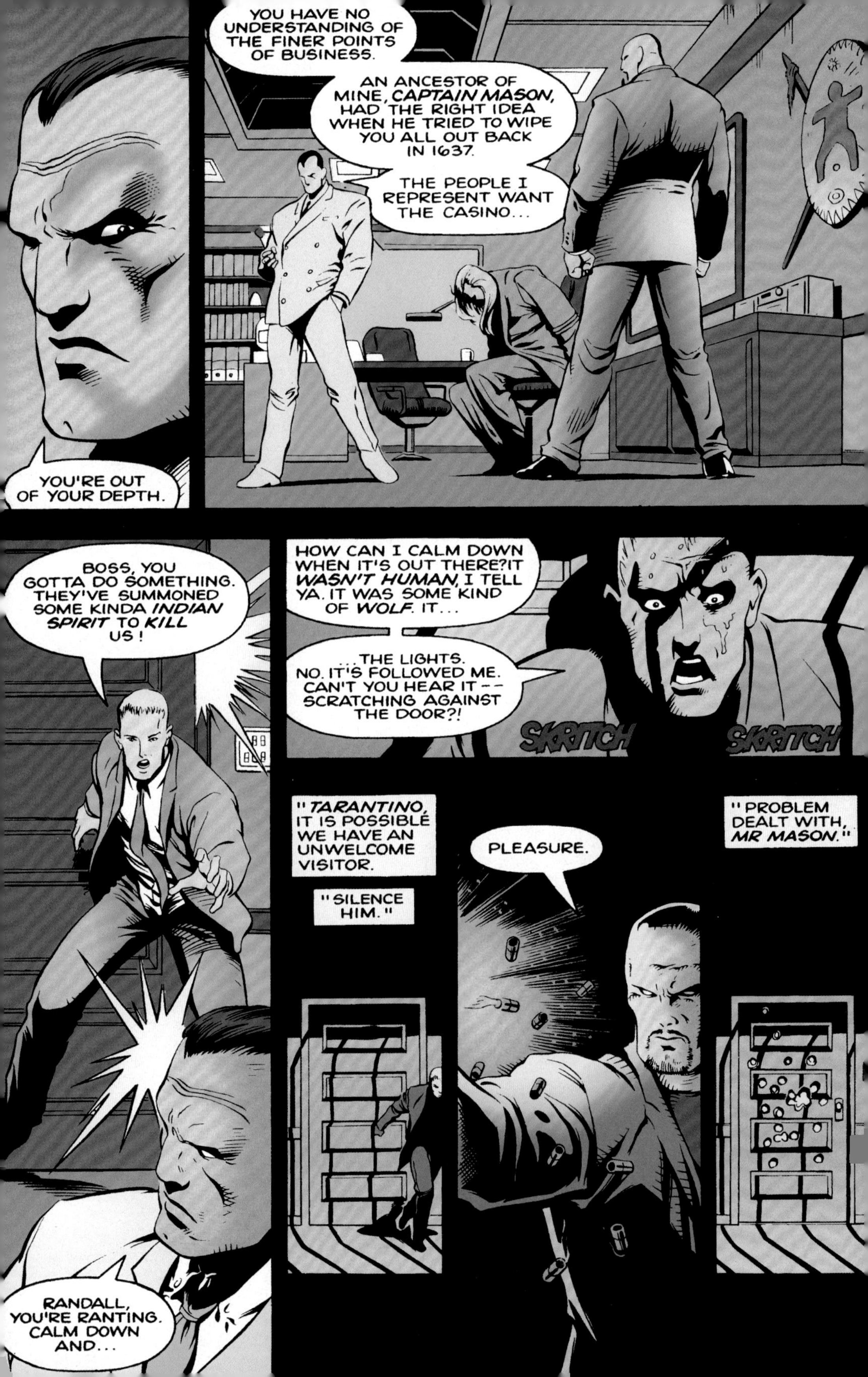

YOU HAVE NO UNDERSTANDING OF THE FINER POINTS OF BUSINESS.
AN ANCESTOR OF MINE, CAPTAIN MASON, HAD THE RIGHT IDEA WHEN HE TRIED TO WIPE YOU ALL OUT BACK IN 1637.
THE PEOPLE I REPRESENT WANT THE CASINO...
YOU'RE OUT OF YOUR DEPTH.
BOSS, YOU GOTTA DO SOMETHING. THEY'VE SUMMONED SOME KINDA INDIAN SPIRIT TO KILL US!
RANDALL, YOU'RE RANTING. CALM DOWN AND...
HOW CAN I CALM DOWN WHEN IT'S OUT THERE?IT WASN'T HUMAN, I TELL YA. IT WAS SOME KIND OF WOLF. IT...
...THE LIGHTS. NO. IT'S FOLLOWED ME. CAN'T YOU HEAR IT -- SCRATCHING AGAINST THE DOOR?!
SKRITCH
SKRITCH
"TARANTINO, IT IS POSSIBLE WE HAVE AN UNWELCOME VISITOR.
"SILENCE HIM."
PLEASURE.
"PROBLEM DEALT WITH, MR MASON."

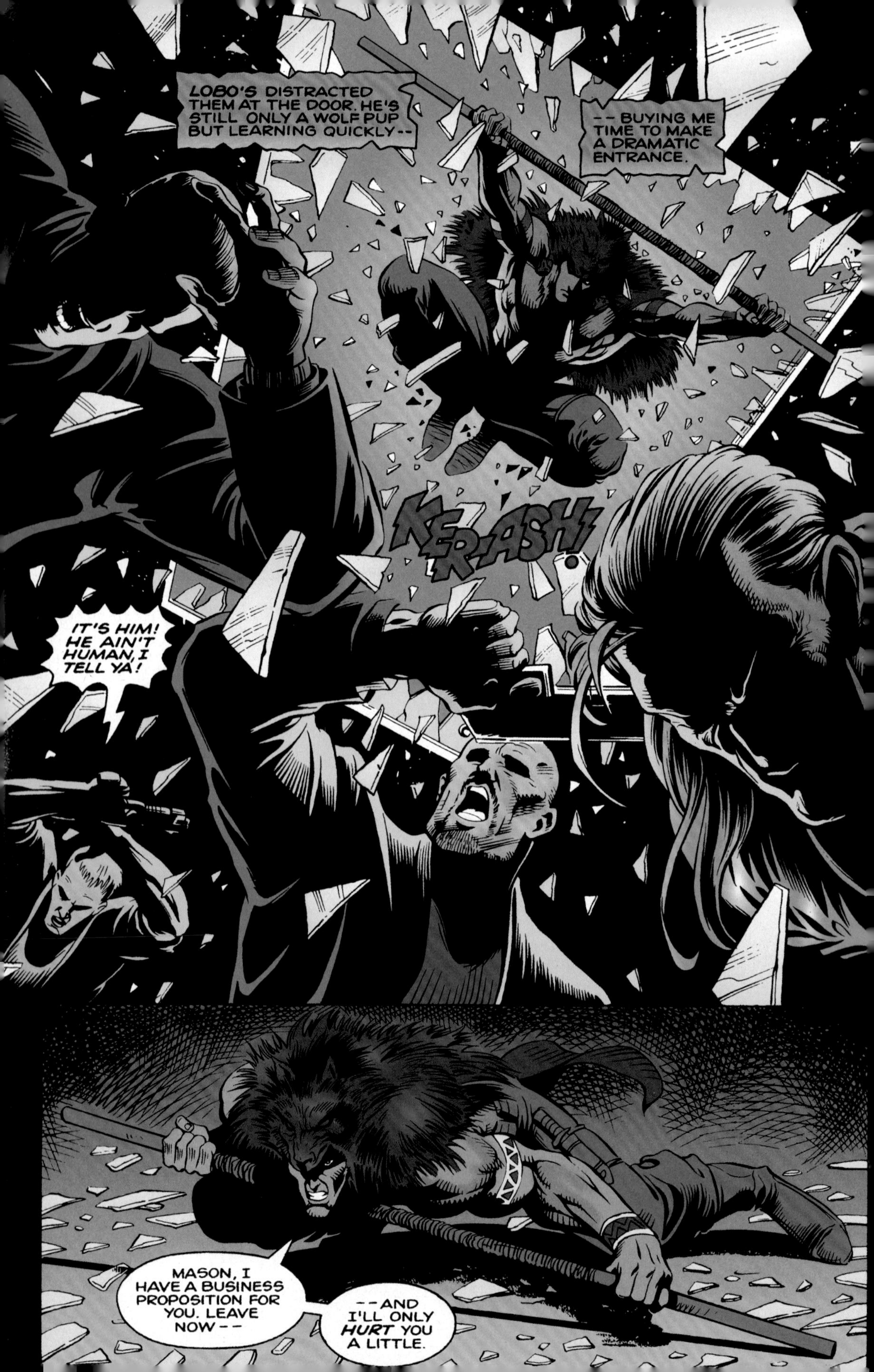

LOBO'S DISTRACTED THEM AT THE DOOR. HE'S STILL ONLY A WOLF PUP BUT LEARNING QUICKLY--
--BUYING ME TIME TO MAKE A DRAMATIC ENTRANCE.
KERASH!
IT'S HIM! HE AIN'T HUMAN, I TELL YA!
MASON, I HAVE A BUSINESS PROPOSITION FOR YOU. LEAVE NOW--
--AND I'LL ONLY HURT YOU A LITTLE.

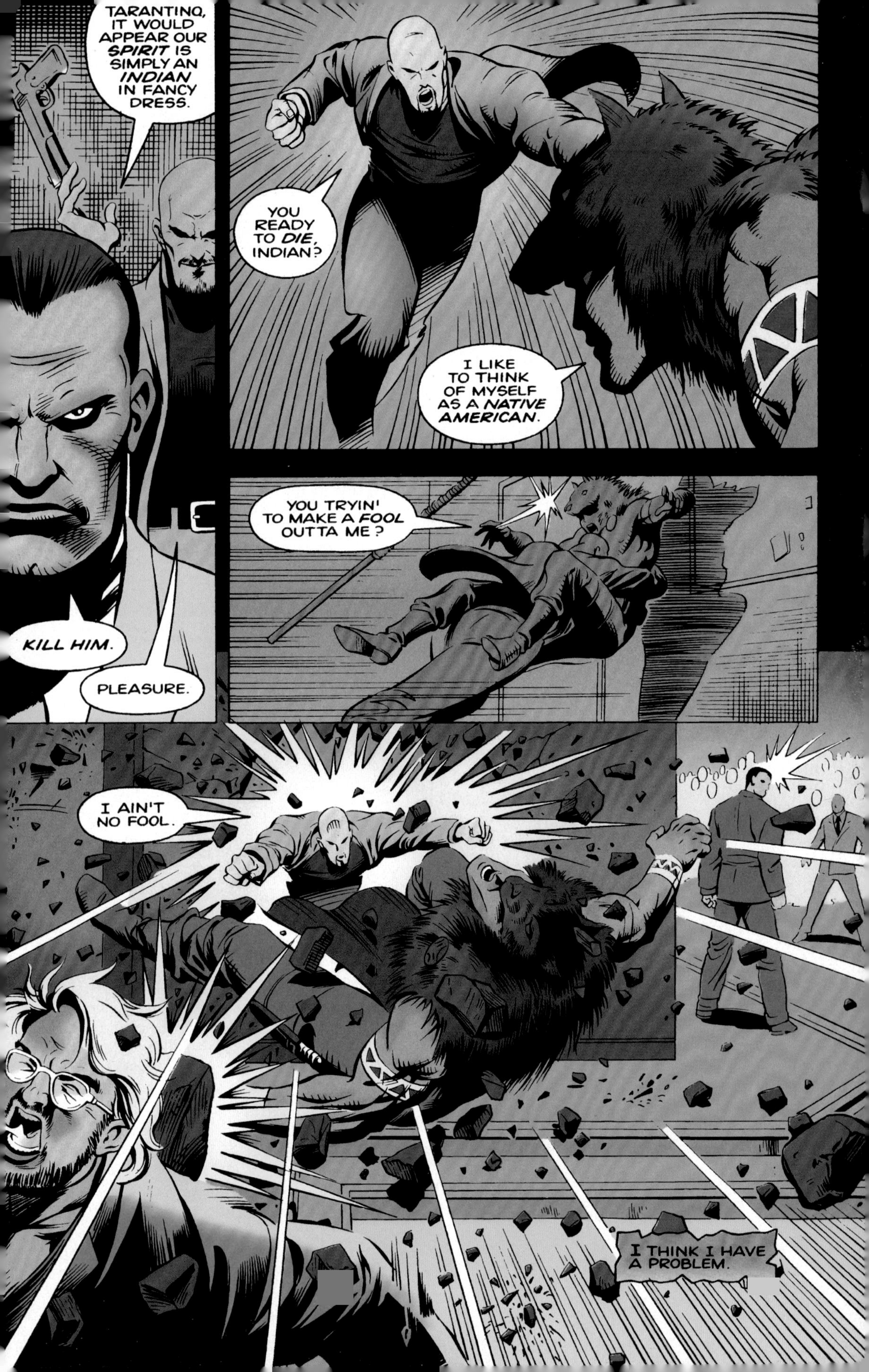
TARANTINO, IT WOULD APPEAR OUR SPIRIT IS SIMPLY AN INDIAN IN FANCY DRESS.
KILL HIM.
PLEASURE.
YOU READY TO DIE, INDIAN?
I LIKE TO THINK OF MYSELF AS A NATIVE AMERICAN.
YOU TRYIN' TO MAKE A FOOL OUTTA ME?
I AIN'T NO FOOL.
I THINK I HAVE A PROBLEM.

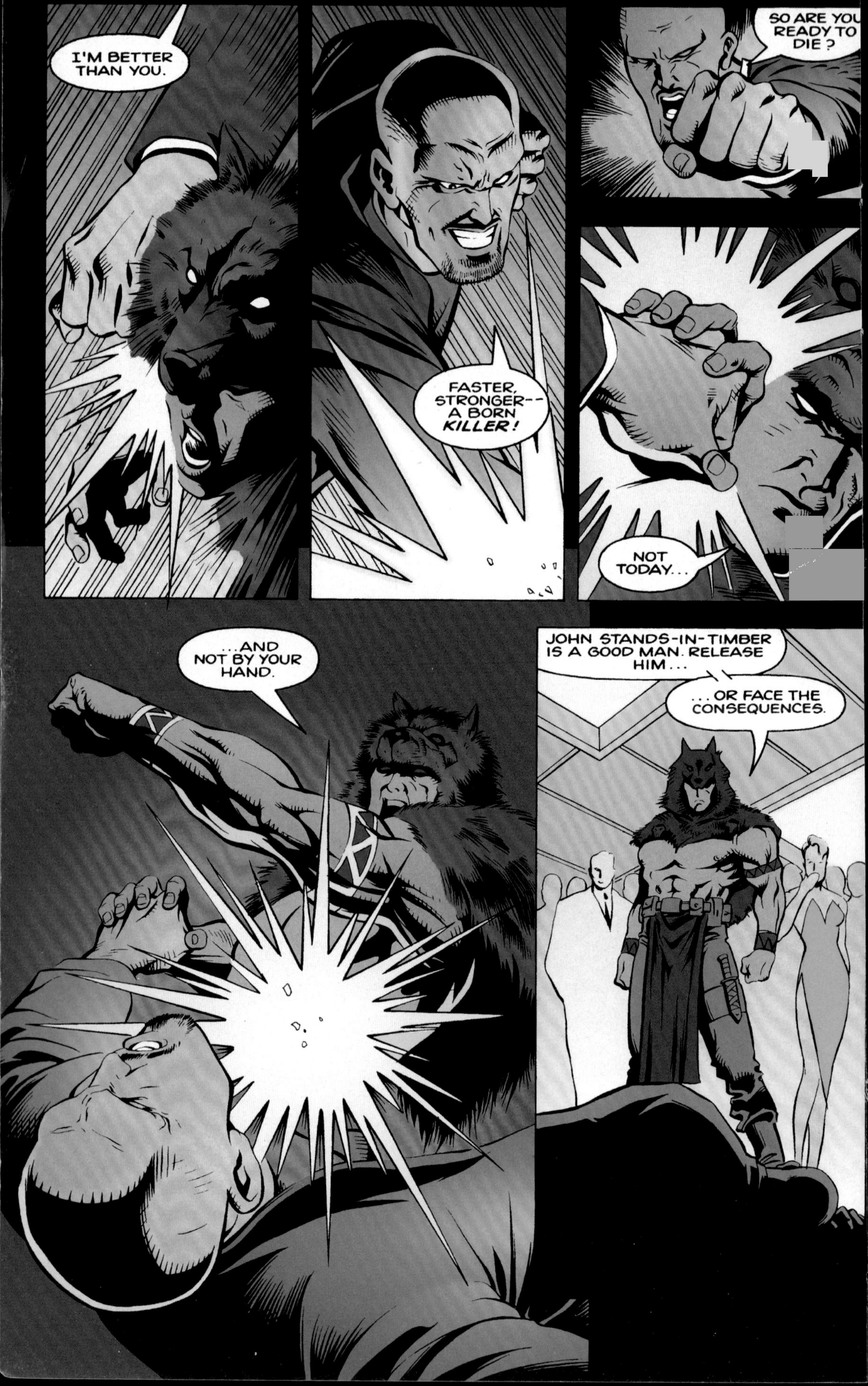
I'M BETTER THAN YOU.
FASTER, STRONGER-- A BORN KILLER!
SO ARE YOU READY TO DIE?
NOT TODAY...
...AND NOT BY YOUR HAND.
JOHN STANDS-IN-TIMBER IS A GOOD MAN. RELEASE HIM...
...OR FACE THE CONSEQUENCES.

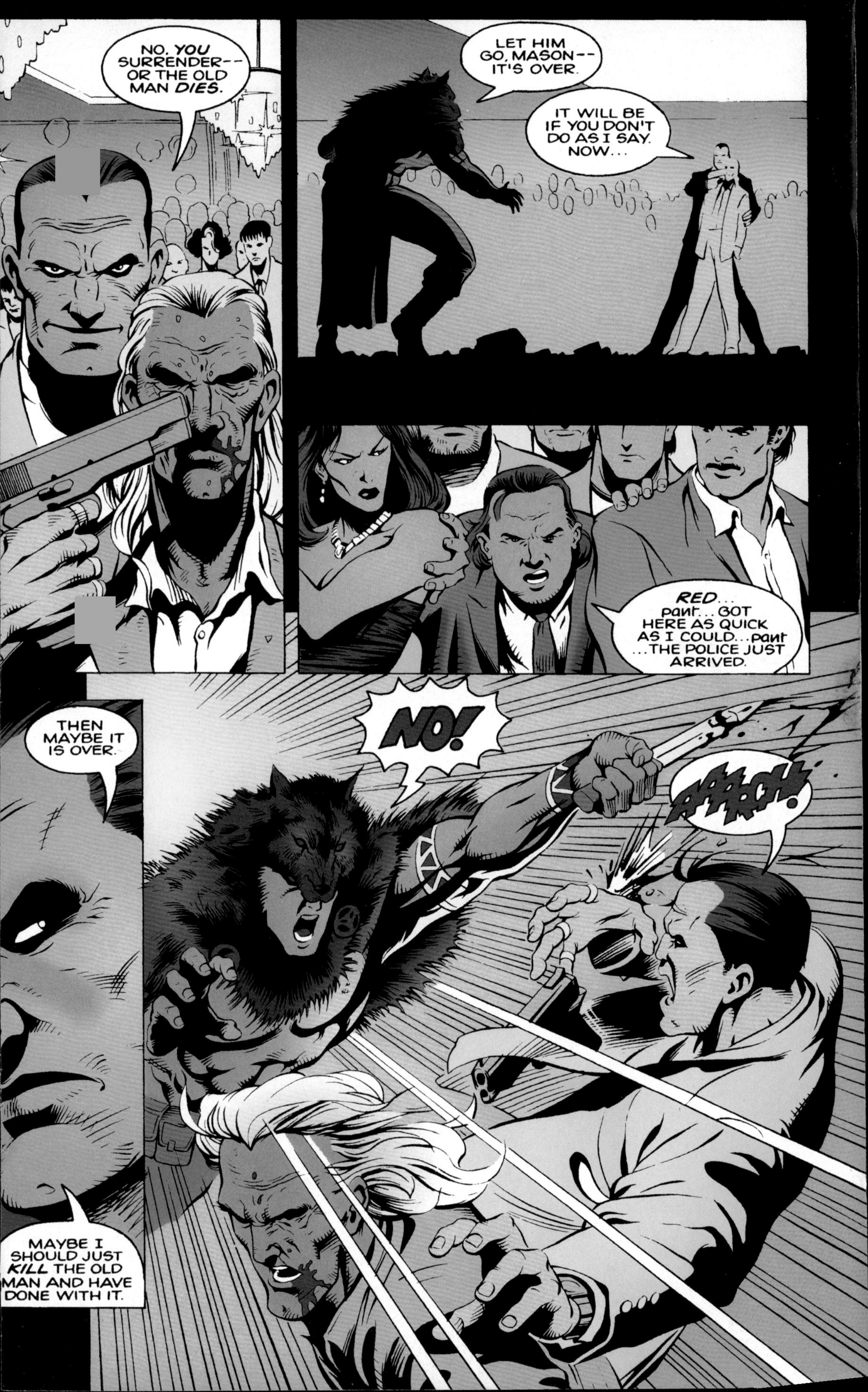
NO, YOU SURRENDER-- OR THE OLD MAN DIES.
LET HIM GO, MASON-- IT'S OVER.
IT WILL BE IF YOU DON'T DO AS I SAY. NOW...
RED... pant... GOT HERE AS QUICK AS I COULD... pant ...THE POLICE JUST ARRIVED.
THEN MAYBE IT IS OVER.
MAYBE I SHOULD JUST KILL THE OLD MAN AND HAVE DONE WITH IT.
NO!
AAARGH!

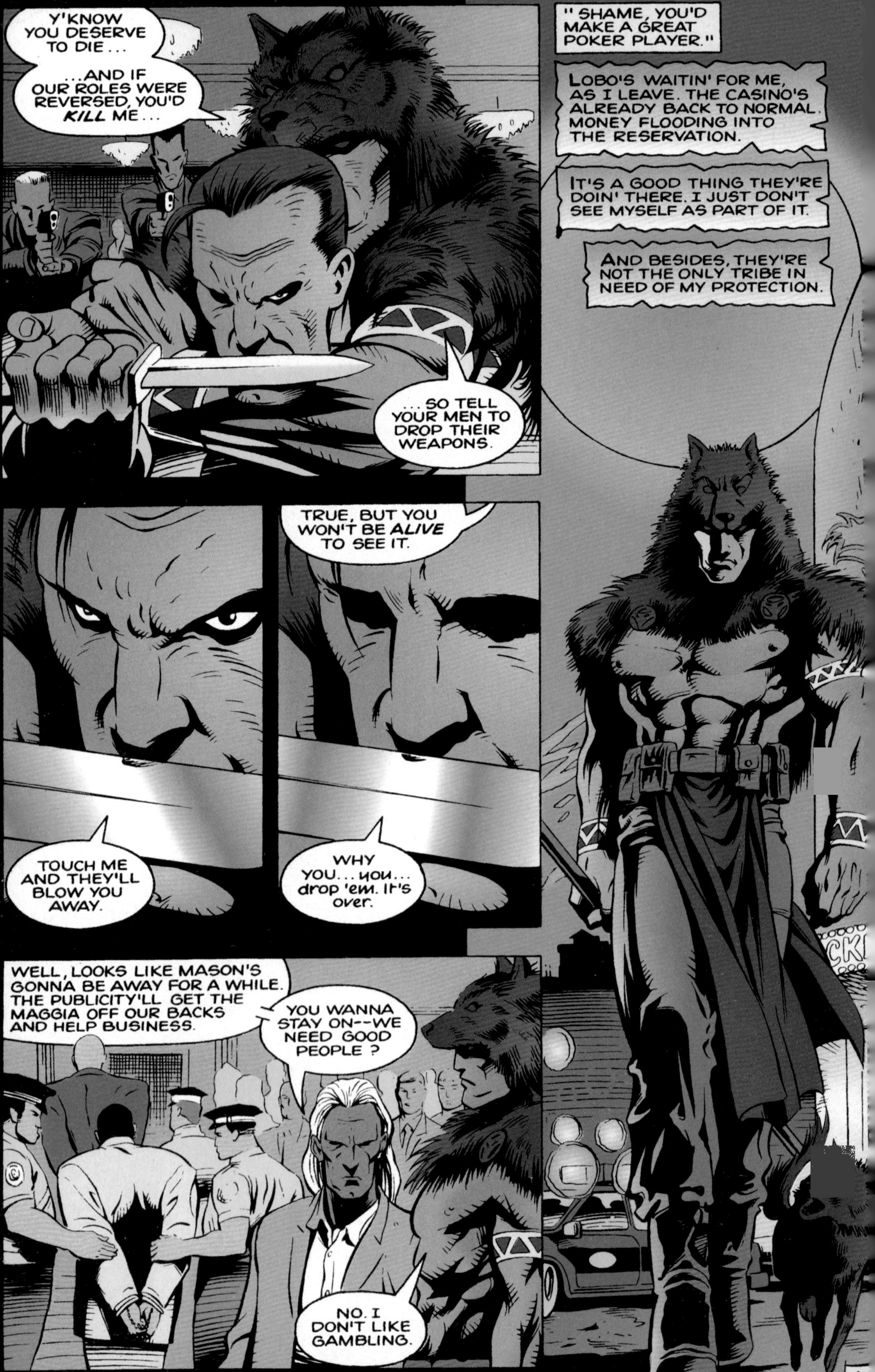

Y'KNOW YOU DESERVE TO DIE...
...AND IF OUR ROLES WERE REVERSED, YOU'D KILL ME...
...SO TELL YOUR MEN TO DROP THEIR WEAPONS.
TOUCH ME AND THEY'LL BLOW YOU AWAY.
TRUE, BUT YOU WON'T BE ALIVE TO SEE IT.
WHY YOU... you... drop 'em. It's over.
WELL, LOOKS LIKE MASON'S GONNA BE AWAY FOR A WHILE. THE PUBLICITY'LL GET THE MAGGIA OFF OUR BACKS AND HELP BUSINESS.
YOU WANNA STAY ON--WE NEED GOOD PEOPLE ?
NO. I DON'T LIKE GAMBLING.
" SHAME, YOU'D MAKE A GREAT POKER PLAYER."
LOBO'S WAITIN' FOR ME, AS I LEAVE. THE CASINO'S ALREADY BACK TO NORMAL. MONEY FLOODING INTO THE RESERVATION.
IT'S A GOOD THING THEY'RE DOIN' THERE. I JUST DON'T SEE MYSELF AS PART OF IT.
AND BESIDES, THEY'RE NOT THE ONLY TRIBE IN NEED OF MY PROTECTION.